Synopsis

A woman's strength makes man look so small, she bites her tongue and tries to help all, be it husband, family or friend, there is only one rod man knows how to bend. Of their governing souls is there no end, to the lies and deceit, the hurt and the pain, that the opposite sex, walk away from time and time again. While women weep, it seems man can only want, what is best for him, and him only!

Introduction

Margaret is warm, loving and loyal; she has the kind of heart that is rarely found in life. This is one woman's story, one woman's strength, the welfare system and the rich man's fence. Her golden heart, breaking every rule, Margaret, has had, and lost it all, yet a woman of stamina, passion and strength, she still stands tall. One minute on top of the world, another buried beneath it all, yet her beautiful soul continues to shine and tolerate it all.

Dedications

This book is dedicated to my eldest brother, Jim Black, whom I love dearly, to both my parents (now deceased) and to all my family, because I believe that family matters. When I was young my mother told me many stories of her life, which remained with me, and which have provided me with some of the material for this book, together with my own memories and experiences, that I, too, would like to pass on to the future generations of my family, who in this modern age in which they live, do not always have the time to listen to the oral tradition of storytelling, but which is, nevertheless, no less important.

Thank you

To the BBC Television Waterloo Road Series and ITV Granada, and the producer of Coronation Street for their excellent and sensitive coverage of the terrible disease, dementia, which has undoubtedly helped to raise public, and government awareness of the issues facing the sufferers of the disease and their families. I would also like to extend my sincere thanks to the medical profession, healthcare workers and carers for the excellent work they do. A special thanks to my sister-in-law, Nula Roberts, for the love and dedication she has always shown to my brother, Jim, in the most difficult of circumstances, that she faced, in supporting him through this difficult time.

Demented

Copyright 2012 by Margaret Johnson

The mortal rights of the owner have been asserted

All rights reserved by Margaret Johnson

No part of this publication may be reproduced, stored in a retrieval system, or transmitted in form, or by any means, without the prior permission of the publisher, not to be otherwise circulated in any form of binding or cover other than which it is published and without a similar condition including this condition being imposed on the subsequent purchaser.

A catalogue record for this book is available from the British Library

ISBN 978-0-9564941-4-6

Printed by Bonker Books in Great Britain

For the Preservation of World Wildlife

Demented

My brother, Jim Black's story

By Margaret Johnson

Contents

PART ONE — *1*
Chapter One — Childhood — *3*
Chapter Two — The Adolescent Years — *19*
Chapter Three — Jim gets his First Camera — *29*

PART TWO — *41*
Chapter One — Crossing the Water — *43*
Chapter Two — Married Life with Fernando — *61*
Chapter Three — The Bad News First Then the Good News — *71*
Chapter Four — Trouble in Paradise — *88*
Chapter Five — The Return of the Prodigal Father — *102*

PART THREE — *109*
Chapter One — The move to Nottingham — *111*
Chapter Two — Trouble in Paradise Again — *136*
Chapter Three — Homeless — *147*
Chapter Four — The Lodgers — *156*
Chapter Five — Time tells all tales — *174*
Chapter Six — Talking of Ex's — *179*
Chapter Seven — Missing Piece in the Jigsaw — *186*

PART FOUR — *201*
Chapter One — Everyone Has Their Price — *203*
Chapter Two — The Car Accident — *221*
Chapter Three — History Repeats Itself — *230*
Chapter Four — The Family reunion — *251*
Chapter Five — The Court Case — *269*
Chapter Six — I Move to Spain — *277*
Chapter Seven — The Edinburgh Fiasco — *287*
Chapter Eight — Jim's Move to Chorley Wood — *291*
Chapter Nine — my Visit to Edinburgh — *293*
Chapter Ten — Jim Moves to Courtlands Lodge — *297*
Chapter Eleven — Nula's Texts — *307*
Chapter Twelve — Friends in High Places — *309*

The moving finger writes; and, having writ moves on: nor all thy piety nor wit shall lure it back to cancel half a line, Nor all thy tears wash out a word of it.

Rubáiyát of Omar Khayyám

This book is dedicated to my eldest brother, Jim Black, who is now sadly unable to tell his own story.

But, mousy, thou art not alone,
in proving foresight may be in vain,
the best laid schemes of mice and men
    go oft astray,
and leave us naught but grief and pain,
    to rend our day

Still thou art blessed compared with me!
The present only touches thee,
but oh, I backward cast my eye
    on prospects drear,
and forward, though I cannot,
    I guess and fear

To a Mouse by Robert Burns

PART ONE

Chapter One

Childhood

My eldest brother, Jim, was born on 24th January 1945, and was christened, James Frances Aloysis Black. I was born three and a half years later on my mother's 25th birthday, 23rd June 1948, in St James' Hospital Balham, London. She would jokingly tell me as I was growing up, that she would never be able to have her 25th birthday without me. My father was from the Broadway area of the Falls Road in Belfast, Northern Ireland and my mother from Armagh City in County Armagh, Northern Ireland. My father's mother, and father, had separated when he, his three brothers (his youngest brother, Joseph, unfortunately died at the age of eighteen from Meningitis) and his two sisters were all grown up, my grandmother remaining in the family home in Amcomri Street. There had never been any scenes of domestic violence or quarrelling, only a strong silence, as they had just stopped speaking to each other. My paternal grandmother, after whom I was named, was a proud, independent, dignified woman, who visited the chapel every day, possibly because it was somewhere to go each day, in much the same way as one goes to work every day, or, possibly, to counteract any feelings of shame or stigma a woman in those days would inevitably have felt living in a small, Catholic community in which divorce was forbidden by the Catholic Church. My mother's father had died on the operating table when she was only eight months old and she was raised by her mother and grandfather until the age of fourteen, when her mother passed away due to cancer of the throat. Her grandfather by all accounts, was quite strict and brought her, as a child, to the early masses every day. She had only one older sister, Mary, who often had to take the responsibility for looking after my mother, which would have proved to be quite a challenge, as my mother was most certainly a free spirit and a bit of a wild child. My mother too, had lost a brother, when he was very young from burns he sustained when he accidently fell into a tin bath of boiling water they would have used for taking a bath. During the war my mother and my father's sister, Bernadette, became good friends while working in an ammunitions factory in London, where my mother was severely reprimanded for lighting up a cigarette in the factory! My Aunt Bernadette, and my mother, went back to Belfast on a holiday and my mother met my father. My mother and my auntie enjoyed their young, carefree days in London, it was war time and the Yanks were over here. They were the glamour girls of their time and very much into style and fashion, especially as my dad's sisters were excellent tailoresses, which is how they also made a living. My dad worked as a fireman during the war, a much more preferable alternative to ever joining the British army. Although my mother could have married a yank, called, Taseman who would have brought her over to America and given her all the "good life" could bestow, so she was to constantly remind my father and us, as we were growing up, that she had settled for my father instead. They married within a few months of meeting one another, on 10th April 1944 and Jim was born on 24th January 1945. Unemployment was high in Belfast and my father, like many Irishmen, "crossed the water" to find work in England. My mother refused to stay with my grandmother in Belfast, saying she was going to be where her husband was and she, Jim and the pram, landed on my father's doorstep, much to my father's surprise. They lived in a rented flat at Gauden road in Balham, and that's how I came to be born in St James' Hospital, Balham, three and a half years after Jim had been born. My mother was good friends with her upstairs neighbour, Rose. There were complaints about the baby's crying, which was put down to me being a yappy baby, the remedy for which was a little nip of whisky in my milk. I kept banging my head against the railings of the cot and it was later discovered that I had a mastoid behind my left ear, which was duly operated on amidst great concern, and then great rejoicing at my discharge from hospital, all safe and sound to go home and have a good night's sleep. I attended a nursery, with, Jim, very often in his role as big brother, even then, often taking care of me, if my mother was working, or not around. My mother and father took the decision to return to Northern Ireland, where "houses that no one wanted" were being advertised, believing that Clapham, which was becoming very overcrowded, was no place to bring up children. We lived for a brief time in a country cottage, outside Armagh. I was still preschool age at this time, but would go down to the little primary school at break time, have my small bottle of milk that school children had in those days, and then go home again. Before meeting my father, or going over to England, my mother had worked in a laundry in Armagh. One day a pair of men's trousers got caught in the large steam rollers and my mother who was laughing, was reprimanded by the manageress in charge, saying.

"Bridget Johnston, would you be laughing if those were your father's trousers?"

The next time a pair of trousers became stuck, my mother, remembering the scolding, tried to rescue the trousers from between the hot rollers and her right hand was severely crushed and burned. She never received the compensation she should rightfully have deserved, but settled out of court. She and my father used this money to buy a bungalow, in Bangor, Northern Ireland. In the period between living in the country outside Armagh and buying the bungalow in Bangor, my father was working as a psychiatric nurse in St Luke's Hospital in Armagh, when my mother suffered what I now believe was a miscarriage. She asked the ambulance men to bring her to St Luke's, and she was kept there on drips until she recovered. My father, unable to cope with it all, arranged for Jim, and I, to go into care in Glenarriff. I remember sitting on a coach beside Jim watching tall pine trees speeding past the window. We arrived at a large grey stone house and were brought into a large, fairly empty room with blackboards on the walls. We were given two green plastic bags with draw-strings containing chalk, which we could use to draw on the blackboards. We both slept in a dormitory with other children, above the door of the dormitory glowed a red night light. We thought this was to let the staff know if we had got out of bed-but we still got out of bed anyway! My father's brothers and sisters were all married, with families of their own by this time, with the exception of my Aunt Bernadette, who remained my maiden Aunt Bernadette until the day she died. My Aunt Bernadette came to see both Jim, and I, at the house, she felt sorry for us and took us home to Belfast with her. Jim was absolutely worshipped by my grandmother and my two aunts, who would spoil him rotten. (My grandmother loved him, but did not believe in spoiling children.) Being the older of the two, Jim formed a very close relationship with my grandmother and totally respected and loved her. I, being the younger, remember my grandmother as an old lady, who had grey hair pulled back in a bun, a little on the stout side and always wearing black.

She would buy us pineapple ice lollies. My father and mother were living in their bungalow in Bangor, when they received the news that my grandmother had died of a stroke. She had baked cakes and bread and was intending to visit us all in Bangor. It was three days before she was discovered by a neighbour, who, suspecting something could be amiss, gained access into the house. My Aunt, Bernadette who was working in England at the time, was unable to make it back in time for the funeral, because she suffered with a terrible phobia of flying and returned home by boat. As all of my father's brothers and sisters were married with their own homes and families, it was agreed that the house in Amcomri Street, previously owned by my grandmother, should be signed over to my Aunt Bernadette, who was the only unmarried sibling. My Aunt, Bernadette wanted to live, and work, in London and agreed to let my mother, father, and Jim, and I, live in the house. They sold their bungalow in Bangor and my father began working, as a progress chaser, in Short Brothers and Harland, the aircraft factory in Belfast. I was now about six years old, and attending Beechmount Avenue Primary School, situated close to my grandmother's house. Just before the death of my grandmother, my mother had given birth to a still born baby, which was perhaps the reason my grandmother was making her way to Bangor and may even have been a contributory factor in bringing on the stroke she had died from. It may even have been the reason for my mother and father's move to my grandmother's house in Belfast; to be close to my father's family. My Aunt Bernadette, returned to Belfast on holiday from England, but received a very cold reception from my mother, who, perhaps, was concerned that my aunt was intending to stay for good and, at best, may want to live with us, or, at worst, may want her house back for herself. So, when my aunt arrived the fire was unlit and the atmosphere unfriendly. Jim, and I, put up the Christmas tree and it was beautifully decorated, with some wrapped Christmas presents already underneath it. My Aunt Bernadette was fiercely independent, but also, like all her family, good natured, warm hearted and very generous. She adored Jim, and both she, and her sister, my Aunt Philomena, either made him, or bought him, the very best clothes, which was their area of expertise: nothing was too good for their golden boy. My aunt, used to living in rented accommodation in London all her working life, bought her own food, which she put in one side of the living room sideboard. One morning as she was making her breakfast, she couldn't find her butter for her toast and asked my mother, if she'd seen her butter? My mother, taking umbrage at the question, said to, Jim, to go round to Bobby Brennan's (the local shop around the corner) and buy a quarter of a pound of butter. When Jim returned with the butter, my mother threw it nastily at, Bernadette, saying, "There's your butter!"

A row inevitably followed, and my mother, who was ironing at the time, had, Bernadette, pinned down on the stairs and was threatening to brand her with the iron. My Aunt Bernadette, unable to remain in the situation went down to her sister's house in Peel Street, off the Falls Road, where she lived with her husband, John, and their children. When my father arrived home from work, he received my mother's version of the story and reacting angrily, he went down to my Aunt Philomena's house and threatened my Aunt Bernadette, in the presence of my Aunt Philomena and her husband. My Aunt Bernadette, clearly unable to return to her own home under the circumstances, was left with no choice but to take legal action against my mother and father in order to have them evicted. My mother and father were given notice of twenty four hours by the court to leave the property. Their belongings were loaded into a small, blue van and we were all moved into the small flat above the dry cleaning shop on Beechmount Avenue, as a temporary, emergency measure to the housing crisis. Shortly after this, Jim, and I, stayed with a friend of my mother's on the Grosvenor Road, which also ran off the Falls Road, as none of my father's family was now on friendly terms with my mother, or father. I don't recall ever seeing either my mother or my father during this time. My mother's friend was cleaning her brown, linoleum covered floors one day and, Jim, and I, had to stay upstairs until the floor had dried. Unable, and afraid to use the toilet, I dirtied myself. Jim helped me to clean myself, in his usual role of protective big brother. After this incident, my mother returned from wherever she was and Jim, and I, went with her to look around Nazareth Lodge, an orphanage in another part of Belfast. My mother was smartly dressed in a blue suit and held my hand while the nun showed us into a large hall, with highly polished wooden floors and lockers on one side. We were all standing in the middle of the hall, when the nun took my hand, and I stood beside her, watching Jim, and my mother, walk the length of the big hall, leaving me alone with the nun. I was about seven years old and it was the first time I had ever had that awful, sick, sinking feeling in the pit of my stomach that indicated to me that all was not well in my childish little world. That night I went to bed at the same time as all the other children in Nazareth Lodge, but I could not stop crying and kept getting out of bed and sitting on the straight back wooden chair, at the side of my bed. The nun came in several times and tried to coax me back into bed, but I was inconsolable. I was teased mercilessly by the other children because of my snoring. All the children would form lines on hair washing day, and any child with nits had their hair shaved off. Once the hair was washed it was rinsed in water smelling of Jeyes Fluid. We were fed bread buttered with margarine and jam, which is a taste I dislike to this day. The older children served out the food to the younger children who were sitting at the table and very often, it was the younger children who received the rotten potatoes. We could go outside to a large grassy area surrounding the orphanage and I would sit alone searching the grass for the four-leafed shamrock that would be the means to having my wish granted to leave that awful place. My mother and father came to visit sometimes, bringing fresh fruit and we gave a banana to the girl with the shaven head. I showed my parents an infected part at the quick of the nail on my thumb, which they brought to the attention of the nun in charge who smacked me across my face once my parents left! Later on I was able to have weekends out with my parents, when we would go by train to visit my mother's sister, Mary, and her husband, John, and their children in Armagh. Other times we would just spend the day out in Belfast, in the large green park area, when I would walk along the low stone walls, holding my father's hand and then jumping off. When these outings ended I hated having to return to Nazareth Lodge and would ask my parents to go to the shop to buy sweets in the hope, that we would miss the bus and that it would be too late to go back to the home. It never worked and it was always with a very heavy heart, that I would hear the bolt on the other side of the heavy wooden, iron studded door being pulled across to open the door to let us back inside, while my parents said goodbye to me in the alcove of the outside door. My parents brought, Jim, and I, to see our new home in Kenard Avenue, showing us the back garden, which backed onto the fields and in full view of the mountain behind. They were so happy and enthusiastic, as they showed us the outside building where the coal would be stored, but they must have been just a little bit dismayed at the moody, sullen seven year old I had become, who could muster no joy, or enthusiasm whatsoever.

The Glen Road was just on the outskirts of the city, at the end of the number twelve bus route. In those days, it was double decker trolley buses and even the smell when passing them, would make me feel sick. The bus terminal ended at St, Teresa's Primary School, which Jim, and I, would attend initially and St Teresa's Catholic Church. The priests' house, a large red brick private property, was also in the church grounds. It was roughly a twenty minute walk to our new home from the bus terminus, if you took the short cut across some fields. Next to Teresa's Primary School was the Reform School run by the Christian Brothers, which had a very long drive up to the building, setting it well back from the main road. Just past the boys' reformatory was the nuns' house, another solid, red brick private house set in beautiful well established gardens with blue and white lilac hanging over the wall. Next to the nuns' house was the Christian Brothers' house, another equally desirable property accommodating those outstanding members of the community, who served the members of their flock living on the other side of the road in their pebble dashed Housing Trust houses. Last, but not least along the Glen Road, was the Ulster Brewery, with its unmistakable aromas of freshly brewed beer emanating around the whole area. It was at the Ulster Brewery that one would cross the road and take the path down to our white pebble dashed Housing Trust Estate, if one opted to take the path rather than cut across the field further down, and jumping the ditch, at the bottom of the path. Jim, and I, attended

St Teresa's Primary School, which was segregated. The boys were treated more harshly than the girls. They would line up in the playground in the morning when the headmaster would inspect their finger nails and shoes. The punishment meted out if either were dirty was severe and they would be slapped on their hands with a short leather strap resembling that used to sharpen an open blade shaving razor. We sat at wooden desks with lift up lids and ink wells, in rows, and we only spoke when asked a question by the teacher, and would be disciplined with a bamboo cane on the hands should it be deemed necessary. However, I was truly blessed with my Primary School Teacher, Miss Ewings. Her sister taught the infants, and often, after I had settled in the school, Miss Ewings would put me in charge of her sister's class, who would be given the task of writing a story. I would stand at the front of the class and when the children would ask me how to spell a particular word, I would write it on the blackboard with a piece of white chalk. I often wonder to this day, if this is what instilled in me my desire to be a teacher. Miss Ewings, taught me right up to sitting the eleven plus, which I would have sat one year later had I been just one week younger. The Eleven Plus was an extremely important examination in those days, as passing it meant proceeding to a Grammar School and failing it meant remaining at the Primary School and sitting the Leaving Certificate. Many of the children were promised bicycles and watches by their parents, if they passed the examination, but my father simply said to me, "Margaret, just do your best, and if you don't pass, then there's something you still have to learn."

This took a tremendous amount of pressure off me and I sat the exam, totally pressure free, and passed it. The headmistress of the school was called Miss O'Reilly and she was required to send off all of the birth certificates of the pupils sitting the examination. As I had been born in London, my mother had to send to London for the birth certificate, which was, therefore, later than all the others. My mother brought the birth certificate to the school, when it arrived, only to be told by Miss O'Reilly, that she had already sent all the others off and it wasn't worth sending it separately, as I wouldn't pass the exam anyway. My mother said, "Well, she'll take her chances like everyone else," and insisted that she send the certificate. Out of a class of forty pupils three passed the exam. One was border line and I was one of the three who passed! Well done mum! I filled in my own application form for the Grammar School of my choice, stating first, second and third choices. In the street around the corner from me were three sisters, who wore the green and white uniform of the Dominican College at Fort William Park, just off the Antrim Road in North Belfast, where most of the professional middle classes lived. It meant a much longer journey, taking two buses, than, if I had opted to attend St Dominic's, on the Falls Road, wearing a wine and white uniform, but I put Fort William as my first choice, as I wanted to attend the same school as the three sisters around the corner from me, as they seemed so much more aloof and middle class, and I wanted to be just like them. I also sat on our brown leather living room settee, just before the exam results, and I recited to Our Lady the Memorare prayer requesting, with a heart-felt passion, that I would pass the exam and my prayers were answered. I didn't seriously expect my first choice of school to be necessarily granted, given the posh area in which it was situated, but I was given a place in the school of my first choice. Miss Ewings gave me the book, "What Katie Did Next," as a leaving present. Passing the Eleven Plus, Examination and attending the Grammar School of my choice in those days, were most definitely, key factors in what Margaret did next. Jim had also passed the Eleven Plus and was attending St Mary's Grammar School, at the bottom of the Falls Road, which was run by the Christian Brothers. The Christian Brothers were renowned for their strictness and I think Jim's Grammar School experience was less happy than mine. My mother took a domestic position at the house occupied by the same Christian Brothers, which I don't think, Jim, found to be helpful to his secondary Grammar School experience, as he believed that it influenced how they perceived him and treated him at school. It was at the age of seven and a half that I stopped believing in Father Christmas. My mother was in hospital as she was expecting my brother, Peter, who was born on 10th January 1956. Jim, and I, found our Christmas presents hidden at the top of the airing cupboard, mine was a nurse's uniform. It didn't spoil the joy and excitement that we felt on Christmas Eve, getting up just after our parents had put the presents into our stockings and had left the room. There were oranges, nuts, and novelty bars of soap, which Jim bit into, thinking it was white chocolate, and we laughed hysterically, when we realized that it was soap. My baby brother came home shortly after Christmas and was the best ever Christmas present for me. He had a head of tight blonde curls, much the same as I myself had had as a baby, and, for me, it like having my own little Tiny Tears doll. I would hold him, and tell my mother that the baby was sweating, except that he wasn't sweating, he was wetting. When he was a little older he would sit on the living room floor and we gave him the pots and wooden spoons, or dried peas in a closed jar to play with. None of us ever saw any shop toys, after Peter, was born, but it never mattered, we knew how to make our own entertainment, that cost nothing and provided us with hours of fun. We had no television, so, instead my mother often listened to programmes and plays on the radio, while she sat clicking away with knitting needles or crocheting. She made baby nightdresses from flannelette material by hand and even made me a dress which had all the capital cities of Europe in the pattern, but this got torn all around the waist, when I went on the gider the boy's had made from a set of pram wheels onto which they had fixed an axle, I was, in fact, a tomboy. All the boys and girls in our street played together, or separately, at times, but we never knew what it was like to be bored. We drew numbers with chalk on the paving stones and played hop-scotch, or using one long skipping rope, formed a line and took our turns at jumping into the turning rope, singing as we played. We played cricket, using the metal plate at the bottom of the lamp post as the wickets that we had to hit with the ball to get the person out. (I was always sent to ask old Mrs Martin, if we could have our ball back, when it went into her garden because she liked me) The boys played hurling, the Irish equivalent of hockey, but with different rules, on the little green in the middle of the street and we played our version of netball, which just involved the girls passing to each other to keep the ball from the boys. We would have running races at the little green, between the boys and girls starting at the lamppost. One would run one way, and the other would run in the opposite direction, to see who got back to the lamppost first. Often, the men, without employment, would stand at their front doors, watching us and cheering us on. I was the fastest runner amongst the girls and, Seamus Corner, who lived three doors down from me, was the fastest amongst the boys. We were very competitive and there was always tremendous cheering and excitement, at these times. We played with hula hoops and spinning tops using the string to keep the top spinning, games of marbles also were popular amongst us all, alongside yo-yos and single skipping ropes, but, most important of all, we all played together and formed our friendships. It was in Kenard Avenue, that I became best friends with Breda Drugan, whose family had moved from Hannahstown further up the Glen Road and we remain best friends to this day. If we weren't playing street games, we were up the back fields jumping across the ditches, or swinging across them with a rope. We lit fires and baked potatoes in the ashes, or climbed the mountain behind us and caught river trout in the mountain streams. We would go to the Half-Moon Lake, which was in a wooded area of small foxgloves and Rhododendrons and catch tadpoles or climb the big horse chestnut tree to gather the chestnuts for the games of conkers, or go into Farmer O Hare's Orchard to nick apples, my cousin, Gerard Black, would later marry his daughter, Anne. We were often rough and played "games" such as pulling one another's hair to see who would give in first or bend each other's fingers back until one would surrender. Our survival skills became finely, and naturally, tuned and we grew in confidence, fitness and strength, we learned to hold our own in any situation. There was one boy in our street, ginger haired, Anthony Rossbottom, who was an only child with over protective parents, who wouldn't let him out to play with the rough children. They would pay us a shilling, (the going rate was a penny for a penny chew,) to go a message, that meant a fifteen minute walk to the main road to the shops and a fifteen minute walk back, just in case Anthony would get run over. One unfortunate day, Anthony was allowed out to play and the boys went to "the six-stitcher," to get conkers. Anthony climbed the tree; he fell, and, unfortunately, suffered permanent brain damage. Even as children, we thought it was better to build ones survival instincts from experiencing all the little knocks, cuts and bruises that the children get while growing. Tragically, two children drowned in the half-moon lake although they weren't from our street. A young brother fell in while catching tadpoles and his older sister jumped in to save him and they both drowned, as neither of them could swim. Ironically, their father had won a silver cup in swimming championships. The Primary School closed on the day of their funeral and we later learned, that the mother never recovered from the loss and tragedy, she continued to wash their clothes and hang them out to dry; she also set the table for their dinner each day. There was also the story of the mad women, who had kept her son in a hen house. When the authorities found the boy, he was unable to talk or stand up straight to walk; he was also imitating the same characteristics as the hens.

My mother went on to have Raymond, eleven months after, Peter, and my sister, Maureen, (Christened, Mary) two years later, and last but not least, my younger sister, Angela, four years after Maureen. The family almost naturally divided into two parts-my father, my mother, Jim and me and "the other four," (the steps and stairs) who were born so close to each other. My mother was never really happy with her life in Kenard Avenue, on a Housing Trust Estate and would always talk about her life in London, with, Jim, and me saying how different and better it had been: she felt she had come down in the world.

*My childhood friend Brenda Drugan and I
in Carnaby Street, London, 1969*

Chapter Two

The Adolescent Years

When I was thirteen years old, my mother bought a piece of material in multiples of blues and pinks, and she sent me down to my Aunt Philomena in Peel Street, to ask her if she would make me a dress from the material. (This was the first time I had seen my Aunt Philomena since my mother's fight with my, Aunt Bernadette.) My Aunt Philomena agreed to make the dress and this was how my mother and my Aunt Philomena became friends again. My mother had also found me a job, during the summer holidays, in the seaside resort of Bangor, in a guest house called Chatsworth House. I would live in and have all my meals and earn £5 per week. I had Thursday afternoons off, when I would travel home to Belfast and give my mother the £5. I never told her about the tips I would get from the guests and would keep these for myself or she'd have had those too! Some Thursdays, I would call into my Aunt Philomena's on the way back to Bangor and stay overnight, getting into the same bed as my three cousins and then go on to Bangor in the morning. I remember on one of these visits back home, making my mother a mint-flavoured instant whip dessert, (similar to Angels' Delight) as she had had all of her teeth taken out at the dentists, because she had pyorrhea of the gums, due to all the Woodbine cigarettes she had smoked all of her life and now needed to be fitted with a new set of false teeth. She was only thirty eight. It was at this time that I, too, thought it might be "cool" to start smoking and bought some Players cigarettes to smoke on the top of the bus on the way home from Bangor. However, I had always heard the other kids say how inhaling the smoke made one turn green and made them sick and so, being afraid, I never did inhale a cigarette and never did get addicted to nicotine. I'd like to say that I had learned a lesson from my mother's experience or that I was health conscious, but it wouldn't be true. When I got home, I was so frightened of being caught with the cigarettes, that I threw them out of the top bedroom window into the back garden. One of the kids found them and brought them into my mother, who thought it was her birthday and smoked them without asking any questions as to how they'd got there in the first place. The guest house was run by two sisters, (one was mentally challenged and threw the odd fit) and another younger girl and myself were the additional staff taken on to help out in the busy summer period. One of the male guests asked me out to go to 'Old Time' dancing taking place at the sea front. I thought this would be good fun and he was very young and handsome and obviously thought, that I was older than I actually was. I agreed to go and got dressed up in the colourful dress my Aunt Philomena had made for me. He never turned up at the arranged time and place and I think someone must have tipped him off as to my real age. I was often hungry with the sea air and the small amounts of food I was given at the guest house, and so I would go in my time off in the evenings to the sea front and buy fish and chips with my tip money and play my favourite songs, "I Don't Know Why I Love You But I Do," by Frogman Henry, and "Halfway to Paradise," by Billy Fury on the juke box. Some Saturdays, Jim, and I would go down to the cinema at Broadway and wait for the exit doors after the first showing to open. We would then bunk in and sit in the front row seats waiting for the next film to come on. We saw Lorna Doone, The Girl with Green Eyes, Snow White and

The Seven Dwarfs and many cowboy and indian films, cheering on the goodies and booing the baddies. It was around this time that I would go to see Bill Haley and the Comets In, "Rock Around the Clock" and the cinema really did rock, as the seats were put up and everyone stood singing, clapping and dancing as Rock and Roll began to take off. I was later to watch Elvis Presley films, each film about eight times, in the same cinema. I pasted pictures of him on the wall on the inside of the built in wardrobe in the bedroom and told the younger siblings, that I was going out with him and that he landed his private plane on the coal shed roof, when he came to pick me up, (and they believed me bless them.)

There was a Kindergarten beside the Grammar School that I attended, my mother got a place there for my brother, Peter, also, so I brought him to school with me, and dropped Raymond, off to my Aunt Philomena, who would be waiting at the bus stop on the Falls Road and pick him up again on my way home from school. I was expected to have the fire lit, the dinner prepared and the house clean and tidy before my mother would return home from the job she had taken in the kitchen of Purdysburn Hospital on the other side of Belfast. It was while she was working in the hospital's kitchen that my mother cut her fingers on her left hand, while using the bread and butter machine. The machine was switched off, but the blades were still going around. The doctor who attended to my mother, on seeing her other hand that had been injured in the laundry accident, and believing that she had not been properly compensated for the injury, got her an Industrial Injuries Pension that remained with her until the day that she died. My dad's father had returned from England and was being nursed by my cousin, Patricia, on my mother's side of the family, in a small hospital in Holywood, Northern Island. He had had his leg amputated due to gangrene and I went with my father to visit him. He was later moved to a large nursing home in Beechmount, close to where my Aunt, Bernadette had her home in Amcomri Street. I went once again to visit him with my dad, who brought him a quarter bottle of Black and White Whisky. My grandfather eventually moved into the home he had shared with my grandmother, which was now Bernadette's home, and Bernadette took care of him until he died. My grandfather's funeral was the first funeral I had ever attended at about the age of thirteen. He was to be buried in Milltown Cemetery, on the Falls Road, where my grandmother had also been buried-united in death, if not in life. There was heavy snow on the ground and the heavy coffin had to be brought into the graveyard on a trailer. I remember standing at the side of the grave and hearing the thud of the small amount of earth that was thrown onto the coffin below. I can remember how all the mourners had assembled at the pub just opposite the graveyard, where the Falls road divides into a fork in the road, and leading up to the Glen Road, where we were now living, and the other to lower road leading up to Andersonstown, waiting for the hearse to arrive. I was sent down to Amcomri Street to stay with my Aunt Bernadette, whom everyone felt should not be alone in the house at this time. I recall her kindness and caring nature, even at this very sad time. She had put white flannelette sheets on my bed and a hot water bottle to make the bed all cosy and warm. She told me the story of how, after her mother had died she was lying in bed one night and she felt the physical weight of her mother in the bed beside her, and when she turned around, she saw her mother crying in the bed beside her. Bernadette gave me a beautiful blue, blazer style woollen jacket as I was leaving. My dad's two sisters were the salt of the earth, with hearts of pure gold. They were the epitome of decency and kindness and I was very happy, that they were back in my life. After my brother, Raymond, was born, when I was about eight and a half, the whole family went on holiday to Tyrella Beach in Northern Ireland, from where it was possible to see the Coast of Scotland on a clear day. My parents had rented a wooden style, self-catering holiday cottage and Jim, and I, played with some of the other children on the beach. They had a black rubber ring which I got into and paddled out into the water with. I mistakenly, believed, that I was paddling towards the shore, when, in fact, I was going further and further out to sea. I began to panic, when I could no longer see the bottom, but only large dark rocks below. When I looked back to the shoreline, my mother was just a speck on the shore, holding my baby brother, Raymond, in her arms. I began shouting to those on the shoreline, "Oh my poor mother, Oh my poor father!" fearing that I might drown and never see them again. Jim, who was about twelve then, and another boy began swimming out in a bid to try and reach me. Two men with a small rowing boat rowed out and picked me up and took me back in the boat. That evening, back in our holiday cottage, we could hear the noise of helicopters overhead. It did occur to me that my little dramatic incident might well make the TV news. Tragically, however, the helicopters were searching for three generations of men from the same family, the grandfather, the father and the son, who had gone out in a small fishing boat which had capsized and all three were drowned. It was said, that they were unable to save themselves, because of the weight of the large fishing boots that they were wearing. I never did learn to swim, as my father would never let me go to the local swimming baths with the boys, fearing for my safety; although he said, it was the problems I had with my sinuses. My father, and Jim, started a little business venture selling tea, coffee, soft drinks and sandwiches from a mobile tea stall, which they parked on the beach. They went out one evening leaving me alone in the caravan! I heard what I took to be footsteps outside the caravan, (which would have been impossible as we were parked on the sandy beach.) I kept telling myself to get up and grab one of the big knives that were being used for the sandwiches so that I could defend myself, if attacked, but I just couldn't move; I was frozen with fear! Then, I heard my father's voice outside calling my name to let me know he would open the door now that he was back. I think, if he had just opened the door, I would have died from fright. The noise I had heard was probably seagulls walking on the roof of the caravan.

When my dad was working in Short Brothers and Harland, (the aircraft factory,) as a progress chaser, every Friday was payday and we would eagerly await his return home. He walked straight and upright and we would see him coming along the street wearing his large Mackintosh coat and we would run to meet him. Once indoors, we would rummage through his pockets to get the big bags of loose sweets he brought home for us every Friday without fail. I started my periods around the age of eleven and my mother must have thought it was the appropriate time for, Jim, and me, to receive proper sex education. My mother brought home two little booklets from the doctor, one for boys and one for girls, and gave them to us to read. The one for girls began, "Our lady was a virgin and a mother," and went on to talk about respect for our bodies, ourselves and the opposite sex. It did make reference to the relevant body parts and the part they played in procreation. All the boys and girls gathered together on the green and the boys read the girls booklets and the girls read the boys booklet just to add further interest to this already interesting topic. I hated Saturday evenings, as it involved all the necessary preparations for Mass on Sundays. Sunday best clothes had to be washed and ironed and all the Sunday best shoes polished. We were all expected to fast from midnight on Saturday until receiving Holy Communion on Sunday. I always attended the last Mass at twelve on Sunday, as I had the joy of seeing all the others off to the earlier masses and then preparing the fresh vegetable soup and the fresh vegetables for the roast Sunday dinner. We never missed Mass because we were afraid the neighbours would talk, if they didn't see us there. It also provided a good opportunity to see someone's new Sunday outfit, or new Sunday hat; it was obligatory to attend Mass with one's head covered. The more fashion conscious of us wore mantillas, which we could throw over our heads before going into the chapel, and take off, just as soon as we came out. I would attend the last Mass every Sunday. As the Mass would be ending, I could hear the priest's voice fading into the distance, as he recited the Hail Holy Queen and I would faint and be carried out of the chapel, sat down on a hard chair and told to hold my head between my legs until I felt better. After returning from Mass we would have a big Sunday breakfast of fried bacon, sausage, eggs, black pudding (which I didn't like) potato bread, soda bread, wheaten bread, scotch pancakes, tomatoes and apples, in fact anything that could be fried for a big fry up!

We would have our fresh vegetable soup made with brisket of beef, barley, leaks, parsnips, celery, carrots and chopped parsley, then our roast Sunday dinner. We always had dessert on Sunday, usually jelly and custard, but not on other days of the week. My mother would do a lot of home baking often making big trays of currant squares, (bread pudding between pastry cut into squares) in order to use any stale bread, that may be left over. Mother made her fruit cakes and small buns, which she one day hid in cake tins under the bed in my room, which she hoped would stop us diving into the cupboards and devouring them all. When I got back from school and went into my bedroom, I could smell the home baked cakes and found them under the bed; I duly helped myself to a large slice of fruit cake and my mother had to find another hiding place. Fridays were always fish days and we would have Ardglass herrings from the seaside town of Ardglass, purchased from the vans that came around the streets. If my mother couldn't afford the herrings, we would have "champ" the name given by the Irish to this traditional Irish dish of boiled mashed potatoes, with lots of butter, milk and chopped scallions, (spring onions) instead. Other vans would come round our streets, delivering bread, and small bread, (soda farls, potato bread, treacle bread) and cakes, (Paris buns, snowballs and iced diamonds) we had these small cakes with cups of tea in lieu of puddings at any time in the day. I was studying Domestic Science at school (as it had seemed the only sensible option, between Science, and Domestic Science, because I was expected to become a good wife and mother at some stage in the future and would be more useful.) I enjoyed the cookery element, but was totally useless at sewing, (I clearly hadn't inherited my aunts' tailoring skills.) I would go down to my Aunt Philomena at the end of the school year, so that she could finish off the blouse or skirt I was making as we were expected to wear and show off the finished item. As I showed an aptitude for cookery, I was then able to help my mother at home and often made the meals we would have. There were a few Republican families, who lived in and around our estate and the notorious Price Sisters, who would go on to bomb The Old Bailey in London, lived in number 39 in our street. Unlike the rest of us, they did Irish dancing and were often seen with their hair in white strips of cloth to make the ringlets for their long blonde hair. On Sunday they would be out in the street in their brightly coloured blue or yellow satin dresses with their ringlets of curls tied up in satin ribbons. Claire Price was the eldest sister, and was the same age as me. She attended St Dominic's Grammar School on the Falls Road. Dolores was the second of the three sisters and was ginger-haired, and, Marion, who was the youngest of the three, had long blonde hair. We all had nick names, and Claire, was given the name Lulu Bells. I had been given the nick name Maggie Geeks and my mother indignantly told the others, that if she had wanted me called Maggie, she would have christened me Maggie! The Price sisters' aunt would visit them wearing black clothes and glasses. It was believed that she had only one hand, having lost the other in a bomb making accident during the last 'Troubles' of The Easter Rising, of 1916. My father never encouraged Nationalist tendencies in, Jim, or I, and would always tread the middle path. Gerry Adams lived around the corner from my Aunt Philomena in Peel Street, off the Falls Road, and my cousin Mary later recalled how she was washing herself at the kitchen sink one day, when Gerry Adams ran past the window over the back yard walls, making his escape from the British Army. She confessed to having a crush on him and was only sorry that he didn't have the time to stop a while and drop in on her.

Chapter Three

Jim Gets his First Camera

Jim had been in trouble a few times that I can remember. Once he had kept two white mice in the electricity cupboard and they made a hole in the corner of the wall and we had to coax them out with a piece of cheese. I accidently walked on one of his mice and killed it. I tried to resuscitate it by putting it in some cold water. I then put the dead mouse back in the Oxo tin in which Jim was keeping it. When Jim found the dead mouse, I found myself on my back on the floor for "having drowned" his mouse! He threw a stone one day breaking one of next doors windows and the neighbour complained to my dad, who apologized, bought a new pane of glass and put the window in for him. Jim would bunk of school some days and on one of these days, I bunked off with him. He also shared the same bedroom as me and one night got into my bed and touched me inappropriately. The following morning I told my two parents. I don't know if it was this incident, or the bunking off school incident, but my dad took the strap to Jim, and there was an almighty row in the house, after which Jim went to stay with my Aunt Bernadette in Amcomri Street. Bernadette bought, Jim, his first Pentax Camera, and Jim, with the help and support of, Father Laverty, a priest in St Teresa's Parish, Jim, began taking professional photographs of the children, who were making their First Holy Communion and selling them to their parents. Jim left St Mary's Grammar School at the age of fifteen without passing the Junior Grammar School Certificate. He went to work for a photography company in Belfast and soon experienced problems in getting an equity card, because of a closed shop union there, closed to Catholics that is. This was his first taste of the religious bigotry and discrimination that existed in Northern Island, mainly due to Northern Ireland politics. Catholic Schools had kept their denominational rights, so there was the segregation of schools, as well as the segregation of housing into Catholic and Protestant areas. Catholics could easily be identified by prospective employers by simply asking, "Which school did you attend, and where do you live?"

To this day, if one Irish person were to ask another Irish person either of these questions, there would be an immediate wariness and suspicion, because it would be viewed as a loaded question. Catholics knew they had to be better educated than Protestants to have any hope of obtaining any kind of employment. Unemployment in Northern Ireland was eleven per cent and there were highly educated bus conductors on the buses in Belfast, and so the Protestant work ethic was inculcated into the Northern Irish people, especially the Catholics. My father, like many of the Catholic men in Northern Ireland, feared the stigma that was associated with joining the dole queue and would go to England, like the many others who, "crossed the water," to seek work and try to keep two homes going. At the age of fifteen, Jim left Belfast and went in the first instance to live with my Uncle John (my father's youngest brother) and his English wife, June, who lived in Woking with their family. Redundancies were also taking place in Short Brothers and Harland and my father opted to jump before he was pushed and went over to England to be with, Jim, who wasn't really happy staying with his relatives in Woking. My sister, Maureen, was born on April 22nd 1959 two months before my eleventh birthday, and with both, Jim, and my father over in England, my mother came more and more to rely on me, the eldest girl, to share the domestic burden. My mother had to rely on the money my father would send from England, together with any money she, herself, could earn from her job in Purdysburn Hospital, and a part time job she obtained, as a domestic help to a doctor, who lived in a private bungalow on the private road which ran parallel to our estate about a fifteen minute walk away. She often brought me with her to the doctor's house, so that I could help her with the domestic chores. I also did some babysitting for a family at the end of our street and earned a few bob too, which all went into the family kitty, without question. My father sent me two pounds in a birthday card from England and that too was confiscated by my mother, who believed that the family kitty took precedence over any birthday present, I could possibly wish to buy. During this period my relationship with my mother became more and more difficult, but I was high spirited and always stood my ground with her. I would say things to her such as, "Hell will never be full until you're in it!"

The sad thing was I meant it. My mother herself must have known that she was not being fair, or reasonable, in fact she was downright demanding and difficult and never satisfied no matter what I did and she would confidently and knowingly admit that I was her "butt." There was one particular day, when I could stand no more and I very calmly, and coolly, took the decision to take an overdose of pills. I took the small brown bottle of pills from the cupboard, I didn't know what they were, possibly paracetamol with a powdery yellow coating, I emptied them from the bottle onto the stairs and swallowed them one by one, until they were all gone, but I just vomited them all up again. The doctor was called and my mother was told that I should rest in bed and have a lot of fluids. My father returned home, and, as was his way with me, we went out for a walk, during which I told him all about the overdose incident. No more was ever said about it, (at least not in my presence) but my father remained at home and Jim remained in England. The times that Jim would come back home for a holiday were always a time of great excitement and rejoicing, just like, The Return of the Prodigal Son. The pot of fresh vegetable soup would be made, the chicken stuffed and roasted, with potatoes and the fresh vegetables prepared and cooked to serve with the roast chicken and gravy. My mother would have baked her cakes and buns before his arrival and there would have been a pudding to follow the dinner. Jim would have been met at the airport by my dad and we would all wait, in excitement and anticipation, for his arrival home. I was sitting my Junior Grammar School Certificate Examinations on one of these occasions, when Jim was back on holiday. Jim arrived home on a Vespa Scooter and thrupence in his pocket. On the day of my French Examination I overslept and would never have made it to school in time to sit the exam, so Jim took me on the back of the scooter in the pouring rain, with brown, muddy water running down the sides of the pavements; nonetheless I made it in time to sit the exam. Had I not sat that exam, I would have failed the whole Grammar School Certificate, as it was one of the required six subjects I had to pass. As it turned out, French was the one subject I passed with a distinction, fortunately for me. After passing the Junior Grammar School Certificate of Northern Ireland in 1963, I returned to the Dominican College at Fort William Park, to study for the Senior Grammar School Certificate, which required that I pass a minimum of five subjects in order to pass the whole examination. My younger sister, Angela, was born on March 24th 1963 and my father had once again returned to

England to work. My mother was suddenly ill with sciatica, and the doctor came out to see her. As I tried to put her clothes on she was in agony. The doctor had her admitted to Musgrove Park Hospital for a period of six weeks of traction, (bed rest on a hard surface the treatment for sciatica at the time.)

I took the six weeks away from school to look after Peter, aged 8, Raymond aged 7, Maureen aged 4, and, Angela aged 8 months. My father wrote asking me, if I wanted him, and Jim, to come home. I wrote back saying no I didn't, as they would only be another two to look after. I made fresh apple tarts with sugar pastry to take to the hospital and bought my mother's twenty Woodbines that she couldn't go without. I had to leave my 8 month old sister, Angela with my 8yr old brother, Peter, as she made strange with everyone else, while I walked the half hour walk to the hospital where I would sit at the side of my mother's bed giving her a detailed account of how I had spent the house keeping money. I would then walk the half hour walk back home again, as there were no buses from where we lived to the hospital, and so, walking was the quickest way to get there. My mother returned home after the six weeks and, as we lay in her double bed together, I told her I was glad she was home, as an intruder had been spotted in the back fields and I was frightened. My mother got out of bed and closed all of the windows in the house, checked all the doors were locked and couldn't get to sleep all night, while I lay snoring my head off, now that she was back home! I decided not to return to school, because I didn't think that I could catch up on all of the subjects that I had missed, especially the Maths, with which I was already struggling, before my six week leave of absence. I felt I would just be wasting two years, which at the age of fifteen seemed like a lifetime because I knew I had to pass all five subjects to pass the examination, and I didn't think that I could do it. When I went to see the nuns at the school to inform them of my decision, and ask them to sign the necessary forms, they tried to persuade me to stay on, but to no avail, my mind was made up. I got a job selling scarfs in a large department store in Royal Avenue, Belfast and on my sixteenth birthday the manageress in charge of the flower department sent me a small bouquet of pink carnations, the first flowers I had ever received in my whole life and I was absolutely thrilled. I had given flowers to my Primary School teacher, Miss Ewings, bunches of lilacs that I had nicked from the gardens of the nuns' house, that were hanging over the garden walls. I'm sure she knew that they were nicked, but graciously accepted them, nevertheless, in the spirit in which they were intended. I was now sixteen, growing up, and had received my first small bouquet of flowers.

My father returned from England, once again, and took me to the Careers' Office, in Belfast. I was adamant, that I did not want to open another text book, or sit in an office; I wanted to be active, not sedentary. I had enjoyed cookery at school, and so it was decided that I would attend an interview at Short Brothers and Harland, (the same place my father had worked, as a progress chaser) as they were taking on three trainee chefs, in their catering kitchens, who would have the opportunity to sit the City and Guilds 147 Examination in Basic Cookery, as well as gaining invaluable experience of working alongside the chefs and cooks, who would be involved in their training. When I arrived for the interview, I was shown into a small, rectangular room, which had hard wooden chairs around each of the four walls, on which sat approximately, forty, sixteen year old boys and girls, who were all hoping to be selected for the three apprenticeships that were being offered.

When the time of the interview arrived, I was shown into a larger room where the three persons, who comprised the panel of interviewers, were seated, a little distance apart from each other. I sat on a hard wooden chair some distance from them, facing the highly polished table, behind which they sat. They took it in turns to ask me different questions, which I answered as honestly as I could; the interview then came to an end. Short Brothers and Harland selected two Catholic apprentices, a boy called Henry, myself, and one Protestant girl, also called Margaret. The catering manager was an Englishman, called, Mr. Price, which is a very likely reason why, two, out of the three apprentices selected that day were Catholics. Had the catering manager been a Northern Irish Protestant, I doubt very much either I, or Henry, would ever have been selected. Mr. Price, being an Englishman, had probably made the selection based on qualifications obtained, and merit, and not on, "where one lived, or which school one had attended."

I began my apprenticeship in the management canteen, earning two pounds eight shillings in the first year, which rose to five pounds at the beginning of the third year of my three year contract. I paid fifteen shillings for my bus fares, per week, gave one pound to my mother for my keep and had the remaining thirteen shillings for myself. It was the first time that I had ever mixed with Protestants, due to the segregated housing policy of Northern Ireland, which was political, as well as being religious. It ensured, that the Protestant Unionist Party, would always hold the majority of seats, in the Stormont Government, because of the Gerrymandering system, that ensured, that even if the Catholics were ever in the majority in Northern Ireland, (and of course this was a strong possibility, as they were breeding like rabbits) they would never obtain a majority of seats in Parliament. Businessmen had ten votes each.

I mixed well with everyone, who worked there, whether Catholic or Protestant and the craic was great. On July 12th the Orangemen made their parades through predominantly Catholic areas wearing their orange sashes and banging their drums, to commemorate King William's crossing the Boyne River and defeating the Catholics. On this same day in the kitchen, the mainly Protestant waitresses would wind up little cottages, that played the Orangemen's upbeat tunes and I sang along with them. They were fine tunes, but what they represented most certainly wasn't fine, especially, to the Catholics, who had to endure these triumphal marches of domination through their areas every year. The apprentices all attended Rupert Stanley College in Belfast, two afternoons a week on day release, and were transported there by mini bus from work. We clocked in by eight o'clock in the morning, if we were late by more than three minutes, the ink on our cards showed up as red. Being late more than three times in a week, meant a visit to Mr. Price to be reprimanded. The vegetable cooks made sure that they always arrived at work very early, and after clocking in, made their breakfast of tea and toast, while others such as, Ellen, one of the cooks, would arrive all flustered, late by a minute or two and start working immediately, giving truth to the saying, "get the name of an early riser and you can sleep all day."

At the age of seventeen, I had started going to the dances in the city, where the big show bands would be playing. My friend, Breda, and I, got very friendly with the Hilton Show Band from Newry, and we became "groupies," who started following them around Ireland, hitchhiking to wherever they were playing. The band would give us a lift back in their bus as far as Newry, and we would hitchhike on to Belfast, arriving in the early hours of the morning. Breda's mother remarked that I looked yellow, as I suffered badly with travel sickness, as well as lack of sleep. The cooks I worked with loved to hear about all our adventures when we were hitchhiking, (there were many that kept us in stitches long afterwards.) One of the cooks, Mary Mcveigh, belonged to the Legion of Mary and was unmarried. If the soup caught or any other problem arose, she would always say, "Oh, well, there's nothing worse than a bad marriage." Mary said that I would make a good nurse, but I knew, that I wouldn't, because I would take the job home with me and couldn't bear to see the suffering of others. The chef was a Catholic, and often hit the cooking sherry bottle and would be very tipsy at work. There were days, when he would be cooking at Mr. Price's private home and the cooks would be trying to get him sober and help him get into his clean white chef's trousers and jacket. The management canteen cooked all the high class food, such as lobster, which would be delivered live and would be walking around the yard with their pincers closed with elastic bands. Before going into the boiler of boiling water, they were hosed down; they were then heard screaming for a few minutes before turning red. Red indicated that they were properly cooked and ready for the beautifully decorated silver platters that they were put upon, ready for the dining room. All the important visitors to Short Brother and Harland were entertained in the management canteen, which had table clothes, good silver cutlery, dining services, and silver service waitresses, I can recall the Admiral of Tokyo being one such V.I.P. Young trainee pilots would often use this dining service and the waitresses would tell me about the young and handsome ones, that would make a perfect match for me.

To me smoked salmon tasted like kippers (then, not now) and I would go down to the workers' canteen, just down the corridor from the management canteen and ask the chef there to keep me a plate of Irish stew that the workers would be getting that day. Some days there would be large trays of roast beef and other nice meats left over; rather than waste it, the chefs would always tell me to wrap it up and take it home, as I came from a big family. My mother was always pleased and grateful to have this food, as it helped feed her ever growing family. Breda, and I, also obtained evening jobs at the weekends in a Wimpy Bar as waitresses. At the end of the evening, we were required to empty out all of the sugar bowls, tomato sauce bottles, salt and pepper pots and ensure that they were all cleaned and filled for the next day. One evening the male teacher from Rupert and Stanley College, which I was attending for my City and Guilds, 147 course, came into the Wimpy Bar while Breda, and I, were working there, I took his order and served him. When he was finished I gave him his bill, but didn't charge him for everything he'd had. At the end of the evening the manageress of the Wimpy Bar, who had checked his bill on leaving, fired me. I told Breda, that I had been fired and she said, "Well, if you're leaving, then I'm leaving too!"

Breda then promptly got her coat. We were very happy not to have to go to the salt and pepper pots and laughed all the way home. I think that was one job that neither of us really minded losing. At that time, Breda was working in a shoe shop in the city, she would tell me how customers would try on a pair of shoes and would then say that they were a little tight. Breda would say that she would take them into the back room and stretch them (by putting the broom handle into the shoe.) Taking the shoes back to the waiting customer, Breda would get them to try them again, and the customer would say that they fitted much better. Breda's boss would say to her,

"I mightn't always be right, but I'm never wrong!"

For Breda, and me, the two years of work, and following the Hilton Band were two of our happiest years in Belfast. My relationship with my mother was still difficult, as often I would try and hide a pair of new shoes that I had bought from her, but she would spot me going up the stairs with them and call, displeased that I was spending money on myself, that she needed. Very often, when I was going out, she would provoke some argument, that would have me in tears and put a downer on the evening, before I'd even left the house. My Aunt Philomena was brilliant, she once measured me and after she had taken the measurements, she would come to visit us and, in a matter of fact way, hand me a beautifully cut dress that she had made from a Vogue pattern and remnant of material purchased from the Protestant Skankill Road she'd have walked to. On one occasion she presented me with one dress in white, and another in navy blue, on another occasion a beautifully tailored grey skirt. I would also buy dresses from catalogues and pay weekly, but much to my embarrassment, going to a dance one particular night, I walked into the dance hall only to come face to face with another girl wearing the same dress with small black spots on a white background. At the age of eighteen I took my City and Guilds 147 Examination; I would sit on the steps at the bottom of our garden path and look up at the lights of the airplanes passing overhead and wonder where they were going. I knew there was a big wide world beyond Belfast and I wanted to know how people in other countries lived. I knew we only had one life, and that we should see as much of life as we could in that one short life that we had. On one of his visits back from England, I was telling, Jim, how I was feeling, and he said, that he would speak to my father, about me moving over to London to stay with him. I didn't think that my father would agree to this, but to my complete and utter surprise, he did. I then thought that Short Brothers and Harland wouldn't release me from my three year contract, as an apprentice with them, but they did, and so I was unbelievably free to cross the water just as my mother, father, and Jim, had done before me.

PART TWO

Chapter One

Crossing the Water

I was to travel with Jim, to Heathrow Airport in November 1966, and, even before I had left, I'd bought, the Tom Jones, record, "The Green, Green Grass of Home," and was playing it over and over again. It was the first time I would travel outside Belfast, as a grown up and the first time I ever flew by plane and didn't suffer from travel sickness, because of the excitement of it all. My Aunt Bernadette was living in a large bedsit on the Kingston Road, Teddington, Middlesex and Jim was living in a bed-sit in a respectable suburban semi-detached house in Twickenham Road, Teddington. Jim had two frying pans, that he used for cooking; one for the eggs, (to keep the oil clean) and one for the bacon. The rest of the time he would eat with his friends from the college he was attending in the evenings (for photography) in Joe's café in Teddington. Initially I stayed with my Aunt Bernadette, who was living in an older property with much bigger rooms and the use of the kitchen. Jim, and I, later rented a flat together in Langham Road, Teddington, which ran parallel to the road where, Bernadette was living. It was the upstairs flat to an Edwardian house, owned by a very genteel, retired Scottish couple. Jim was working in a photographic company of printers, doing lithographic work and attending evening college. The company was just around the corner from where we were living, close to Teddington Lock. Jim took me to the Department of Employment to help me find a job. I accepted a job at Barclay's Bank Training Centre on Teddington Bridge as a vegetable cook. The salary of ten pounds a week was double what I had been earning at Short Brothers and Harland and seemed like a fortune in comparison by me. I started work doing the vegetables and would look out of the window from the top floor of the building at the people below crossing over the bridge and would envy them their freedom. I was asked to clean out the two big ovens and steamers and decided on the spot to leave the job. Jim, on hearing what I had done taught me the first of his many golden rules, (similar to those of Scott FitzGerald's, "Great Gatsby," trying to achieve his American Dream,) that, you don't leave one job until you have got another. I got a job in Kingston Hospital, as a diet cook and had day release to attend Ealing College, at Ealing, to do the 150 City and Guilds Course. Meanwhile I had heard from my friend in Rupert Stanley College, Belfast, that not only had I passed the City and Guilds 147 Course, but I had obtained the highest marks in Northern Ireland and the college received a cup for that year. I would have been pleased just to pass the exam. Bernadette was working in Esso's Social Club in Teddington and I went there with her to work, too, sometimes. I asked an Irish woman working there how long she had been living in England, and she said, "Twenty-two years!"

I was surprised, that she hadn't lost her accent; I was also surprised that she had managed to survive twenty two years of living in England: (little did I suspect, that I would end up living over forty years in England) I had moved to England in November and Jim said, that we couldn't afford to go back to Belfast for Christmas and buy Christmas presents for all the family. So we opted to buy Christmas presents and go home for Easter instead. Jim had invited a girl from where he worked, who would otherwise have been on her own for Christmas, to spend Christmas with us. On Christmas morning my father telephoned us to wish us a Happy

Christmas, and I just felt a big lump come into my throat, and I couldn't speak. Jim took the phone and said that I was just overwhelmed and to ring back later. My dad rang back later and I spoke to him, after the call my spirits lifted, I went to make the Christmas dinner for Jim, his friend, her sister and myself. I was homesick during the first six months at Teddington; I would look out of the window of our top floor flat at the roofs of the Edwardian houses facing us and ask myself what I was doing there. Jim's friends from the college where he was attending evening classes, became frequent visitors in the evenings and I would cook the evening meal for all of us. In the morning, I would wake up to full ashtrays of cigarette butts and rooms that smelt of stale smoke. I would do all the housekeeping, shopping, washing and ironing, unquestioningly, (as well as paying half of all the bills) as it was unheard of in Irish culture for the male of the species to ever do what was traditionally considered to be "Women's Work!" They'd rather have been seen dead than pushing a pram. Jim's friends all commented that they certainly didn't have sisters like his and the elderly Scottish couple, who lived in the flat downstairs, also said they'd never seen a brother and sister, who got on so well and that we were more like a married couple than a brother and sister.

Jim thought nothing of changing his shirt three times in one day, and when I commented on the amount of washing and ironing this created, (as washing had to be done at the launderette) Jim replied, that he didn't know what all the fuss was about, it was simply a matter of water and soap passing through clothes. I still recall the lovely, elderly Scottish gentleman, downstairs saying to me one day, when I must have been having a bit of a moan, that, if a women didn't have a complaint, then that was her complaint. I walked up Teddington High Street one day with his wife, talking all the way, when she said that she had to pop into the Post Office, and took her leave of me. It was only sometime later, that I learned, that she couldn't understand a word I was saying, because of my broad Belfast accent, and was just nodding and smiling in what she considered, to be all the right places and made the excuse of nipping into the Post Office to escape the embarrassment of the situation (and she spoke with a Scottish accent!)

Jim, and I, would go to the cinema, or out for an Indian meal in Twickenham and walk back to Teddington afterwards, with me giggling all the way, because I'd drunk the whole bottle of Beaujolais in the restaurant, because Jim didn't like it. As each person would pass us on the way back, he would nudge me with his elbow, mimicking Aunt Bernadette, who viewed every stranger with suspicion, and I would go into fits of laughter. Even when we were children and we would go to my cousins' house in Armagh, Jim would just have to wriggle his little finger at the breakfast table and my cousin, Patricia, and I, would start laughing uncontrollably. Patricia, who had just taken a mouthful of tea, found the tea coming out of her nose, instead of its intended journey down to her stomach. I had got an evening job in Pope's Grotto, a large pub by the riverside, in Twickenham cooking the pub meals that they served. An Irish waiter, called, Tom, offered to walk me home one evening. When we arrived at the flat, I bought him in to introduce him to, Jim, saying, "This is Tom, who works with me at Pope's Grotto."

Jim very curtly replied, "Congratulations!" and then walked out of the room. I lost my job at Pope's Grotto, because the manageress walked in and caught me eating a bowl of strawberries and cream, which were clearly intended for the paying customers, and not the staff. The waitress, who was supposed to be keeping a lookout, was unable to warn me, because the shoes she was wearing were of the mule variety and didn't connect very well with the kitchen door. Jim, and I, both had a joint bank account, into which our wages were paid and could, therefore, be used to pay the rent, electric and food bill. If I wanted to buy anything for myself, I needed Jim's signature on the cheque too. Wanting to buy a new handbag one day, I caught, Jim, early in the morning while he was still in bed half asleep and asked him to sign a blank cheque; I then withdrew the money from the bank and bought the handbag. I was later told another of Jim's golden rules, "You don't spend the rent money."

I was earning as much, if not more than Jim, due to the two jobs I had, as well as doing all the housekeeping, entertaining his friends, and paying half the bills. I told Jim, that I thought it would be better, if we had separate bank accounts and I have never had a joint bank account with anyone, from that day to this. As planned, we went home at Easter time; afterwards we returned to Teddington and my father came over to visit us. The son of the Scottish couple was planning to sell the property and my father discussed the possibility of renting the whole house with him, thereby enabling his parents to proceed with their own plans at this time. So it was, that one year after I moved to Teddington, my father moved the whole family there, as he had no wish to watch all of his children grow up and one by one, "cross the water." When my mother, father, and the other four arrived over, I used what money I had to buy the pyjamas and clothing for my younger brothers and sisters. Jim was now dating a girl called, Tina, from Hyde in Hants, Jim spent the two hundred pounds he had to buy a second hand mini, which he used to travel down to see, Tina, and her family. Although, Jim was now living back with the family, he did not believe that he should pay keep, or take any financial responsibility for the family. He did discuss with my father a plan for saving the money to get the deposit he needed to buy a house, which then, as now, was an expensive undertaking, as London properties have always been more expensive than other parts of the country. My brother, Peter, aged eleven at the time began keeping white mice as pets in a proper hutch in a shed at the bottom of the garden (as opposed to the electricity cupboard.) One day, Jim took, Peter's, mice down to the river at Teddington Lock and set them all free. Peter was absolutely devastated and broken hearted at losing his pet mice, and I was dismayed, that Jim had forgotten how he was as a boy. Jim would often pull my mother up in quite a condescending way about her shoddy housekeeping skills, pulling out socks, that would have been put into the drawer of the large antique dresser in the kitchen; holding them up, he would ask her what they were doing there. Tina often came up at weekends to stay, and so, on top of the four young ones and, Jim, and I, we had an added guest to cater for. I began to experience some of the social life and culture of London, when I went out with, Tom Mills, an educated black University Student who had his own house in New Malden, Surrey. Tom worked part time at Kingston Hospital to earn some extra money. He played tennis and enjoyed classical music and we attended the Last Night of the Proms and the Boat Show at Earls Court. Tom would bring me little presents into work; pairs of tights and Callard and Bowsers nougat coated with sugar paper that I quickly discovered was edible. Tom was a real cultured gentleman and I went out with him, as a friend, and good friends we were. I brought him home to meet the family and, although he would have liked to have been more than friends, it never went any further. I started dating one of Jim's friends, Stuart, who also did photography and worked at the National Physical Laboratory in Teddington. Stuart, owned a little Robin Reliant and was much shorter than me, what he lacked in height, he made up for in intelligence and personality. When I would go out for a walk with him by Teddington Lock, my youngest sister, Angela, would come with us. One day, as I walked along smiling at my four year old sister, who ran ahead of us, he took a photograph of me without me knowing, from the top of the river bank. On Valentine's Day, he presented me with a large blown up black and white photograph of myself wearing my brown calf length suede coat with the willow tree branches overhead and the sunlight glistening on the water smiling at my four year old sister, who was not in the picture. It was mounted on a black background and was to be the most beautiful Valentine's card that I was ever to receive. It remains in the family to this day. I went with Stuart to a pub in London to meet his father, who was a squadron leader in the RAF and was based in Scotland. It was all very polite and civil, but I was most definitely in the company of a very different social class to the one I'd always known. I remember going to Richmond Theatre with Stuart to see Ballet Rambert, it was the first time I had ever been in a theatre and I found the whole experience exhilarating and breathtakingly unreal. When I was going out to dances in Belfast with, Breda, and meeting different boys, some who would break my heart, and some whose hearts I broke, it would never have occurred to any of us to consider getting married. We were enjoying our youth, but were always aware that marriage was the last thing that any of us wanted. We knew, that once entered into marriage, it really was death, that would ever part us and there would be no way out. We were in no hurry to have the same lives as the women we saw around us; very few of whom went out to work, as there wasn't enough work even for the men, and having as many children as God blessed them with, bringing them up as best they could no matter what the circumstances. It was certainly not something to be entered into lightly. In England however, I was surprised at how easy it would be to marry the boys one dated, and at how many would actually want to get married. Greater opportunities presented greater possibilities and at this time, Stuart and I were considering getting engaged. My father had got employment at Kingston College in Cranberry Park Gardens, and my mother was able to work in a care home just around the corner from where we were living in Teddington. If I were free to do so, sometimes, I would cover her weekend shift. My father, aware that, Jim, and I, were likely to get married sometime in the near future, made enquiries about obtaining a mortgage to buy a house for my mother, himself, and the other four. He was advised that due to his age, and the age of my mother, he would qualify for a council mortgage of £3,500, at the fixed interest rate of 8%. My father needed a thousand pounds to put down, as a deposit on a house he wanted to buy in King's Road, Kingston-Upon-Thames. He was able to borrow five hundred pounds from the son of the owners' of the house we were renting in Teddington, to be paid back within a year, at the interest rate of 25%. However, we still needed the other £500. I was the only family member with a bank account still in credit, so my father and I, went to see my bank manager. We met with the manager and explained the situation, and so it was decided, that he would lend us the money, which would be secured with a life insurance policy in my name. My father and I came out of the bank and stood in Teddington High Street, hugging one another out of sheer joy and relief. We moved to King's Road, Kingston-Upon-Thames, Surrey, on January 1st 1969, New Year's Day. I brought my four brothers and sisters up to Richmond Park, where we walked through virgin snow that had completely covered the park making the only footprints in the snow that day. Jim was not around the day we moved, as he had gone down to Tina's home in Hants, and his little yellow mini had broken down. It was so cold, that we put all the beds into the one big front bedroom, so that we could all keep warm in the heart of one bedroom, just until we got the rest of the house sorted out. I had by this time already ended my relationship with, Stuart, as I had met, Fernando. Fernando came to work in the hospital, as a kitchen porter, having obtained the necessary work visa required at this time. I was putting the food, which was to go to the wards, into the heated trolleys, and, on looking up, saw him grinning down at me. "What a cheeky face he has!" I thought to myself.

Fernando said to the other Italian kitchen porters in Italian, "What a beautiful girl," which he thought I wouldn't understand, but I did. Sometimes, I would do a double shift, if any of the Italian chefs were taking their extended holidays: time that they had saved up by working Christmas Day, and all the other Bank Holidays which gave them double time and a day off in lieu. This enabled them to go off to Italy for long periods of time. If I were working a double shift, I would finish the first one at around 2 and then have a two hour break, which I would spend in the staff room. When, Fernando walked into the staffroom I was absolutely breathless, he was so dark and handsome, I was totally bowled over. He began talking to me and he wrote in French, on my white cook's coat, "Would you like to go for a walk with me this evening?"

As I had ended my relationship with Stuart, I began going out with, Fernando. My father had become good friends with, Stuart, and, on hearing the news, said that he was going to start a club for my ex-boyfriends. When I would come home, after being out with, Fernando, my father would think, that I'd been drinking, because my eyes were absolutely shining. Fernando, and I, were planning to get married and went to see the priest, in the Catholic Church in Teddington to arrange it. As I wasn't yet twenty one, I would need my parents' consent. We were discussing the details, such as flowers for the church and an organist, when Fernando turned around and asked the priest, "And how much is all that going to cost?"

His tone of voice was quite abrupt and the priest turned and asked him, if, he wanted to get married or not. I was absolutely shocked at Fernando's question to the priest as it shattered all the romantic notions I had of getting married. We went to the cinema that night I was still numb and in a state of disbelief, that he had raised the subject of money and cost for something as important as getting married. I decided that I wasn't going to get married after all. A few weeks later, my father returned from Sunday Mass at the chapel and told me I had better go and tell the priest that I wasn't getting married. They had read the Banns out at Mass two Sundays in a row and would be reading them out again the following Sunday for the third, and last Sunday. I went round to see the priest and told him that I wasn't getting married after all and he certainly didn't try to talk me out of my decision! After we had moved to King's Road in Kingston-Upon-Thames, my mother met Bernadette at a bus stop in Kingston and invited her around to the house. Bernadette came with her, and their argument, over fourteen years ago, was, if never totally forgiven or forgotten, temporarily put behind them. Jim returned home with Tina, after his Christmas holiday with her family and announced that they were getting married, and that, Tina, would be working in Kingston, as a secretary, and staying with us, so that they could save up for the wedding. My mother, father, Jim, Tina, and Aunt Bernadette all smoked at that time, (I was the only non-smoker,) and Tina, would always accept any cigarette, that was passed around by the others, but never passed hers around; she would simply take one from her own box of cigarettes, without offering the others one, and smoke it. This was the first time, that I had ever witnessed this kind of behaviour. My father had often quoted, "What's yours is mine, and what's mine is my own." Tina had the same philosophy.

Jim, and Tina, were to be married around April; they were about one week away from the wedding, when, Jim, did a disappearing act for three days. No one knew where he was, not even Tina. A letter arrived for, Tina, and after reading it, she put it inside her handbag announcing to my parents, that she wouldn't marry, Jim, now, not even if he were the last man on earth. We never did learn exactly what was said in the letter, but one day, soon after, Tina, had taken her leave of us and returned back home, her mother, dressed in an expensive fur coat, landed on our doorstep and told my mother she would be taking legal action for Breach of Promise. My mother, standing in the doorway, told her to go ahead, but she might hear things about her daughter, that she didn't want to hear. Tina's mother left and we heard nothing more. Soon after this, Fernando returned from Spain, where he had gone after I ended our relationship and called off the wedding. He had been writing to me from Spain, but the letters were going to the wrong house, number 8, instead of 81, (the one obviously being mistaken for a comma) and being returned to him as, "not known at this address." By this time we had settled into King's Road and I was feeling like Polly Flinders sitting among the cinders. I started going out with Fernando, again, who was now working on a work visa, once again as a waiter, in the Mitre Hotel, opposite Hampton Court Palace. There, he served famous people such as, actor, Donald Pleasance, and tennis player, Anne Jones. Fernando was living in staff accommodation, provided by the hotel, in a hostel in Hampton Wick. We decided once again to get married, but I promised my father, that I would remain at home for the year until the end of his heavy financial commitments and continue paying my salary into the family's bank account. I got an evening job in the Bird's Nest Pub in Twickenham, which was to help pay towards the wedding costs. Fernando, didn't like me working in Kingston Hospital because of the shift work involved, and I got a job as a stock control clerk in Meredith and Drew, (the biscuit people) in Kingston Bridge House just over Kingston Bridge in Hampton Wick. One of the "other four" would meet me on my way home with, Fernando, saying my mother needed a pound, which I would give to them from the money I was earning from the bar job. Fernando would sometimes bring me into Bentall's department store in Kingston and buy me some new pairs of tights, as the ones I would be wearing would be laddered. If we went window shopping around Kingston and I remarked how lovely a little tea set was in the window, the next day he would go and buy it, and present me with it. So, I learned to stop saying that I found everything in the shop windows lovely. Fernando would buy the things we needed for the wedding, the ring one week, the bridesmaid dresses for my sisters, Maureen and Angela, another week and so on. An Irish girl called, Mary Rudd, with whom I worked in Meredith and Drew, had got married just a few months before and lent me her wedding dress which I got dry-cleaned. Mary was much shorter than me, but I was much slimmer than she was and so the Princess line dress fitted beautifully.

My Aunt Bernadette was working at the Mitre Hotel, at the same time as Fernando, making open sandwiches for the customers, who wished to have lighter meals outside by the riverside with its scenic views of Hampton Court Bridge and the boats on the River Thames, going from London all the way up the river. I would go with my aunt some weekends to help her and a German chef, who worked in the hotel with, Fernando, couldn't believe that I was going to marry Fernando, and would ask Bernadette, if she couldn't talk me out of it. Bernadette did try, but she didn't succeed. The only good thing my aunt could find to say about, Fernando, was, that he was immaculate. Fernando was extremely handsome, his family consisted of only his widowed mother, who had given birth to him at around the age of forty and was being kept an eye on by his older married brother, who had two sons of his own and lived in Leon, in Northern Spain. This enabled him to always buy the best clothes, shoes, jackets, watches and wallets for himself. No doubt, Fernando would send money to his mother, as there was no welfare state in Spain at that time, but he was still relatively free to just look after himself. I always used to love seeing his white shirt collar against his dark black hair. My father was unhappy about the forthcoming marriage, and one day asked me, if I'd ever confided anything to, Fernando, because of a conversation that they had had. It seemed Fernando told my father that he was still a virgin, and my father, said that he was sure that I was a "good girl," too, to which Fernando, replied that he didn't know his daughter. My father knew me better than anyone in the world, but his definition of "good" would have differed entirely to that of Fernando's and the question of whether or not I was still a virgin, would not have changed his feelings towards me one iota. My father was a broad minded liberal man of the world, who always put the health, welfare and happiness of his family above everything else including Catholic, religious dogma. I think his fears and concerns were more to do with his awareness that I would be going into a marriage with a man who did not hold the same tolerant, liberal views rather than whether or not I was a virgin. He was in his usual diplomatic way, trying to warn me about this puritanical attitude of, Fernando, and said, perhaps based on his own experience of marriage, that marriage was the one thing we did without the benefit of hindsight. However, I was now living in England, not Kenard Avenue, and I, somewhere, deep down knew, that, although I was going into marriage for all the right reasons and truly believed it was, "until death do us part," that if it did not work out, I would be in a better position to leave it, than if I were still living back in Belfast, where social and religious conformity was the norm, rather than the exception. Jim was also opposed to the marriage and tried to put me off by saying that, in Spain, they shit on their hunkers, (squatted) and the women gave birth in the fields and just got up and carried on working! I think my father, and, Jim, both believed, that, if they didn't actively support the plans for the wedding, that I wouldn't go through with it. Fernando, and I, carried on making the arrangements. The priest at St Agatha's Church, also in King's Road, said he would put the flowers on the altar and, Fernando, and I booked a sit down meal for around fourteen people. Red and white wine bottles on the table would accompany the meal, (no bar and no evening buffet or disco) in the upstairs restaurant of the hotel situated at the entrance to Bushy Park, and facing Hampton Court Palace. We brought the date of the wedding forward to the 16th of August, and as the day of the wedding grew nearer, my father began to do work on the front living room in readiness to receive wedding guests and make it presentable for me to leave home. He had suggested that Fernando and I, live in one of our upstairs bedrooms that had a large sink in the room. I said no, if the marriage didn't work out, I didn't want it to be because we had opted to live with my parents. On the day of the wedding, I went to my Italian hairdresser in the Market Square in Kingston at nine o'clock in the morning with my two sisters to have our hair done, the wedding was at noon. She did my sisters' hair fairly quickly and they sat patiently waiting for me to have mine done. I was having a hair piece fitted in order to have the Grecian curls look. The hairdresser was also doing the hairs of some of the other customers and I was afraid to say anything at all, in case she got all temperamental and didn't do my hair properly.

We ended up leaving the hairdressers at five minutes to twelve and opted to walk, (or should I say run) back home, as it was the quickest way to get back. As we made our mad dash through Kingston, I felt sure, that Fernando would pass us in a car from his place in Hounslow, where he was living with friends, a Spanish woman and her Jamaican husband, on his way to the church. We all arrived back at the house and I was told that my father was in hospital, as he had gone to the doctor that morning suffering with pains in his chest. I said I didn't have time to stop, and pulled on the wedding dress, quickly fitted the veil and slapped on some make up. Maureen, and, Angela, put on their bridesmaid dresses, one yellow and one blue and we discovered, that Maureen's dress, which had been a perfect fit when we went to the shop and hadn't needed altering, was now calf length. Angela's had been altered and fitted perfectly. The husband of, Mary Rudd, who was to be a guest at the wedding, said that he would give me away, and, on learning that there were no wedding cars booked, quickly put some ribbons on his car, so that we could make the short drive to the church. On hearing that I was late due to my father being in hospital, Fernando said that he wouldn't be the only one in hospital, if I didn't turn up. His best man was a Spanish friend called, Pin, who lived in central London with his wife, who did a domestic live in job in a large private house. I arrived very late at the church and the priest carried out the wedding service with two altar boys by his side. I had never been to a Catholic wedding service in a Catholic church before. The priest had arranged the organist, as well as providing the flowers for the beautifully decorated altar, from where he read the twenty third psalm. "The lord's my shepherd I shall not want."

The reading was from the Book of Ruth. When the priest read the words, "and may he give you the wisdom of Ruth" and said the words, "may you live to see your children's children," I found the words so moving that the tears began to flow down my cheeks and the two young altar boys were embarrassed and didn't know where to look. The priest quietly whispered to me to cheer up, but it wasn't until after we had gone into the vestry to sign the register and I came out again, that I could raise a smile. As I walked down the aisle, I remember thinking that I didn't feel any different as a person, although I thought I should do. However, although I was still the same person, marriage brought a big psychological difference. Jim wasn't at the wedding, I don't know why. It didn't occur to me to go and see my father in hospital and see how he was. It turned out that he had been put on an ECG and had suffered, "a nervous lock." He was always able to say to Fernando after that, that he had never given me away. After the meal in the restaurant at Hampton Court, Fernando's best man, Pin, drove us to a small hotel in Godalming, Surrey, which had been booked for two nights. By the time we reached the hotel, I was suffering from car sickness so Fernando had tea and sandwiches sent up to the room while he had his evening meal alone in the hotel's dining room. On Monday morning we caught the bus back to Hounslow, where we were to live with his Spanish friend, and her Jamaican husband, with only the bus fare in our pockets. At the time Fernando was working, as a hospital porter in West Middlesex Hospital in Hounslow.

Chapter Two

Married Life with Fernando

Fernando, now a British citizen no longer needed a work visa and was free to work wherever he pleased. We went together to the offices in London that dealt with immigration and I was appalled to see how the security officials outside the building treated those standing in the queue. The very long queue went right around the outside of the building as those in it waited to go inside and have their papers processed. They spoke to them in a rough tone of voice, as if they were herd of cattle and told them to move along. Once free to work without the restrictions attached to the work visa, Fernando got a job in Bentall's Department Store in Kingston-Upon-Thames, as a men's hairdresser. We were in rented accommodation in the home of a Spanish family, who lived in the next street. Maureen, and, Angela, would often come round to the house on a Saturday morning to see if I would take them into Kingston. As our kitchen was between the bathroom the Spanish family also used and the rest of our accommodation, he would complain sternly, to, Fernando, if I ever left anything on the kitchen table before leaving the house, so we decided to look for another place to rent. My father, Fernando and I went up Kingston Hill, just opposite Kingston Hospital, looking at a property to rent in Brunswick Avenue. It was one of the big, older houses, that lead up to the Kingston Gate entrance to Richmond Park. As we arrived, my black friend, Tom Mill's, saw us. He began chatting to us, happy to see us all, when my father discreetly slipped into the conversation that we were out flat hunting, for the two newlyweds. The expression on Tom's face changed instantly to one of shock and disappointment and he very quickly took his leave of us. We moved to the flat in Brunswick Avenue, which was owned by an elderly couple, who were to live in the flat below. However, the accommodation that we had viewed was not the accommodation that they allocated us and we were living on two levels instead of one, in rooms that had problems. I told Fernando, that I wasn't prepared to have them, "put their hand into us," (con us and rip us off!) I told him to look for another property. Fernando found a downstairs flat, in a large house owned by an Italian woman, which had a large, open plan front living, room that looked out onto the main road. It also had an adjoining large bedroom and a small kitchen, which had been converted from a small utility room, off the bedroom. The kitchen led into the back garden and the bathroom was off the hallway that led into the front room. The flat was in Gibbon Road, just two streets away from King's Road, where my family still lived. My friend, Mary Rudd, and her husband had paid five hundred pounds for their wedding reception, which was obviously a big affair, complete with evening buffet and disco, as well as the main reception. They then rented a flat in a road off Tolworth Broadway, and I never could understand their reasoning. If I had had five hundred pounds available to me when I got married, I would have used it for the deposit on a house instead and bought my own home. Just before I got married to, Fernando, my mother's sister, my Aunt Mary called to see us; she was now living with her husband, John Cravaghan, and her family in Littlehampton. During a conversation with me, she said, that once I got married and left home, Jim, too would also leave home. I said, that I didn't think that this would be the case, as I suspected, that Jim would be only too pleased not to have to share the pecking order in the family with me. However, Mary's, words turned out to be true; once I was married, Jim, found a flat for himself and moved out. Well, he was twenty four by then. Jim had applied to the BBC for the trainee position of camera man and had been rejected. He applied a second time and was successful and his career in television was about to start. I was still working as a stock control clerk at Meredith and Drew's. I had attended Kingston College of Further Education in the evenings to obtain GCE O' levels in order to apply for teacher training, which was what I had always wanted to do. The teacher training college at Twickenham would only recognize the Senior Grammar School Certificate, but would accept six O' levels. Unable to return to Northern Ireland and pass the Senior Certificate, I elected to obtain the O' level certificates in the required subjects at evening classes. I passed the examinations and was offered a place at Gypsy Hill Teacher's Training College in Twickenham, which I turned down, because I didn't believe, that I should pursue a professional career, now that I was married to Fernando, or that it would be right to be more educated than him, which might offend his already strong, male ego. My younger sister, Angela, was six years old when I got married and she innocently thought that babies just automatically came with marriage. She would ask me when I was going to have a baby and I would say to her, that every time I went up to the hospital to get one, there was too big a queue for them. She replied that the next time that I was going up, she would come with me and that we would just push in and get one. I was equally as innocent as my sister, Angela, and was not using any form of contraception, in true Catholic tradition. Almost a year after our marriage, I was still not pregnant and went to see the doctor to see if there was anything wrong.

Fernando, and I, had planned to go to Spain to meet his family for the first time. The doctor advised me to go on the holiday and come and see him, when I got back to carry out some tests. Fernando wanted us to spend five weeks there. It would be my first time to go anywhere outside of the UK. Meredith and Drew agreed to let me have the extra three weeks holiday, as unpaid leave, but said that I would have to again, start building my benefits, as though I had just started the company. I felt that this was really unfair, and left the job. While I was working at Meredith and Drew, I was in a section of really bitchy women and developed a rash on my hands, which I thought may have been caused by the carbon on the van sales men's receipts. When I went to the doctor he prescribed Librium, for my nerves. I told him that I was only twenty one, and didn't expect to suffer with my nerves at such a young age. He told me that it was nothing to do with age, but more to do with the stresses of modern life, and so I started taking what I jokingly called, "my happiness pills."

Fernando, and I, flew to Madrid, where we stayed with his, Aunt Lola, the widowed wife of his dead father's brother, who was a nurse. She was looking after her elderly mother, and had a male lodger also. She had a son, also called, Fernando, who was studying to be heart specialist, and a daughter called, Lollie, who was a teacher with two young sons, that her mother looked after, so that she could continue working. Fernando, and I, would go out with Lollie and Miguel, to the bars in Puerto Del Sol on a bar crawl drinking glasses of red wine and eating tapas. I didn't really drink then, but the alcohol was very cheap and I would have Bacardi and Coke and was totally astonished at the size of the measurements of the Bacardi, which was poured into about a third of a tumbler sized glass, straight from the bottle. I was introduced to grilled prawns, fried green peppers and Parma ham. In the Puerto Del Sol, I was shown the spot which marked the exact middle of Spain. It was during one of these days out, I went to use the toilet in one of the bars and saw the hole in the ground and the two places on the tiled surround, where one placed one's feet, I recalled Jim's words, "They shit on their hunkers in Spain."

They were very friendly, hospitable and keen for me to experience everything that was typically Spanish. We would have chocolate with chorros in the morning for breakfast, but there were days, when I could have murdered a boiled egg and toast. One day we ate soft, warm, black pudding, which I didn't know was black pudding at the time, and I was running for the toilet for days afterwards and felt really sick. Fernando's aunt gave us a meal served with fresh green beans, which she dressed with lemon juice and asked him, if I like them, I said, that I did. She said, "When you're hungry, the bread's never hard."

I am pleased to say that I have never known a hungry day in my whole life, and I am grateful for that. We went to a bullfight one Sunday afternoon and I would have liked to have left after just one of the bulls was killed, rather than stay and watch the rest die. We made a trip to the Palacio Real and another, by car, to see a church built on top of a mountain outside Madrid. It is clearly visible, because of the giant cross outside the church that is carved into the mountainside. At the feet of the crucified Christ, are figures so big that just the little finger of one of them is about one foot long. Inside the church is a beautifully painted ceiling to commemorate the Civil War, displayed around the walls, the stations of the cross. I was absolutely amazed to see Fernando, kneeling at the golden altar rail in prayer, as he never put his foot inside a church back in

England. He even stopped me going to Mass on Sundays, insisting that I stay in bed. It was all obviously a show, put on to impress his aunt! We were to go to La Baneza, in the north of Spain, to visit Fernando's mother, and to Leon, to visit his brother and family. Fernando took me to El Corte Ingles Department Store in Madrid and we bought some material, so that Fernando's sister-in-law could make a suit for me. Fernando's, aunt kept referring to "La Baneza" as "el coulo del mundo," (the asshole of the world,) which I didn't particularly like, as it not only marked a certain kind of arrogance, but was also very disrespectful to Fernando's mother, and to, Fernando, himself, who grew up there. His parents had been very well off, before the Civil War and had lost everything, when it ended. Like so many countries, Spain didn't have a class system; it just had rich and poor. I never believed that poverty was anything to be ashamed of. We took the train to go North, and, when we couldn't find a seat, Fernando told one of the male passengers, that his wife was pregnant and the man gave me his seat, (mocking is catching.) We went to visit his brother in Leon first and, once again, the hospitality extended to me was very warm and friendly. Fernando's sister-in-law measured me, just as my, Aunt Philomena, had done. She made a pattern out of a newspaper and made the material into a two piece suit that I had described to her; the jacket with long sleeves and round at the neck, with no collar, and a short mini skirt; it fitted perfectly. We ate traditional Spanish soup made with chorizo sausage, tomato, onions, garlic and beans. As we made the journey to Baneza, through farming countryside I was shocked at the poverty of the people and the houses which they lived in, houses I thought would be better suited to keeping animals in. We arrived at La Baneza and went straight to meet a young couple, who were friends of

Fernandos. They owned a jeweller's shop in the village and lived in an apartment in a block that their parents owned. Their parents lived on the ground floor and, Fernando, and I, stayed in the apartment above them, but we had all our meals with the young couple. Fernando's friend told him, that his mother was absolutely wild with joy and happiness that he was coming to visit her. Fernando was intending to buy me a gold Certina watch and spoke to his friend about it. His friend could sell him the Certina watch, but did not have a strap big enough to fit my large-boned, wrist. Although I was slim, I was also big boned and needed longer straps than smaller, petite women. They agreed it would be better to buy the strap for the watch, when we returned to Madrid, which we did. We were to have dinner at Fernando's, mother's house the following day and Fernando gave her four thousand pesetas to buy prawns to put into the paella she was going to make for us. Her house was just a short walk from his friends apartment block, and we walked over to have dinner with his mother. She was a small woman, dressed completely in black, as was the Spanish tradition for widowed Spanish women whose husbands had passed away. Although she was only around sixty three years of age, she looked much older than sixty three year old women back in England. She reminded me of my grandmother and the other old women, who had lived in her street. All her top front teeth were missing and she would walk up and down past me, unable to keep her eyes from me, not knowing what to make of me. I don't expect that they saw many twenty one year old Irish women, wearing a mini dress and speaking English, in that little village, and, to her, I must have looked like someone from another planet. A young Spanish girl from one of the neighbouring houses was absolutely fascinated by me and kept asking, Fernando, to get me to say something. Fernando's mother's, house was one of a small row of single storey houses, which had corrugated roof tops. Inside there was only one large main room, which contained a highly ornately decorated brass bed. The room had a long wooden table and chairs and a wooden floor, it was simple and basic; but immaculately clean. Fernando's mother had cooked the paella outside the back of the house, where she also kept some chickens. As we were eating the paella, Fernando whispered to me not to eat a certain piece of white fish, as he thought I wouldn't like it, (it was octopus, and cheaper than prawns.) I put it to the side of the plate; there wasn't a prawn to be seen. Fernando's mother was a woman after my own heart and not prepared to put on the style for anyone, and no doubt needed the prawn money for more important things. She had failing eyesight and yet she made the me a truly beautiful, soft, white, fluffy, woollen stole, which reminded me of a similar multi coloured tartan stole, Stuart, had brought me from Scotland, but which only sat in the drawer, as there was nowhere I could have worn it. I told, Fernando's, mother, that the stole was absolutely beautiful and asked, Fernando, to ask her, if she would be able to sell it. I asked him to explain to her, that I wouldn't ever be going anywhere that I could wear it and it was too beautiful just to sit in a drawer. She said she could, and I think she understood that I very much appreciated the trouble and effort, (and expense,) that had gone into making the present, for someone she had never even met before. She also appreciated that, I, like her, was pragmatic and wanted things to be put to good use. I had always been impressed with the generous spirit of the poor, and this was a gesture that would remain with me forever. We returned to Leon and collected the two piece suit, Fernando's, sister-in-law had made up and it fitted perfectly. Like my Aunt Philomena, she knew her trade. On our return to Madrid we went to a wholesale jewellers Fernando's friend had recommended and bought the longer 18 carat gold bracelet to fit the Certina watch. We said our goodbyes to Fernando's family in Madrid and returned to our flat in Kingston once again.

Chapter Three

The Bad News First Then the Good News

On arriving home, I was on my way round to see my parents and met my sister, Maureen, out riding her bicycle in the street, who told me that my mother was in hospital. At first, I thought she meant the General Hospital at Epsom. My mother had gone to Mass one Sunday morning and had suffered a nervous breakdown during the Mass. I went to see her at the hospital and brought her the little statue of, "Our Lady," that I had bought back from Spain for her.

She said to me, "You'll never see another period," I told her she was wrong, because I was already having one. I had been nine days overdue and had thought that I was pregnant. When my period came on I broke down and cried from sheer disappointment. Social workers called to our home in King's Road, as, "the other four," were, of course, a cause for concern. Peter was fourteen years old, Raymond thirteen, Maureen eleven and, Angela seven. I told the social worker, that we would be fine, as I would look after the home, and my brothers and sisters until my mother was better. I began at the top of the house, taking each room in turn and threw out all the old clothes, such as vests with holes in them and clothes that were too small and would no longer fit anyone. I cleaned the house from top to bottom and brought some sort of order and stability to our family home. I bought the school uniforms my brothers and sisters needed to return to school, (this had always been a stressful time for my mother and I had often been sent to Robb's Department Store in Belfast, to buy the uniforms, at the beginning of the school year, using the vouchers my mother received from the Social Services Department and saw, that they all returned to school. The four would sit around the kitchen table, when I had made the dinner and, egged on by brother, Peter, would start to play up, just as they had probably been used to playing my mother up. One day, I grabbed, Peter, and, opening the cellar door that led from the kitchen, I threatened to throw him down the cellar stairs. He began to cry and call out for my mother and I told him his mother, wasn't here, but I was, and he was going to behave himself. I had no more trouble from the "other four" after that, with peace and order restored to our home, they would sit beside me on the living room settee and snuggle up to watch television. During this period, Jim was moving flats and had cleared his clothes out altogether, with those he'd removed from the drawers and wardrobe and I was given the job of washing them. I bought them round to the launderette and put them into the larger washing machine, dried them in the driers and brought them home, where they were then ironed and folded. I later received a complaint from my father, that, Jim's, good jumper should have been hand washed! That's gratitude for you. My mother was soon allowed weekend visits home, in readiness for her visits home for good, and I would go up to the hospital, on the bus to collect her. One day, as she was walking down the long road with me, that led up to the hospital, she began coming out with all this religious mumbo jumbo. I stopped walking and firmly told her, that, if she didn't stop talking all of this religious stuff, I would take her right back to the hospital. She went very quiet and didn't say another word, and so we went home together. After nine weeks, my mother was allowed home for good and she slept in the back room downstairs, which was used as a bedroom. I continued looking after things, until one particular morning. I made "the other four," their breakfast and sent them all off to school. I was just about to prepare breakfast for my mother, when she came out of the bedroom making a clicking noise with her thumb and middle finger, and said nastily to me, "You wouldn't do *that* for me!"

With that, I went into the kitchen, collected my good dinner plates I had brought round, gathered up my belongings and told her, I was going home and that she could now takeover herself. To all intents and purposes, my mother's nervous breakdown was brought on by exhaustion and financial worry. She was working night shifts in a care home, as a care assistant, and was getting very little sleep during the day. She had overheard a telephone conversation between my father and our previous landlord, who had not been repaid the loan within the year and was now worried about just trying to make ends meet. She always blamed my father for gambling the money, even when I was a child, and Jim would also jump on this particular band wagon too. However, although my father did like a little flutter on the horses, it didn't take an Einstein to work out, that the wages of my two unskilled parents together, trying to pay a mortgage and the other loans, as well as the everyday living expenses of a family of six, did not leave much money for the luxuries of life or for putting on the style, which so many of the others, who came into our family wanted to do. My father, whenever he had a little flutter on the horses, would do an accumulator or an each way treble, hoping to get a big return from a small stake. He enjoyed the world of horse racing-but then, so did the Queen Mother and the Queen, who attended the Derby at Epsom race course on Derby Day and Royal Ascot. We were surrounded by race courses: Sandown, Kempton Park, Epsom, Windsor and Ascot. For us it was a good day out, unlike the seedy little world of smoky betting shops that my mother, and, Jim, would have had us all believe. My father may have placed his little bets in a betting shop; but his interest in the world of horse racing was much wider, extending to his knowledge of trainers and stables and horse breeders and, if he ever did have a win on the horses, we would all know about it, as he shared it with my mother and treated all of the family. I applied for another job through an employment agency in Kingston and was sent for an interview at the Norwich Union in Kingston, who were looking for a cashier. The manager of the branch asked me, if I was intending to start a family and I told him it was in the hands of the Almighty. I suppose my honesty, rather than my naivety was seen to be a positive attribute and I was offered the job, which I accepted. It was certainly a better position than the one I had left, with Meredith and Drew, and offered better pay and conditions too.

Taken when my parents retired to Piltown near Waterford, Eire

The other colleagues in the office, men and women, rather than all women, were much better to work with too. I didn't have to handle much money, only payments which may have been made over the counter. The job mainly involved paying the commission due to insurance agents and converting ledgers from pounds shillings and pence to decimals, which were written in red, above the old figures. There was a good social life, as the office also organized social events. I became good friends with an Irish girl called, Liz, who was originally from Dublin, and was married to a trombone player from Derry in Northern Ireland, who was playing with the, Ray Mc Vey Show Band in the Grosvenor House Hotel in London. Fernando, and I, were invited to a party in the home of Company Director's secretary, Kate, in a block of purpose built flats called, King's Keep on the border between Kingston and Surbiton for which the Norwich Union was the management company. Norwich Union staff had priority should any of these flats come up for rental at a subsided rental. When Fernando saw how lovely, Kate's, flat was and learned that, as an employee of the Norwich Union, I would be eligible to put my name down on the list for one of the flats, he asked me to do so. I was surprised at this, as deep down I always felt, that Fernando wasn't looking to settle permanently in England, and was hoping, one day, to return to Spain. Nevertheless, I was delighted to put my name down, as it would mean no longer having to rent property in a shared house belonging to a private landlord and would afford us greater security at a more affordable rent. I missed a period and went to see my doctor, who confirmed that I was pregnant. I was absolutely overjoyed at the news, and Fernando would tell everyone that it was definitely a boy, because he always shot straight bullets. He'd always said that, if I gave him a son, he would give me the sun the moon and the stars. The name was already decided before the baby was even born; it was to be, David, after, Fernando's, father. I had no problems with either of these, as I liked the name, David, and I, also wanted a boy. I had very bad morning sickness and could not put my foot on the floor without having a piece of dried toast first. When I went shopping in Sainsbury's, just across the road from our office, I would look at all the raw meat, feel sick, and come home again without buying anything for, Fernando's, dinner. I would go to Leyland's home bakery and buy French sticks, which I would have half eaten before leaving the office to go home. The smell of passing the fish and chip shop on the Richmond Road on the way home would make me feel sick too, but it was often where Fernando had to go to get his evening meal. I had a craving for cashew nuts and bitter lemon and it was always just before the pubs were closing. Fernando would run round quickly to buy them for me just before the pub closed. At the Norwich Union, we would receive luncheon vouchers, which we would use in the nearby Chinese restaurant, where I would eat most days at lunchtime. I found the bland Chinese food very settling for my stomach and the others would jokingly say, "That child's going to be born wearing a Coolie hat," and we would all laugh. This was one place of work I was sad to leave, when the time for maternity leave arrived, as the atmosphere was great, and the people very easy to get along with. I didn't like being at home all day on my own and was quite anxious about giving birth for the first time, especially after seeing a film I watched in the ante natal class I was attending with, Fernando. I came out more scared than when I went in. During this waiting period, Fernando would come home from Bentall's and if I was not all smiles and, "Hello, darling, have you had a nice day?" he would just say nothing, turn on his heel and walk out again, without saying, where he was going or, when he would be back. Sometimes I would just go and visit my family, just for the company. My Aunt Bernadette had lent my father some money and, in return, she came to live with them, rent free. She had bought a new brown leather sofa, which she moved into the top back bedroom, where she would also sleep. She had been living with a lovely Italian family in Teddington, but I think, after years of living in bed-sits, she preferred to be close to her own family. I went up to Kingston Hospital for what I believed was my six month pre natal check-up. They found sugar in my urine and said that they were keeping me in. They would not allow me to go home and get a nightdress and said that I was two weeks away from having the baby and must have got my dates wrong. I was adamant about my dates, because of the period I had had, when I had returned from my holiday in Spain. They kept me in and did a glucose tolerance test, which involved inserting a needle attached to a small tube into my hand, where it stayed, and having me drink glasses of glucose, after which they would draw off blood using the needle in my hand and send the blood for tests. Fernando and my dad came to visit me and brought the nightdresses and toiletries that I needed. My father looked worried and anxious. I thought I was in Butlins, as I was able to have a good rest in bed, have meals brought to me and a relaxing bath, when I wanted one. I hadn't realized just how tired I had become, until I got into that hospital bed. The hospital carried out an X-ray to determine the length of the pregnancy and it was one of the most beautiful pictures I have ever looked at in my whole life. It showed my spine and the little spine of the baby together with the head already engaged. I would not buy anything before the birth of the baby, fearing I might jinx it. I was two weeks from having the baby and I left the hospital after one week to go home and await its arrival. The baby was one week overdue, and, tired of waiting, I told, Angela, and, Maureen, that I would go into Kingston with them on the Saturday morning. I was sitting on the settee in my parents' living room, when the waters broke and my trip into Kingston had to be abandoned. I immediately called an ambulance, as I preferred to be in the hospital, with all the doctors, nurses and right facilities around me. The ambulance men decided that they would drive around Richmond Park and go over a few bumps to bring on the contractions. I was put into the hospital bed, but still wasn't having any contractions. I remember looking out of the window at the green leaves on the trees outside unable to believe, that I would soon be holding my very own baby. The contractions still didn't come, and, on examining me, the doctors found that I was so many centimeters dilated and that the baby was in distress. They decided to induce the baby, and were taking bets, as to what time it would arrive. David was born at nine o'clock that evening. Fernando was at the birth and when the nurses handed me this crying little baby, I said to him, "There Touche, don't cry," and Fernando would always call him, Touche, after that. They put David in the little glass cot in the labour ward and I looked across at him and thought, it's a real baby! I had so much milk, that the nurses would come and express it for the premature babies in the ward. They would jokingly say, "We've come for a pint of gold top!"

David was jaundiced and had a sticky eye and I would cry at the thought, that anything could be wrong with him; obviously suffering the baby blues. I left hospital one week after the birth. Fernando had bought the pram and other things the baby needed, while I was in hospital. His Aunt Lola came over from Spain the week after I came out of hospital, to be, David's, Godmother, and her son, also called Fernando, was to be Godfather by Proxy. The day after David was born, my father came up to the hospital to see us both and I now knew what the expression, "tickled pink," meant literally. His face was the happiest I had ever seen it, and when he looked at us both his face was literally pink in colour, proud, and delighted at the birth of his first grandson. He told me he would never forgive me for making him a granddad, but both of us knew it was not true. Maureen, aged twelve, and, Angela, aged eight, the same age I had been when my brother, Peter, was born, came to the flat to visit us once I had arrived home. They were thrilled and excited by the new arrival and, when they put their heads into the pram to look at, David, Fernando told, Maureen, off, because her long hair was falling into the pram. Fernando's aunt had bought a gold St Christopher and chain, as a present for David. Fernando went to work as usual, and left his aunt with David, and me, as the extra pair of hands. It was really difficult, as she couldn't speak any English and I couldn't speak any Spanish. Nevertheless, we did our best to communicate with each other and would go out to Kingston market, taking David in the pram to buy hake for the evening meal, which she cooked. She sat knitting little woollen jackets for David; the Mother Care, ones would follow later. As she was a nurse in Spain, I didn't go to the baby care clinic with, David. My breast milk wasn't satisfying David, who was a big baby, and I found myself feeding him nearly every two hours around the clock.

I told, Fernando, that I was thinking of putting him onto a bottle, but his aunt said, that it would only upset his digestive system, if I changed him to a bottle, before he was four weeks old. Being a new mother, I accepted the advice of the "expert," as I had no wish to harm my new baby. I would put baby grows on, David, and lie him on a Mother Care plastic changing mat on the floor to allow him to kick and move his arms around freely. Fernando's aunt said that this wasn't right and that he should be wrapped tightly in a sheet. If David cried at all, even if we were having our dinner, I was expected to immediately put down my knife and fork and feed him. I would go around to my parents' house for a break from the conversations that were taking place in Spanish, leaving, David, with, Fernando, and his aunt. When I returned, they would look at me, as if I were a bad mother, who had abandoned her baby. Fernando's aunt told him, that his mother wasn't expected to live long, as she was suffering from breast cancer and had refused to have the breast removed. Fernando had been exempt from doing National Service in Spain, as he was the younger, unmarried son and it was deemed, that he would be needed to look after his widowed mother. Fernando's aunt said that, if she died, he would have to return to Spain to do his National Service, in order to be able to return to Spain to work there or carry out any form of business. The National Service would be for two years. I asked, Fernando, to ask his aunt what I would be expected to do, having just had my first baby, while he was doing his National Service. She said, that I could live with my parents, (just as they did in Spain at that time I presume.) I told, Fernando, to tell his aunt that if he returned to Spain for two years leaving me with a new born baby, while he cleaned the Colonel's boots, not to bother coming back again! Fernando's aunt was absolutely horrified and said it was not the way a good wife and mother should behave. (In Spain, perhaps, but I was living in England!) David was christened in St Agatha's Church, with Aunt Lola, as Godmother, and all the family present: that is to say, my father, mother, brothers, Peter and Raymond, sisters, Maureen, and, Angela, who were all living in King's Road. Aunt Lola returned to Spain and I continued breast feeding David, until sleep deprivation proved just too exhausting and I went to see my doctor. His receptionist asked me, if it were an emergency and, fearing that I would not get in to see the doctor, I lied, and said I had an abscess on my breast. The doctor told me to put, David, on the bottle. He prescribed me some Mogadon sleeping tablets for a good night's rest and said, if need be, let the baby cry. That night I took the sleeping tablets and, when David cried in the middle of the night, and Fernando elbowed me to get up and feed him, I went for him. He smacked me across the face and I walked out and went down to the River Thames at Kingston. I sat on one of the benches just soaking up the peace and quiet. I seriously thought about jumping into the river and, being a non-swimmer, I would most certainly have drowned. Only the thought of, David, stopped me. I kept seeing his little face in my mind; I resolved to leave, Fernando, and not go back. I walked from Kingston right down the riverbank to Central London and went up and down the underground with all the homeless persons of the night, before returning to my mother's house in King's Road. When I arrived there, she was in the bed in the downstairs room, having completed her nightshift in the care home. I told her I had left, Fernando, and wasn't going back; she pulled the bedclothes back and told me to get into bed with her, which I did. Later that day, Fernando wheeled, David, round with his things on the baby tray underneath and pushed him through the front door with a smug smirk on his face. David was born on 15th May 1971, and on 24th June 1971, the day after my twenty third birthday, we received a telephone call from Fernando's friend in Hounslow to tell us that Fernando's mother had died and could we let him know, that he was to catch a flight at ten o'clock that evening to attend the funeral. I went round and when he opened the door and saw me, he began to say, "Huh, I knew you'd be back," but, seeing the expression on my face, he stopped. I told him that his mother had died and he began to say, that we would just concentrate on ourselves now, but, when I went on to say, that his aunt had booked for him a flight for ten that night, he immediately began to gather his passport and things that he would need to catch the flight. Fernando had walked out of his job at Bentall's and, when I asked him why, he said, that he had cut the collar of a customer's shirt while cutting his hair; the customer had complained and he had just walked out. I accepted this explanation at the time, although I thought it was somewhat irresponsible with a wife and new born to support. (The real reason would be revealed some twelve years later!)

My brother, Jim, was now working as a cameraman on Panorama with the BBC and travelling the world. He had bought a motor boat and had plans to use it for a skiing business venture, in Spain, which, Fernando was to run for him. While Fernando was in Spain, my mother continued with her job in the care home and I found myself not only looking after, David, but the whole household. My mother would get herself dressed in my best clothes and go out, hair done, carrying my straw wicker basket, leaving me to cook the dinner for us all, as well as doing all the housework. Fernando phoned to say, that his Aunt Lola's mother had also died, while he was in Spain. I received a letter from the Norwich Union saying, that a flat at King's Keep, in Surbiton, had now become available and, that, Fernando, and I were to go to their offices in London, on a particular day and time, to sign the tenancy agreement. I began to worry that we would lose the flat, as Fernando was not in a steady job and was about to embark upon some hair brained venture of Jim's, (Who had a good job and no children.) The next time he phoned, I told him, that the flat had come up and he needed to be back in England, as soon as possible, or we could lose it. When I put the phone down, I just sat in the hall and cried from sheer exhaustion and frustration. My Aunt Bernadette, who was living in the house at the time, stopped on her way out and asked me what was wrong and I told her. On hearing that Fernando's aunt's mother had died, now leaving Fernando's aunt free of caring for her, my father told me to keep a close eye on, David, fearing, that Fernando may try to take him back to Spain for his Aunt to care for. Justifiable fears given the attitudes expressed, while she had been over for the christening. My mother was going to give, David, a bath in the front room; now I had been taught to put the cold water in the bath first, then add the hot water and test it with my elbow. I went into a panic, as I saw steam coming out of the bath and my mother undressing, David. I stepped in and said, that the water was too hot, and took over bathing him.

Fernando returned from Spain and that night I sat up in bed and said, "What a wicked, wicked thing to do," (the thought, that Fernando could possibly take the baby to Spain playing on my mind.) I asked, Fernando, to go and get my father from the downstairs bedroom, as I really thought that I was dying. My father came into the bedroom and I put my arms around him, and told him that I loved him; with that I passed out. When I was wakened in the morning, I couldn't move anything, but my mind was racing. I kept telling my little finger to move, but it didn't. I could hear everything being said, but couldn't move. My mother brought up a full fried breakfast with tinned tomatoes, which was left on top of the bedside chest of drawers and I couldn't eat it. I could hear my father tell my mother, that she had better go over the road and fetch a doctor. When the doctor came, he prescribed a liquid medicine, which I had to take every time I wakened up to put me asleep again. I was sedated around the clock for three days. When my father came into the bedroom to see me, he always had worried concerned expressions upon his face. When, Fernando came in he was smiling, light-hearted, trying to get me to eat some grapes. When my mother came into the room, I jumped in panic. Jim had telephoned when Fernando, was in Spain. He told my father, to tell, Fernando, to go to the Commissioner of Marinas, to get a licence to use the boat for water skiing, to which my father replied, "For God sake, he's burying his mother!" When I was ill, I could hear, Jim, who had gone ahead to Spain, with my fifteen year old brother, Peter, telephoning from Spain, because the engine in the boat had broken down and he wanted my father to get another one and send it out. I could hear my father telling him, that I was ill in bed. During this telephone conversation, I was squirming all over the bed! I slowly regained my strength. My mother had warmed a large bottle of fresh milk for, David, saying he was starving, which didn't seem to have done him any harm. David would be put in his pram and put out into the back garden and Bernadette would remark how you could tell from his little cries, now and again that he was seeking attention. I would lie in the front room bedroom and look up at the bedroom ceiling. I felt that I was far down below, and, that life was way up there, just like the ceiling, and was the place I had to reach once again. When I could finally get up and go downstairs, I would sit at the long table in the kitchen to eat dinner with the rest of the family. One day I said to my father, "I think I am mad."

My father replied, "If you are mad, Margaret, then the whole world is mad!"

I would often break into tears during meal times, and, on one occasion, when I did eventually go out, I saw a male colleague from the Norwich Union, a little distance away and thought that he had deliberately ignored me. Fernando abandoned his plan to carry out the water skiing business in Spain and got a job in the stock room of Hawker Siddley, which built the Harrier Hawks' engines on the Richmond Road at Kingston-Upon-Thames. The date for signing our lease for the flat at King's Keep arrived and I was well enough to go with, Fernando, to London, to complete the necessary formalities. We took possession of the keys and left the home of my parents in King's Road, with, David, in the pram. We walked the whole way from Kingston, to King's Keep, to begin again in our secure, rent controlled, purpose built flat, on the Surbiton Kingston border, ten minutes away from my friend, Liz, and about a half hour's bus journey from my parents in Kingston. The doctor told me, that powdered baby milk was just as good as mothers' breast milk, especially, if the mothers' growing baby is not getting enough. He also said, that the idea of not putting the baby on the bottle before it was a month old was very old fashioned and probably suggested, because the powdered milk in Spain was not as good as ours. He advised me not to have another baby, not, at least, until David was two years old and out of nappies. His nurse had to spend a very long time convincing me, that it was safe to take the contraceptive pill, (I think too the Catholic teaching against contraception was strongly and deeply ingrained in me at that time.) I finally agreed to take the prescription to the chemist and get the pill; I took the first one that night. The next day I read an article in the Daily Mirror, which said, that a young woman had died and her death was being attributed to her use of the contraceptive pill. That was all the justification I needed to stop taking the pill. I naively thought that, as it had taken one year to fall pregnant with David, that I didn't fall pregnant easily. I had gained a stone during the pregnancy with, David, and began to go to Weight Watchers to attempt to lose it. David was five months old, when I became pregnant with my second son, James. The nurse at the baby clinic insisted I stop the Weight Watchers' diet, as I continued to lose weight after I was pregnant. I never knew the having, of my second son, who was born on the 17th of July 1972, as I had my own home and, having had my first baby, I took having the second one in my stride. I was more relaxed and confident and much more in control of the whole situation.

Chapter Four

Trouble in Paradise

Managing a fourteen month old toddler and a new born baby was not easy, but I had reasoned that having another baby meant company for, David, and I would get all of the nappies out of the way in one go. (Had I had a girl, I would have been happy to have had one of each.) I lost no time in having an IUD fitted, as I knew that I would be having no more children. David was jealous of the new arrival and, if I were bathing the new baby and talking soothingly to him, he would stand screaming loudly without stopping or pull everything out of the kitchen drawers to get my attention. I would change, feed and wind the baby and put him down in his cot, because I was afraid David might try to harm him. I steeled myself to let the baby cry for ten minutes, after which I would go in to check that everything was alright, but, invariably, he would go off to sleep, before ten minutes was up. I breast fed him just as I had done with David, until I could see he was full to the gills, and, as soon as I thought, that he wasn't getting enough breast milk, I put him straight on the bottle. As soon as I thought he was ready for solids, Farley's Rusks, or an egg yolk, went into the milk too. Once he was on solids, he would be fed custard, creamed potatoes or anything suitable, that we would be having, and he thrived on it. I was most certainly less neurotic than when I had had, David, and I was not going to have history repeat itself. David would play in a square wooden playpen with no floor in it and every time the front door would open in the flat, he would try to make a dash for it to get outside, but the size of the playpen would stop him getting it through the door. Sometimes it took all day trying to synchronize the needs of a toddler with the needs of a baby, and there were days, when I had not even managed to change out of my nightdress, by the time the evening came. When the baby reached the age of five months, I remember sitting on the living chair, totally exhausted, wondering how I would find the energy for the next week, never mind the rest of my life. I put, David, now nineteen months, into a nursery for half a day, two days a week, just to try to get a break. By the time the baby was ten months old, David was two years old and could go full time to a nursery, if he were toilet trained. I went to a nursery in King Charles Road, Surbiton, where my friend, Liz, lived, which was in a church hall and closer to King's Keep to enquire about David attending full time. The lady running the nursery was called, Pat, and obviously very good with the children. While I was speaking to her, I noticed that she had a baby of about ten months in a pram and I asked, if she would also take my younger son, she said she would. My brother Peter had been godfather to my younger son, who had been christened, James, after my father, in St Raphael's Church in Kingston. I always thought that name, James, was too formal and stuffy for a small baby and so I always referred to him as "as the baby," whenever Pat, asked me his name I explained my reasons. She said, that she would call him, Jamie, and, to this day, I still call him Jamie.

. After explaining my reasons she said, that she would call him, Jamie, and to this day, I still call him, Jamie. Having obtained places for both, David, and, Jamie, at the nursery, I went with an employment agency to see how things would work out, taking a temporary job in the Royal Guardian Exchange Insurance Company in Surbiton, just around the corner from the nursery. At first, David would scream when I left him but had settled down by the time I came to pick him up again and we all soon settled into a daily routine. Pat said, when David was naughty, she would put him into the next room, where she kept drawers filled with spare clothes for the children and, when she would go in all the clothes were out of the drawers on the floor. Far from this being a deterrent for the other children, they began to misbehave too, so that they could go into the room with David too! Older women at work would say to me,

"I don't know how you leave those two children all day?"

When I said this to my father, he simply replied, "The rich never reared their children, Margaret."

I thought, if these women tried coping with these two children all day in a flat with no garden, they would soon see for themselves how I could leave them all day! The nursery and temping was for a trial period, and although I soon realized that I was actually doing two jobs, by the time I got us all ready and pushed the pram with the two children in it up the steep hill to the nursery. I knew that I wouldn't take the children out of the nursery, as they were benefitting so much from being there, socializing with other children and settling into a structured routine, which would prepare them for school. I also enjoyed being back in the routine, that work offered and socializing with adults once again. I knew I could not face another year of going around to the little park with the other mothers talking about fabric conditioner and the price of potatoes, or witnessing, if David picked up another child's ball, him getting pushed down by the other child for touching it in the first place. Fernando said, that he would buy me an old banger for taking the kids to the nursery which would first mean, that I would have to have driving lessons and pass my driving test. It was at this time, that my father's company was relocating from Kingston to Banbury in Oxfordshire; employees who wanted to relocate with them would be eligible for a council house in Banbury. My father had bought Kings Road in Kingston for £4,600 and sold it for £12,500. The £8,000 equity would have bought him a similar, private red brick house in Banbury, with no mortgage, which is what I thought he should have done, as he still had the "other four" to think about. Having left one council estate in Andersonstown Belfast, I had no wish to ever live in another one, or bring my children up in one. I think my parents were tired of making do, and money being tight, so, they took the option of the council house giving them some breathing space and money to spend in their pockets. My father asked me to go on holiday with my mother and two sisters to Torre Blanca, just outside Torremolinas, while he made the arrangements for the move to Banbury. Another friend, Liz, with whom I had worked with in Kingston Hospital, who was married to an Italian, said she would look after, Jamie, for me and I would take, David, to Spain with me. The holiday, paid for by my father went well, and, when we returned, everything was settled for the move to Banbury. Meanwhile, Jim, had met, Carol, who was a doctor at the beginning of her medical career, while he was filming, "Inside Medicine."

Xmas at Jim and Carol's house in Caversham, Reading

Carol was a few years older than Jim, and already had a degree in History, which she had taught in the Gilbert Islands, as a volunteer with V.S.O. Carol had lost her parents and was befriended by another doctor, who, when she died had left Carol, a house and some money in her will. Jim had bought a house in Tilehurst in Reading and arrived one day at my parents' home and took the wardrobes and chest of drawers, as he was intending to put the house up for rental. Jim took, Peter, up to the house to do the work it required and bought him an old car, as payment for the work. Carol converted to Catholicism in order to marry Jim. Fernando and I were not invited to the wedding; I think my parents were the only ones from the family, who were there. Jim and Carol wanted to buy a large character house in Caversham, which had a preservation order attached to it. Jim persuaded my father to split the equity money from the sale of King's Road, in order to help him, and Carol buy the property. That Christmas, when Jamie was seventeen months, old we were invited to the new house in Caversham for a big family Christmas. My father drove me, Fernando, and the children, from Kingston to Reading, as neither of us had a car or could even drive. I had gone around Kingston buying small token Christmas presents, which was all we could afford. My father had a bit of motorway phobia then and, as we drove along the M4, I kept talking to him from the front passenger seat of the car to try to take his mind from it. Carol's housekeeper had prepared a lot of the food and left it in the freezer. I peeled the frozen boiled potatoes for roasting but would have found it easier to peel fresh ones. My brother, Raymond, almost seventeen now, had turned up with his girlfriend, Denise, much to, Jim's, annoyance, as it was supposed to be a family affair, and Denise had not been invited. My father was very nervous and jittery and accidently knocked over a glass of wine, making him even more nervous and uncomfortable. The house was a large stone built detached property surrounded by countryside. It had a big open hearth in the heart of the living room with the chimney going up to the ceiling. We all sat down at the long dining table for dinner in the beautifully decorated living room and we all helped with the making and serving of the dinner, as well as the washing up afterwards. There were presents for everyone. Jim and Carol had bought, Fernando and I, a painting of an angelic little boy with golden curls. Jim took photographs and I still have a treasured one of, Jamie, his hand reaching up for an orange in the fruit bowl but his eyes on the camera the whole time. There is also one of ten year old, Angela, outside by a fence, with, David, and, Jamie. At the end of the day, Jim began to complain, that his wife was tired. Fernando and I, and the two children were going to be driven back to Kingston by, Jim, and, Carol, which was fine with me, as I preferred to be in my own home, in my own bed, for when the children wakened up in the morning. Anyway, it was, after all, a traditional Christmas and there was obviously no room at the inn; preservation order or no preservation order. Jim, who had had a bit to drink during the day, kept going on about people and their small, petty lives. Carol, to her credit, said that she didn't think that there was anything small, or petty, about the problems that came with rearing two small children. I added that not everyone enjoyed the luxury of jet setting to other countries. We arrived back home safely to our own home and, "our small petty lives," and I, for one, thought there was no place like home. A few months later my brother Peter was going to book driving lessons in Kingston and I asked him to book some for me, while he was there. I wanted to learn to drive and thought it would be another interest for me as well. Back then, driving lessons were £1 per hour, I asked Peter to book one a week for me. The first lessons were to be in an assimilator. Peter booked the lesson and left the card on the mantelpiece. I went to the first lesson in the assimilator, and Fernando came marching in during the lesson, all annoyed and angry, and said, "Do you do nothing I tell you?"

When we returned home, my father, trying to smooth over troubled waters, said, that he had said, that he would pay for the driving lessons, (he had done no such thing!) I told my father, that a wife did not need her husband's permission to have a driving lesson. Even though Fernando had said, that he would buy me a runaround, he was now going on about how the next thing I would want would be a car. What Fernando really meant was that, if I had a car, it would give me too much freedom. When my father and Peter left, Fernando put on his best brown suede leather jacket, his gold watch and put his passport and wallet in his inside jacket pocket and left the marital home without saying, where he was going, or, when he would be back. I began to realize, that I could be left to raise two small children on my own and I began to get pains in my chest and worry about keeping face with my family and friends. It was at that point, that I knew, that I had to continue working and rely solely on myself to bring up my two children; the trust in my marriage was gone. I had naively thought, that marrying a catholic, I would have a passport through married life, which would guarantee the happy ever after; the until death do us part with someone, who shared the same faith and values, that came with it, as me. Fernando returned three days later, having gone to Spain to discuss the situation with his Aunt Lola, at a cost of £65 for a scheduled flight to Madrid, (sixty five driving lessons and almost six weeks wages for him!) He told me his aunt had told him to return to England and make it all legal. He said he would remain in the home, until he had saved up enough money to repay some money he had borrowed from, Hughie, one of our friends, for his flight and other expenses. Needless to say, the atmosphere in the home was far from happy and a state of tension existed between us. I obtained a permanent position, as a Motor Insurance Clerk in Stewart Wrightson UK, a firm of underwriters, with connections to Lloyds, in London. I could not believe that any father of two children would just be legally allowed to leave the country and must surely be prevented from running away from his responsibilities to his children. I spoke with a solicitor in Kingston, who told me, that all I could do was let him go and then divorce him on the grounds of desertion. There was that big ugly word divorce, forbidden, like contraception, to Catholics. One Saturday morning, I needed fifty pence to go to the launderette and looked through Fernando's pockets in his jackets, which were hanging up in the wardrobe. I found forty pounds in his wallet and took it, in the belief, that I would need it more for myself and the children than he would. I rolled the notes up and hid them in the hem of the living room curtain and just waited for Fernando to discover, that the money from his wallet was missing. The inevitable argument followed the discovery of the missing money, after I had gone to bed that evening. Fernando swore on his mother's life, that the money was to pay, Hughie, money he had borrowed from her. I told him, he didn't take many chances, as his mother was already dead. The row escalated to a point where Fernando, placed his thumbs on my Adam's apple and pressed it for a good few seconds. Still in my nightdress, I jumped out of the bedroom window of our ground floor flat and ran down the road. Fernando ran after me and said to a passing couple, that his wife was sick. I said to the couple, who could clearly see, that I was distressed and upset, that I was not sick and that my husband had just tried to strangle me, and could they please call the police. Fernando ran off and I returned to the flat and was sitting in the armchair in the foetal position, when two policemen arrived with, Fernando, and his friend, Jim, whose hair Fernando cut privately and, who tipped him well. Jim asked me, where Fernando was going to stay, to which I said, I didn't care, where he stayed anymore but it wasn't going to be in our flat. The police told Fernando to leave and said, that they would circle round to ensure, that he didn't return. My father came down from Banbury and I told him I couldn't face people, as I felt they would all know my marriage was over and would be talking about me. My father told me to go into work and shake it off, which I did. Normally, I had been a lively bubbly person at work but, for the first few days after

I returned I was very quiet. I worked alongside a male colleague, with whom I was on good friendly terms, as well as in a mixed section of female and male colleagues, who were both understanding and supportive and it wasn't long before I was back to my old self. I shared my father's and brother's fear of the dole queue and the stigma attached to claiming benefits, so I wrote to the DSS detailing my change of circumstances and asking, if I were entitled to any benefits. I received a reply saying that I was entitled to a rate rebate, a rent rebate, and the nursery fees for the children were reduced from £80 per week to £8 per week. I received £40 to buy a new cooker, which I hand not a snowball's chance in hell of ever getting from, Fernando. I quickly came to the realization, when all my financial obligations were consolidated, that I was financially better off without him. I could not believe, that I was receiving all of this financial support and it was being given without any attitude or conditions attached. A short time after I had stabilized my situation, I received a letter from, Fernando, now living in Spain with his aunt while my father was staying with me. The letter said that he was living in Spain, that he was going to be happy and that he wanted the two children. I showed the letter to my father and asked him how he would like to receive a letter like that on his way out to work to support himself and his two children? My father told me to call Fernando's bluff; he told me to write back and say, that he could have one of the two children and that I would have the other; this I did. I wrote saying, that I could see Fernando wanted to fulfil his responsibilities, as a father, to his two children and, that I was willing to let him have one, and I would have the other, (Over my dead body!) I asked him to let me know, which of the two children, that he wanted and, if he would send me the plane fare, after which I would send him as an accompanied passenger, with an air hostess and he could pick him up at the Madrid airport. I didn't have to wait long for his reply, which began, "I think a child should be with its mother." And for once we were in agreement.

As I was now in the benefit system, I had to begin legal proceedings. I went to see the same solicitor, a Mr. Munsy, of Bell's Solicitors, in Kingston, who advised me, that, as Fernando was out of the country, we would have to wait two years to have a divorce by agreement or five years, if there were no agreement. In the meantime, Jim, and Carol were selling all four of their houses and buying one character house in Ealing, so that Carol could be closer to her job in Hammersmith Hospital and Jim would be closer to the television studios of the BBC in Wood Lane. The house needed a lot of work and was to be completely renovated to exactly how they wanted it, which meant that they had to live in a virtual building site, as the work took place around them. My father and Jim argued, when my father wanted his money back, that he had lent them, in order to buy a corner shop with a flat above it, in Tolworth, close to Surbiton. My father only ever said, that Jim had said something that stuck in his craw. He never said exactly what Jim had said to make him so angry, but I guessed it might have been something to do with my father's interest in gambling, and, that he couldn't be trusted with the money. Jim and Carol's house in Ealing was finally completed. They had bought the carpets for it from Harrod's sale and asked them to keep them for them until all the work had been completed. Carol was a good homemaker and, although she and Jim believed in buying the best, she was also very frugal and no spendthrift. It was soon discovered that Jim and Carol were unable to have children, because Jim, had a low sperm count, and because Carol was older than him. (It was thought, that his chances may have increased, had he married a much younger, fertile woman.) I knew this would be devastating for, Jim, as, when we were younger, we had both wanted children of our own, but Jim had always maintained that he would never have children, until he had the perfect career, the perfect wife and the perfect home for his children, who would no doubt have been perfect children too! Jim stopped smoking, drinking alcohol and black coffee and did all the things recommended to try to increase his sperm count. The news was equally devastating, as Jim was the eldest son in the family, as well as being, "the golden boy," who could do no wrong and it was an enormous blow to his male ego. My mother went into denial, as, for an Irish Catholic, it carried a bit of a stigma. Jim was reading International Relations, as an external student, at the London School of Economics, while still working as a cameraman for Panorama with the BBC. He began to develop a phobia of flying, which was totally out of character for him, as he had always loved travelling and said that flying was the best form of travel. He would take medication to help him overcome his phobia and in his third year of studying at the L.S.E, he left the BBC and became an internal student in order to complete his degree. While I was still working at Stewart Wrightson, John Johnson, joined the company as a trainee manager, going around all the different departments in turn to gain work experience. He was shown around our department one day; I saw this tall, thin long faced young man wearing a grey suit with a green shirt and tie. He was friendly, but shy as he had not long left Manchester University, where he had obtained a Joint First Class Honour's Degree in Maths and Management. He came from Amersbury in Wiltshire and was living in a bedsit in Thames Ditton, close to Kingston-Upon- Thames. Like me, he enjoyed tennis and two of my colleagues arranged a doubles tennis match with him and me after work one evening. I had no trouble finding a babysitter as, Maureen, or Angela, or my friend, Liz's, sister, Sally, were always happy to babysit for me. After the tennis match, my two colleagues made their excuses and left, leaving me talking to John Johnson. We got on well, although it wasn't that breathless instant attraction, I'd felt when I first met Fernando, (because he was dark and handsome and different.) John was calm and placid in temperament and could also be nervous and shy at times. He was the exact opposite of Fernando, and, although only twenty three, (I was twenty seven) he was really mature, which I put down to his education. He was affable and well liked and would be teased, because of his West Country accent.

We started going out together and would take, David, and, Jamie, in his car. On the way down the A3, David, would ask, if they could go and play in that park; he was referring the fields either side of us and I realized just how confined their young lives were. We would take them both to Richmond Park and the two boys would run off, like two dogs that had just been let off their leads. John was absolutely brilliant with the two boys. He was into cricket and we would bring the two boys to Bushy Park, where he taught them to play cricket properly, or sit on the swings with them in the playground. John got on well with my mum and dad and shared my dad's love of horseracing. One evening, all four of us went out to the dog racing at Wimbledon. My mum and I sat talking while John, and my dad, went around the bookies, checking the odds and placing their bets. In order to have an interest in the last race, I asked my mother to pick just two numbers; she picked 2 and 6. I went and put 50 pence reverse forecast on numbers 2 and 6 for her and just did the same bet for myself. When the meeting was over, John and my dad came back to where they had left us, just in time for the last race. It was obvious from the expressions on their two faces that they had not won. Numbers 2 and 6 won first and second place and the four of us went up to collect our winnings. As they paid the money out on my mum's ticket, my dad and John were smiling at the irony of it and they positively stared in disbelief, as they then paid out the same amount of money on my ticket. Unlike Fernando, John liked a pint and my dad enjoyed his company, as we could sit in a pub and relax. Fernando, if we ever went out together, would have half a lager and then begin pacing up and down, impatient to go; he just couldn't sit still and relax and neither could anyone else in his company.

Chapter Five

The Return of the Prodigal Father

John, and I, were in my flat one day when we received a telephone call from, Fernando, to say that he was in London and wanted to come to the flat to talk to me about something important. I arranged a time, allowing for the half hour train journey from London to Surbiton. I later learned that he was calling from Hughie's flat and had been brought up to date about everything in my life from the day he had left, including, John Johnson. Fernando was looking out of Hughie's window as John left, so that the meeting could take place in private. He arrived wearing a pinstriped black suit, striped shirt and spotted tie. He told me, that his Aunt Lola, had made him go to evening classes to gain business qualifications and that he was working in an office with a Spanish boss, who would bark orders to his employees and expect them to obey instantly. Two traders had flown from their London offices to his office in Spain and, Fernando had spoken to them about coming to work for them in London. He said, that he could earn a good salary and, that we would be able to buy a house in the future. I decided that his time in Spain had probably helped him to get Spain out of his system and to realize that his two sons were the most important thing in his life. I agreed to have him back and to make a go of things for the sake of our children. I knew that I would have been wracked with guilt, if I didn't give it another try. I spoke to, John, that evening, explaining to him, that I was going to give it another try with, Fernando, as he was the boys' father and, that I owed it to them to try and make the marriage work.

John was understanding and accepted the situation without protest, and so, Fernando moved back in. The two children were now attending a private nursery in Grove Crescent, a five minute walk from where we lived, as Pat's nursery had closed down. Social services agreed to leave the nursery fees at £8 per week for both of the children, to give the marriage every chance of working again. One evening, soon after Fernando had moved back in, I went to see my friend, Liz, in King Charles Road, in Surbiton, some ten minutes away. While I was in Liz's house, Fernando rang and asked to speak to me. I took the phone and listened to him. The next day, John phoned me at Surrey County Council's County Hall, where I was now working, as a wages clerk. John asked me if everything was okay, I asked him why he thought it wouldn't be, to which he replied, that Fernando had rung his landlady in Thames Ditton and asked to speak to him. John knew it was, Fernando, because his landlady said, that the caller had a foreign accent. So, Fernando was checking up on me. I was angry, because it meant that he had gone through my bag to get the number! Fernando said, that he wouldn't want to speak to 'anyone like that,' to which I quickly replied that, that person had been there for me and his two children all the time he had been living away with his aunt in Spain. The row continued and it became clear, that this reconciliation wasn't going to work. My mother was in the living room one day, when Fernando said that I wouldn't see the light of day and my mother went for him. My father came around and he told, Fernando, that he hadn't reared his daughter to be a chattel for him. Fernando brought, Father Sullivan, from St Raphael's Church, to tell me to do my duty. Father Sullivan told him he would have to be very patient with me, as I had been very hurt, to which Fernando replied, "I can be patient all my life if..."

Father Sullivan, to my surprise, replied, "I wouldn't place such a burden on you Fernando."

He had obviously got the measure of Fernando, and everything he was ever going to do would be conditional. I went to social services, as I really did feel, that he would try to take the two children back to Spain. A social worker, who had been married to an Argentinian man, came to the flat and began speaking to us. She told me I would have to try to understand the Spanish culture, but I felt, that I had already made every effort to do that. I had learned to cook Spanish food and had been to conversational Spanish lessons to learn Spanish. The social worker began to speak to, Fernando, in Spanish and at the end of the conversation she angrily exclaimed to him in English.

"Who do you think you are, God?"

I don't think God has a mentality fixed in stone. The social worker brought to my attention the effect that the atmosphere was having on, David, when he appeared with his book all torn up. Fernando told me, that he would come and go, as he pleased, but I would take the two children with me everywhere I went like two balls and chains around my ankles. This wasn't an attempt at reconciliation; this was revenge and Fernando made it clear, that he wasn't leaving a second time. I went to see the solicitor again, who, unsympathetically, said to me, "What do you want me to do? You let him back in again."

I told him why and he spelt out my options.

1. I could leave him and take the children with me.

2. I could stay with him and just put up with it.

3. I could leave, and leave the children with him.

He continued to say, that from what he knew of, Fernando, the latter option was the most likely to prove successful in getting Fernando to leave the matrimonial home, and did I have anyone, that I could go and stay with? John, and I, had helped a girl called Lorraine, to move her furniture from North Wales to New Malden, near Kingston, all of which Fernando knew from Hughie. So, I arranged to stay with, Lorraine, in New Malden and leave the two children with Fernando. It was an agonizing wait and I found it hard to concentrate on anything, but, after about two weeks, I received a telephone call from, Liz, saying, that Fernando was willing to leave the flat and let me return to the two children. I rang social services to ask, if they had been informed of this decision, to which they said, that, as far as they were aware, he was going for custody of the two children. The children were both still attending the nursery in Grove Crescent, Fernando, having arranged for a young girl, the daughter of the previous child minder, to take them to the nursery and then to collect them again. I arrived at the nursery before the girl and collected the two children. I telephoned, John, and asked him, if he would take me and the two children to my parents' house in Banbury, in the car. He said that he was in a meeting until 5pm, but would take us afterwards. When we arrived at my parents' home in Banbury, Fernando was already there. John dropped us off and left. Fernando said that he was going for custody of the two children, as I was an unfit mother! I went for him, and, if not for my father intervening, would have done him a serious injury. The next day my father drove me, and the two children back to the flat. When we arrived, Fernando had gone, and he wasn't going to be let in a second time. I went to see the solicitor again and he once again spelt out my options. I once again, thought that he could resolve all of my problems, without mentioning the word Divorce but I now had to face the fact, that this was the only option. The solicitor said, that Fernando could counter file for a divorce on the grounds of adultery, to which I replied, that I, now, didn't care, what the grounds were, just as long as the marriage ended. To Fernando's claim, that I was an unfit mother, the solicitor replied, "who has been bringing them up while he was in Spain?"

We filed for divorce on the grounds of mental cruelty, nowdays referred to as unreasonable behaviour. It meant going into the witness box in a court of law, before a judge, and proving the grounds for the divorce. On March 24th 1975, my sister, Angela's 12th birthday, I attended the court in Kingston-Upon- Thames and answered the questions put to me by the barrister. I found it difficult to talk to strangers about private, family matters but the barrister took me through it and the decree nisi was granted. Fernando didn't appear, or contest, the divorce. My sister, Angela, was most put out that her 12th birthday had been overshadowed by the divorce proceedings. John, and I, went for a drink that evening and, although I was pleased to be divorced from Fernando, there was also the feeling of an anti-climax. My Catholic beliefs about marriage had been totally turned on their head but my reason had begun to prevail over dogma and I was totally unconcerned, as to whether or not, I was now ex-communicated from the Catholic Church. I was still of the opinion, that we only have one life and like Mary McVeigh, the cook in Short Brothers and Harland, who ironically had never married, I was now of the opinion that there is nothing worse than a bad marriage. The decree absolute was granted some six weeks later. I was awarded £5 per week maintenance for each of the children, as this was easier to enforce, in case of default, and six pence per week maintenance for myself, just to keep my claim open in case of any financial changes in the future. Fernando said, that, if it ever came to paying the maintenance he would fly, which is just what he did. The only problem was he would one day fly back again. I continued to see, John, and, because he was so reliable, dependable and responsible (everything Fernando wasn't) I came to realize, that I couldn't really see a life without him in it. Although I didn't really feel any immediate need to get married again, John wanted us to get married. We fixed a date to marry at Kingston registry office on 25th September 1975. It was a small, but very happy affair. John had taken my father to the pub for a drink and showed him the respect due to him by asking for his blessing for the marriage. My father told him that, although he couldn't be expected to love, David, and, Jamie, as their natural family did, that he would always have the support of the family in bringing them up. My mother, father, brother, Peter, sisters, Maureen, and, Angela, all came to the wedding ceremony together with my friends, Liz, and her sister, Sally. Breda, and her husband, Peter, Johns' mother and father, (who had been in bed for three days after the shock of hearing the news.) John's sister, who paired up with my brother, Peter, and John's friend, Martin Telfer and Adge, who would marry a month later, with John, as their best man, and all of John's friends from Stewart Wrightson. We had the reception in a pub in Berrylands, Surbiton, a set sit down meal with wine and drinks from the bar. John looked happy and relaxed standing against the bar talking to his old friends. John, and I, spent our honeymoon in Martin Telfer's parents' mobile home in Great Yarmouth and went to see Love Story starring Ryan O'Neil and Ali McGraw. We went putting and John couldn't believe it, when I did a hole in one, so I did it again. We visited Norwich Cathedral and spent a day at Newmarket races. All the way to the racecourse, John kept saying that he was going to have a bet on a grey horse called, Pasty. When we got there and saw Lester Piggott's horse, Kangol, walking around the parade paddock looking in great shape, John changed to Kangol. Unfortunately, as luck would have it, Pasty won.

A lady I worked with in County Hall insisted, that I should have a wedding cake and made the cake and iced it for us. It was beautiful; I got the recipe from her and used it for my cakes every Christmas afterwards. It had been a small, simple, but happy occasion, and, when the week of our honeymoon was over, we returned to the flat at King's Keep to start our married life together.

PART THREE

Chapter One

The Move to Nottingham

Stewart Wrightson was sponsoring a three year Research Fellowship at Nottingham University, and John was advised to apply. He was told that, although he was an employee of Stewart Wrightson, it would not give him any advantage over any of the other candidates. I went with him on the day of the interview to provide some moral support. It was to be a whole day affair, which involved meeting the Head of the Department, the other members of staff and having lunch before the actual formal interview in the afternoon. We arranged that I would look around the shops in the centre of Nottingham and meet, John, in the Bell Pub after his interview. John was told on the day that he had been successful and we were both delighted, as we both felt it would give us a fresh start. We decided to buy a house which was cheaper, by almost 50% than in the London area. We found a semi-detached house on the main road, just outside the village of Draycott, between Derby and Nottingham. It had a small front garden with a willow tree growing just inside the front wall, and a large back garden The village itself was mainly one street, with little two up two down red brick terraced houses, that at one time had all been owned by the factory owner in the village and were rented out to his employees. There was a village shop, a village pub and a clothing factory, as well as a village primary school, that the two boys attended. We had the opportunity of buying our King's Keep flat at the reduced rate for sitting tenants, of £3,600, or just continuing to rent it on the controlled rent basis. I suggested to, John, that we keep the flat on and let my Aunt Bernadette, who was living in a large bedsit five minutes away from the flat, live in the flat. John rejected the idea thinking it would be better to cut our ties with the area, and to the past, I suppose. John, and I, married on September 25th and two months later in November, during the doctor's strike of that year, he became so ill that I called my doctor out. John had a really high temperature, was vomiting had a red rash on his toes and feet and couldn't bear the light in his eyes, not even the small chink, that passed through the drawn bedroom curtains. My GP, Doctor Riley, whose practice was in Berrylands, Surbiton was due to soon retire and was none too pleased at being called out during a flu epidemic in the middle of a doctors' strike, especially when the patient wasn't even on his patient list. He examined, John, and said that he had flu and asked him to sign the necessary form, that would include him on his list of patients. John was complaining about his left eye, which I thought had become infected due to the fact that he was so weak and hadn't been washing his hands properly after struggling to the toilet. I went to the local chemist and explained all the problems John was having with his eye to the pharmacist. The pharmacist gave me an eye wash to bath the eye, some antiseptic cream to apply after bathing it and an eye patch to protect it from the light. My mother called in during this week and suggested, that I should take, John, to Surbiton Eye Hospital, but, still believing John was suffering from flu, I couldn't envisage him sitting in the outpatients of Surbiton Hospital in the state he was in. I also didn't think that he would receive a friendly welcome in the middle of a doctors' strike. I told my mother that I would wait until he had recovered from the flu and take him to the Eye Hospital, if it was still no better by then. A few days later, when our friend Lorraine was due to marry, at Kingston Registry

Office, I removed the eye patch and looked at John's eye. It now looked so badly infected, that I took the risk of once again incurring the wrath of Dr. Riley. I called the emergency service and asked if he would come out and see, John, again. I told, John, that I would go to Lorraine's wedding service and return home straight away afterwards, missing the reception. When I got back from the service, my sister, who had stayed with, John, said, that he had been rushed into the intensive care unit of Kingston Hospital. I immediately went to the hospital where, John had been given an injection of antibiotics straight into the eye and was being put through several tests to establish the cause of his illness. The doctor at the hospital said, that the only time he had ever seen anything similar had been in India and asked, if we had been abroad or eaten any shell fish, to which I said, that we hadn't. John told me, that they had asked him some very personal and probing questions regarding his sex life. The doctor said, that he had found some evidence of TB in one of the cultures they'd grown, but it was too small to be significant. When the infection was brought under control, John, was transferred to Surbiton Eye Hospital, where I would later speak with a consultant, who told me, that, John would not only lose the sight in his left eye, but would lose the eye itself! I told the consultant, that he had just obtained a position, as a Research Fellow, at Nottingham University and, that we were due to move to a new house in February. I asked his advice about even making the move at all, as we both had jobs in Kingston and I did not want, John, to have the additional responsibility for my two sons, or to put any extra strain on the other eye, from all the reading involved with his new position. The consultant advised me to go ahead with the proposed move to Nottingham, as it would probably be better for, John, as it would be a new challenge providing a positive distraction from the problem of his eye. The nurse told me, that eyes are very strong and that, in cases of glass in the eye, after car crashes for example, that they are able to remove the glass very successfully, but, in John's case, in which the cause was due to an infection, they were unable to do anything. She advised me that, if my children were ever to suffer a similar problem with their eyes, not to delay, but to take them straight to the Eye Hospital, as an emergency. She said I would have to be very strong for, John, in the future. I rang my father from the Eye Hospital, and, when I began to tell him what the consultant had said, I began to choke with tears and couldn't speak. Knowing me as he did, my father just asked me where I was and told me to stay there, because he was coming to collect us. When we got home, I just sat on the living room floor and let the floods of tears I could no longer contain flow unchecked. One of the most difficult things to accept was the not knowing what had actually been the cause of the devastating illness in the first place. Many years later, however, I watched a television programme on meningitis and I am certain, that that was what John had contracted and was not spotted by either, Dr. Riley or the pharmacist, as it can be mistaken for flu. John had had all the classic symptoms of meningitis, which strikes the weakest area of the body, does the damage and is gone within twenty four hours. I would certainly recognize the symptoms, if I were ever to see them again and be straight up the accident and emergency of the nearest hospital. John, and I, went to spend Christmas with his parents at their council house in Amesbury in Wiltshire. John's mother was house proud to the point of neurosis. She had linoleum on the three bedroom floors upstairs, which she washed, brushed and polished every day. The milk bottles were washed, before being put into the fridge and she never baked, because of the mess it would make. John had never had a homemade roast dinner in his entire life, because his mother couldn't cook and they had the frozen roast dinners that went straight into the oven instead. She made salads, and as she herself said, there would be no risk of burning them. She made apple crumble pudding, the crumble made from a packet of short crust pastry mix with more sugar added to it. She read tea cups, handwriting, and the whole family was into the Ouija board; not surprising, I suppose, as they lived so close to Stonehenge. His father, unlike, John, who was over 6ft, was of medium height and a bit of a wimp, I thought. His mother would wash the dishes and his father would dry them with the tea towel and put them away. They stopped me washing the dishes, when they saw me rinsing them under running hot water, which they thought was a terrible waste and would result in an increased electricity bill. John's dad had been in the army and was now working in Boscombe Down. He had the typical stereotype manner one associates with someone, who works for the military. John's sister, Vanessa, who was dating my brother, Peter, whom she'd met at our wedding, was friendly and outgoing, but a little bit spoilt. Although John's mother and father lived in a council estate, they liked to think, that they were better than everyone else and admitted, that they had never allowed, John, to play out with all the other 'rough' kids on the estate. Instead, they had kept him confined to the garden.

    John and Martin had become best friends and Martin's mother was a real outgoing, friendly country woman. However, it turned out, that, just before his wedding, Martin discovered, that he had been adopted by the two parents, whom he had always thought were his natural ones. The discovery gave him a real identity crisis.

Before we were married, John, and I had gone on holiday to Benidorm and John had got very drunk and started pushing me away. That very same night in bed, he kept saying, "Don't go Sylvia. Don't go!"

As he had never mentioned any, Sylvia, before, I wondered, who the hell she was. I asked John's sister, who Sylvia, was. She told me, that, Sylvia was one of three sisters, who lived in one of the big private houses in the road leading into the council estate. John and she had gone out together and, just as John had finished his degree course at Manchester University, she was awarded a scholarship at The Royal School of Music, in London, as she was a talented piano player. Vanessa said, that Sylvia had long blonde hair, which she put some braids through, but none of the family liked her. We had Christmas dinner and I was given a whole small turkey leg, along with the usual Christmas trimmings. After the Christmas dinner we sat talking in the living room and John's father kept making noises, that John needed to convalesce after his illness, hinting, that he would get very little rest with two young children running around. I had to return to work to do the weekly paid Christmas pay roll and, wishing to appease his parents, tried to convince, John, to stay with them and get some rest. John really didn't want to stay in Amesbury with his parents, but wanted to return to Kingston with me and the two children. He was feeling so low, that he actually started to cry. I eventually persuaded him to stay in Amesbury, promising to return with my brother, Peter, for the New Year Celebrations at Boscombe Down. As I was leaving in the car with my brother, Peter, who had come to collect me, and to see, Vanessa, John's father made a point of saying, that John had a joint First Class Honours Degree. I must confess, that it really didn't mean that much to me at the time, but I did respond by saying, that I had had a place at a Teacher Training College, that I hadn't taken up, but I did want to train as a teacher one day. The opinion of John's parents was, that I was very capable, and I think that is how a lot of people saw me. (Have to, is a good master.) I telephoned John's parents from work and they told me, that he was eating like a horse, (he was on tablets to build him up again, as he had been very run down.) I tried to reassure his parents by saying, that it was a good thing, that he was now married, although I'm not sure they totally agreed with me. I bought lots of bacon, sausages and eggs to take up to Amesbury at the New Year. My brother, Peter, was coming with me and would drive me up there. When we arrived Peter, John, Vanessa, and I went into Salisbury to look around and, John just seemed like a total stranger to me, as if we had never been married three months earlier. We all went to the New Year's Dinner at Boscombe Down and were all seated at a long dinner table, when the message was passed along the table, by John's father, that Peter should put his tie back on. The following day, Vanessa, Peter, and I were sitting in the kitchen and wanted to have a go at the Ouija board. For me it was just a bit of fun; I didn't believe in it, or take it seriously. John was standing in the doorway of the kitchen and we asked him to join in, but he stubbornly refused and, in spite of all our attempts to get the glass to move, it wouldn't budge and we had to abandon the game. Anytime we had done the Ouija board before, John was affected and his nose would begin to run. He once told me, that an Irishman, at Stewart Wrightson had told him one day, while they were playing the game in the pub, that they shouldn't do it, because, when you called up a spirit from the dead, you had no say in whether it was good or evil. I wondered, if John thought, that an evil spirit was responsible for causing the, as yet, still unexplained, damage to his eye. I also wondered whether or not his sudden coldness towards me was somehow an indication, that he now believed that I was the evil spirit, who was responsible for his, now, badly disfigured eye. John had always been very self-conscious about wearing his glasses for short-sightedness and would look like Mr. Magoo, because he wouldn't put them on. One day, I had unexpectedly run into him in Kingston wearing a pair of brown rimmed glasses, much to his embarrassment. We later bought him a pair of blue tinted, gold rimmed glasses and I made great comments about how attractive he looked in them to try and get him to overcome his self-consciousness, which he did. He never had a problem wearing his glasses after that. Peter, John and I took our leave of John's parents and, Vanessa and returned to Kingston, glad to leave the world of superstition and spirits in Amesbury and Stonehenge, where they belonged. On February 9th 1996, Martin Telfer, and Adge, helped John, and I, to move to our new home in Draycott Road in Draycott, Derbyshire. As I passed, John, on the stairs, I asked him, if we could go down to the village to see, if we could buy some bread and other groceries. He coldly turned to me and said quite nastily, "Fuck off!"

I said to him, "How dare you speak to me like that!" As if I, was something that he had just picked up from the street.

Our notice on the flat in Kingston wasn't up, until 16th February and there were to be many occasions in the future, when I wished I had asked Martin, and Adge, to put the furniture back in the van and take the kids and me back to Kingston, leaving, John, to his new house, and new job in Nottingham University. I enrolled, David, and, Jamie, in the village school and they ran down the road, both excited and eager to start their new school. They would climb into the willow tree and jump out at anyone passing by, like someone let out, unused to such freedom after the confines of the flat. John and I took them up to the foothills of the Peak District and when they saw some cows standing still in a byre they asked us, if they were real. How different their childhood then had been to mine, spent exploring the natural countryside, unlike, where we had lived in Kenard Avenue, and to, John's, in the countryside of Wiltshire. I made friends with the Pakistani man, who owned the village shop and was surprised to hear his teenage daughter, obviously Pakistani, speaking English with a Derbyshire accent. She had been born and educated in England, but she was still expected to follow the customs and traditions of the Pakistani culture. She was to have an arranged marriage and her father had bought her, and her Pakistani husband, a small house in the village. He would not have his family work for any employer, but would provide employment for them. At first, it was strange going into the little village pub, as the locals would just sit staring at us village new comers. There was a friendly young couple in the house next to ours, whose mother would ride along the road on her bicycle and call out to the two boys, "Ay up me ducks!" The boys thought this was hilarious and would run down the road crying out, "Ay up me ducks."

I thought I was in a time warp, when a young mother, who had just put her five year old son into school for the first time, was feeling lonely and depressed and wanted to take a part time job, as a machinist, in the local factory. Her husband expected his dinner to be on the table, as soon as he got in from work, but was always the first to be standing outside the pub doors, waiting for them to open. I did a part time job in an office in the village, and another in a pub in the village, making pub lunches. I applied for other jobs in Derby and was horrified at the salary they paid, and what one was expected to do for it, which was, essentially, everything in the office. I would also have had to have paid the fares to Derby and the job wouldn't really have been a viable position, even if they had offered it to me. I applied for a job, as a cook in a school in Long Eaton, just to get back into work. On the day of the interview, John, had gone to London, "on some work related business," and was staying overnight. I invited my next door neighbour in for a drink and bought a bottle of martini, as that was what she drank. When I didn't even get the school cook's job, which went to a younger newly qualified candidate, I was really down. My neighbour called in but wouldn't have anything to drink, as she was suffering from a bad cold and went home early. I drank nearly all the bottle of martini, and ate loads of biscuits. I had to crawl across the floor to turn off the television and crawled up the stairs to bed, as I couldn't stand up. The next morning, I had a massive hangover and knew that I couldn't cope with the two boys all day. I handed them a sock, as they were getting dressed, and then turn around and be sick in the toilet. I got the boys off to school and, when, John, arrived back home, that evening, the boys told him how mum had been sick in the living room, sick on the stairs, sick in the sink and sick in the toilet. I have never been able to look at another bottle of martini, let alone drink one, from that day to this, without feeling sick in my stomach. John spoke with the Personnel Officer, at the university, about the possibility of a job for me there. I was offered the job as an Admissions Clerk in the Arts Faculty, which I readily accepted, promising to do a typing course enabling me to type in the addresses on the standard forms in the office. There was a young typist called, Yvonne, in the office, who was an experienced typist. She sat head down over the typewriter all day, doing all the letters that were a lot more urgent. Another older lady called, Nora, also worked in the office and suffered with neuralgia on one side of her face. The manager of the Arts Faculty's Admission's Office was a man, slightly older than me, in his mid-thirties. He had a wicked sense of humour and told me, that the other most boring job he had ever been in was in a cornflake factory, picking out the burnt cornflakes off the conveyor belt. He left soon after I started and was replaced by a young woman, who was also married to an academic and who suffered with irritable bowel syndrome, she was often absent, so that she could attend the hospital for tests. Mary Foley was in overall charge of both the Science Faculty's and the Arts Faculty's admissions offices and would go between the two. She had the almost nun like, quiet demeanour of an academic, when she came into the office to give the timid, Yvonne, her typing for the day. The most interesting people, who came into the office, were the academics from the departments, who would be sending out the offers and their conditions to the students or the invitations to attend an interview. The academic from the French department, a Dr. King, one day told me, during a humorous exchange of banter, that I was paranoid. I asked him what it meant, and he said when you thought people were persecuting you. I told him, that I didn't think people were persecuting me, I knew they were! Another interesting lot who came were the older group of male students who were from St John's College and were studying Theology. There was nothing God-like or Saint-like about them; they seemed a real, fun loving group of people. When I looked at the application forms from the students applying for courses in the Arts Faculty, I began to think I should be thinking about furthering my own education once again and enquired to Trent Polytechnic, as to the entry requirements for teacher training courses. I was advised, that, as a mature student, with previous work experience, I could apply for the course, if I could obtain one A' Level. I immediately went to The Further Education College in Long Eaton and enrolled on the English A' Level course for Language and literature. I wanted to study History as well, but the teacher advised me not to attempt two A' Level subjects between January and June, as I would only give myself a nervous breakdown. I said I would make up the Shakespeare element of the course, that I'd missed in the autumn term on my own. I attended the college on two evenings a week, between January and June, and passed with a disappointing D grade. Nevertheless, it was enough to get me onto the course, once I had successfully passed the interview. I would begin the course in September 1977 and was no worse off financially than, if I were working. Having worked full time three years before the course, I got a larger mature student's grant and there were no tuition fees in those days. Rodney, a friend of, John's, who lectured in Accountancy at the university, suggested, that we buy a house in the Park in Nottingham. At first I thought he was referring to a park, like Richmond Park, but he was referring to the prestigious Park Estate, the only private estate in the country, beside Nottingham Castle. The private estate consisted of large Victorian houses, built in the 19th century for the wealthy lace manufacturers of Nottingham. John and I looked at a six bedroom Victorian corner house, at no 1 Peveril Drive, built in 1865, that had been owned by an elderly lady and was still in its original state. It was on the market at £11,000 and I asked the estate agent, if it would fall down around us the day after we moved in, but he assured us, that they were solid, well built, brick houses. We obtained a mortgage to buy the property and an improvement loan to carry out the necessary renovations and move into the property in 1977, before I would start my teacher training course in September. When we moved to Draycott, John wanted to legally adopt, David, and, Jamie. I agreed with the idea, as I wanted the children to have a stable and secure life, free of any dramas, that would most certainly, have taken place had, Fernando, continued to do his usual disappearing act, when it suited him, disrupting all of our lives. John, and I, spoke with a solicitor in Long Eaton, who told us it was very unusual for a court to grant an Adoption Order, without the natural parent's consent, if the natural parent were still alive. We advised, Fernando, that, John, wanted to adopt the two boys and tried to get his consent. He refused to give it, saying that, if anything happened to John, and I, he did not want to lose his rights, as the boys' natural father. John and I were both in my father's living room while my father spoke to, Fernando, on the telephone. John had asked my father to ask, Fernando, about the maintenance payments for the children, as he had never attempted to make any of the payments. Fernando, lying as usual, told my father, that he had made the payments, John, and I, unknown to Fernando, were sat on the settee listening. My father said to Fernando, "Well, I'm sure, that you will have the receipts to prove that."

My mother told me, that, Fernando, had told her, that, John, had his wife, and his children, and, that he could pay for them. The solicitor said that he would apply to the courts for the Adoption Order, without, Fernando's, consent, on the grounds, that he had proved to be an irresponsible father. He had made no attempt to pay any of the maintenance ordered by the court, nor had he made any attempt to see his children. A social worker called to the house in Draycott to assess both, John, and me, as suitable parents for adoption. Even though I was the children's natural mother, because I was now in a new relationship, I had to apply to adopt them too. She made a thorough assessment of our home, and financial situation and sent her report to the court in support of our application. It struck me at the time, that, if natural parents had to go through the same stringent assessment, that many of them would never be allowed to have children. We got a date for the hearing, while we were still living in Draycott and John, and I, together with the two boys, attended the hearing in front of a judge in the Family Division of Derby County Court. The Adoption Order was granted and the boys' names were changed to, Johnson, and a new birth certificate issued for both of them. It was in 1976, that, Abba's song, Fernando, was released and one day, as it was playing on the radio, David, said, "We used to know someone called Fernando, didn't we?"

I looked at his little face all puzzled, and frowning, and I thought to myself, "He is going to have the carefree childhood that I want for him," and I said, "Yes, that was a friend of Hughie's."

Satisfied with the answer, the puzzled frown left his face, and Fernando, was never mentioned again. My sons did not have to go to school, wondering why they had a different name to their parents and were going to have a good, secure, settled home life, which was no more than they deserved. My mother came up to Draycott and looked after the two boys while John, and I, had a week's holiday in Tenerife. On our return, my mother told us that, David, had lit a candle under the bed, apparently he wanted to read his book instead of going to sleep. The flame had caught the horse hair filled base and had smoldered slowly. My distraught mother had to drag the bed down the stairs and out of the house, fearing it would burst into flames and set the house on fire, and John, and I, would have no house to come back to, or the children and, perhaps, even mother, too! David received a beating from my mother, who never read Dr. Spock or Super nanny, but simply reacted to events. John, and I, took my mother, out to the Peak District and she attempted to climb the foothills. She was just a little way up, when she went into a total panic, and couldn't move. We thought it really funny and told her to just sit down, which she did, and she came down on her bottom all of the way. It was then that we realized that she suffered from vertigo and a fear of heights. The Victorian house in Nottingham proved to be a good buy. Because of the money borrowed for the Home Improvements Loan, I got my first ever washing machine, when, David, and, Jamie, were five and six. Workmen, who came to work on the house, said it was an absolute joy to work on the house, because of the craftsmanship, that had gone into it, when it was built. The brickwork was 18 inches thick and all of the rooms had high ceilings, which had the original rose in the centre and original Victorian coving around the ceiling. The two large living rooms had marble fireplaces with the servant bells at the side, which still ring on the board in the kitchen when pressed. The wood was all seasoned and the doors, stairway and banisters were all made of the original solid pine. The basement was where the servant quarters had been. There were Victorian tiles in the hallway, which had a small fireplace, and three steps leading to the kitchen. The kitchen actually had a well for water in it and a large, Belfast sink, with a rickety old shelf above, with hooks attached and a Thurland Range, with built in cupboards to the side with pine doors. It occurred to me, that, if we took a picture of the kitchen sink, we could use it on a poster for a "Shelter Advertisement." Upstairs, on the first floor, there was one large, high ceilinged bedroom to the front, with a small dressing room off it, the size of a single bedroom .Next to that, was a second, large bedroom, that faced onto the street, that led up to Peveril Drive. The bathroom was off the landing on this floor and the third smaller bedroom was next to the bathroom. On the second floor were two large attic rooms, one looking onto Peveril Drive and the other onto the street leading to it. The house had a small back, and side garden, and a garden at the front with a gate and path leading up to the front door. The wooden, front door opened into a small hallway, with a door to the side, that had small, square yellow Victorian window panes, and this door led into the main hallway leading to the rest of the house. Outside was a Victorian gas lamppost, that they would come round and light in the evenings. We were the corner house and could be seen from the ramparts of Nottingham Castle, which was just around the corner from us. Beside the castle, was the Brewhouse Yard, which was a Victorian museum containing a Victoria schoolroom, not unlike St Teresa's Primary School, that I had attended and the Trip to Jerusalem Pub, the oldest pub in England, which was built into the castle rock that was made of bunter sandstone. There were caves in the rock in which people had lived at one time, because they were so dry. They had lots of underground tunnels, that lead all over Nottingham. The Park Estate had been built for the wealthy lace manufacturers of Nottingham and the properties were all leasehold and owned by Lord Nuffield and the Nuffield Trust, who later sold the leaseholds to the owners, in order to build halls of residence for the students of Oxford University. The land had originally belonged to the castle, until it passed to Lord Nuffield. The houses were built in concentric circles, like the canals in Amsterdam, in order to give a sense of space, and a requirement was, that they should be good quality houses. At the top of the Park was the Ropewalk, just off Derby Road, which had large houses containing caves with cave drawings, such as, Daniel, in the Lion's Den. There was Gladstone House, where the Prime Minister stayed, when he visited Nottingham, and was used by the judges, when they were sitting in the courts. The Davis cup was played in the tennis courts in the park, before it changed venues, and I watched Jeremy Bates, playing there, when he was just at the start of his tennis career, I noticed, that he had the killer instinct in him required to win.

We knocked the wall down in the kitchen, making it into one long kitchen, and covered over the well, concreting over the kitchen floor. We removed the Belfast, kitchen sink and shelf and replaced it with a modern sink unit. John painstakingly renovated the Thurland Range, painting it black and the edges with a thin red trim. We bought a long, wooden, pine, table, with benches at the sides from Neale's auctions on the Mansfield Road, as it was cheap to buy, big old antique furniture, that wouldn't fit into smaller houses. We had to replace the whole of the wooden floor in one of the main living rooms, as it had damp rot coming up from the basement that had no ventilation. The necessary work to cure the damp rot in the cellar was carried out and ventilation installed. We lived in one room, lighting the fire in the marble fireplace that took one whole bucket of coal at a time, while the floor in the other room was replaced. The decorators prepared the walls with embossed wallpaper and did decorative panelling, painting the walls burgundy and the panelled areas grey, lending warmth and richness to the rooms. Although they said they would strip and varnish the pine banister on the stairs, and the doors, by hand, in the end, they sand blasted it, while the house was still empty of furniture to complete the job quickly. Much to, John's, annoyance, they would often disappear to go off and do other small jobs. We had central heating installed and the place then began to feel like home. We were close to Trent Bridge Cricket Ground, and would go there often with the two boys, as it made for a good day out in the fresh air. We would also go to the one day John Player Matches and the Nottingham Forest Football Ground when Nottingham Forest was playing. Other times, we would take the two boys out to the Peak District, stopping at country pubs for lunch and a drink, sitting in the garden, and, John, would tell the boys not to go beyond the fallen tree a little way from where we were sitting. Typically, the boys ran straight for the fallen tree, testing the boundaries. The boys attended St Mary's Primary School on Derby Road, next to St Barnabas' Cathedral. Although, John was not a Catholic, he was hands on with the boys' education, and would attend the parents' evenings and Mass on Sunday. When, David, was due to make his First Holy Communion, he had to first make his First Confession. John, and I, went to the Cathedral with, David, and, Jamie, so that he could make his First Confession. We waited outside the confession box and when I saw, David, hesitate, when it came to his turn, I just pushed him through the door and closed it. We came out and were walking down Maid Marion Way, on our way to buy, David, and, Jamie, sweets. Ordeal over, David, ran ahead of us skipping light heartedly and singing, "I've got a sparkling soul," over and over again and we all laughed. Canon Cummins at St Barnabas Cathedral spoke to, John, about converting to Catholicism, and, to his credit, John, agreed to attend instruction sessions with him, but I don't think he ever did convert. As for myself, I had never attended confession after my last confession, which was the day before I married, Fernando, when I went to confession in a different area to the one in which we were living in. I always said that, after I married him, I never got the chance to sin. I started my Teacher Training Course at Trent Polytechnic in September and during the First Freshers Week, the lecturers arranged a four mile hike in the Peak District, so that the students could all get to know each other. There were three other mature students, about the same age as me, (29) with husbands and families, who were having a second chance to obtain professional qualifications. We would walk and talk a while, we then had a lunch of stilton cheese and onion sandwiches in a friendly country pub. The lecturers were friendly and informal, telling us, that they saw us as future colleagues. They particularly liked having mature students in the lectures, as they were closer in age to them and felt that they created a sort of balance, with the younger students. Between the two academic worlds of the University and Trent Polytechnic, John, and, I made good friends and had a good social life. John, would often remark, that he wished he'd done his Degree as a mature student, as he'd have gotten so much more out of it. The Teacher Training Course fitted in well with the school holidays and the relaxed atmosphere of both places enabled, John, or I, to bring the boys into our respective departments should the need ever arise. I would do the Summer Schools during the school holidays and take the two boys with me. During our first year in Draycott, John's moods would get me down, he would lie sleeping in the bed like a coiled spring having nightmares and I would be afraid to awaken him, fearing what his reaction might be. I went to the doctor about myself and he told me to tell John, that if he valued his marriage, he should come with me to see him, which he did. I said to the doctor, that although, John, had lost his sight in one eye, he could still drive and play cricket and do his job okay and, John, said, "But not as well as before." He was a perfectionist.

The doctor told him, that he had to adapt to the new circumstances and should take up a hobby like shooting, which involved closing one eye. I felt, that the prospect of having his eye removed was, not surprisingly, playing upon his mind; he was, after all, only twenty four. He asked the doctor too if he would make an appointment for us to see a consultant at the hospital, which he did. We went to Nottingham Hospital and saw the consultant, who examined John's eye and told us that, although the eye had shrunk, it was now holding its own and wouldn't have to be removed. He said he would arrange for a lens to made, similar to a contact lens that, John, could wear to cover over the eye. I was absolutely delighted, and relieved, to receive this news, knowing it would lift a tremendous weight off John's mind. I completed my first year of teacher training, which was for Primary School teachers and decided that I wanted to transfer to the University of Nottingham Teacher Training Course, because I found the CNNA course too child-centred and generalist. I really wanted to go further in my own education and be a specialist teacher, rather than having to study more general subjects, required for Primary School teachers. We would go into the Primary Schools and fit the theory to the practice and I found the teachers were sometimes more petty than the children over things like blackboard dusters and similar items. I had a meeting with the Dean of the College, who was somewhat amused, when I said I was 29 and wanted to qualify as soon as possible, before I was too old to begin a career in teaching. My first year on the CNNA counted as two A' Levels and enabled me to transfer to the University of Nottingham, BEd (Bachelor of

Education) course which required two A' Levels. I knew I wanted to teach English and the choice of second teaching subject was between Religious Education and History. The lecturer said, that the R.E department was almost agnostic and that clinched it for me. I felt I owed it to myself to study Religious Education, having been brought up, as a Catholic, in an environment, that taught, that it was a sin to even go into a protestant church, even to attend a wedding service, and that Catholics were infallibly right about everything and all the other religions were wrong. This was one of the best decisions I ever made in my life; the course was a real eye and mind opener. It was really interesting covering the five world religions, philosophers, humanists, such as Bertrand Russell, as well as debates on morals and ethics. I never taught Religious Education, except on teaching practice, but I never regretted doing the course. The English course was equally interesting and broad and included Drama. The education element comprised of Psychology, Philosophy, Sociology and History of Education. These were all new subjects for me and were both interesting and broadening. I chose two other options, Integrated Studies and Educational Technology. One of the lecturers in, John's department was leaving and, John was invited to apply for the position, which would be permanent, as opposed to The Research Fellowship, which was for three years. John, once again, had to compete with two other applicants and, once again, was successful in obtaining the position. His mother, father, aunt and uncle, (who were over on holiday from Australia,) came to visit as well. John's father told me, that nothing they had shown his aunt and uncle had impressed them, until they saw Chatsworth House and Haddon Hall. They were also impressed with our house in Peveril Drive, but, John's mother was horrified, at how I could possibly clean such a big house. Surprisingly, a large house, with lots of space for everyone, is much easier to clean, than a small house full of clutter. At the end of the first year of my CNAA Generalist Course, the college organized a field trip to Angelsey for the tutors, students and some disadvantaged children from inner city homes, a group of physically and mentally challenged children from a Special Needs' School, and their teachers, who would be responsible for supervising them. We organized ourselves into groups of four, as we would be sharing a tent and I said I didn't think I'd survive a camping trip, as I was too old and used to sleeping in my own comfortable bed and having all my comforts. When we arrived in our mini bus to Anglesey, we erected the sleeping tents in one field, with a catering tent beside each tent, where we would cater for ourselves, and the tutors, in turn. The children and their teachers had their tents in the field next to ours. We also erected one big marquis tent in our field, which was used as a big, communal place, in which everyone could come together in the evenings. The activities that were organized for the children were stimulating and interesting and a wonderfully creative way for Primary School children to both learn, and socialize, together. Needless to say, that my catering experience was fully appreciated by my group and the tutors, who remarked, that should we run out of money, they would send me out to sell clothes pegs. I felt I was on an island in paradise; the whole experience was so amazingly brilliant. A talent competition was organized for the children in the large marquis and was won by the children in the Special Needs' School, who formed a group and played lots of different musical instruments. Everyone clapped and cheered, when they received their prize, including all the other children, who were on the trip. Once the children went off with their teachers to their tents in the evenings, we were free to go to the local pub for the evening, where we had a great time. One evening, we all gathered in the large marquis and sang songs. One tutor remarked that I had a very expressive face, when he saw the expression on it, as all the younger students sat singing, "Peter Rabbit," doing the actions to the song. Large quantities of alcohol were consumed and I fell asleep, where I lay, on the grass and wakened in the morning to find myself completely surrounded by empty bottles, (not all mine, I might add.)

In the mini bus on the way home, the next day, I felt, that I could just put out my arms and I'd be able to fly home or, that I'd be completely topped up again, if I drank just one half pint of lager. When we arrived back in Nottingham, my friend, Diane, told me, that, when she had telephoned her husband, Paul, (John wouldn't allow us a telephone in the house on the grounds of cost) he had told her, that, John, had been admitted into Nottingham General Hospital, as he had contracted mumps and his testicles had swollen. He had never had mumps as a child, and had probably caught them off, David, who had them at that time; Rodney had had the good sense to stay away from the house, fearing he might catch them. I asked, Diane, why she hadn't told me this, when we were in Anglesey and she said, that I was having such a good time and that she felt I needed the break and didn't want to spoil it for me. My sister, Angela, and her friend, Sue Darcy, had come up to Nottingham to help, John, with the boys and they looked after, David, and, Jamie. John's testicles were put into a truss to help support them and the secretaries in his department visited him in the hospital, bringing him pornographic magazines, which they thought was hilarious. There was the concern, however, that the mumps in an older man could cause him to become sterile. John, and I, never talked about the possibility of having children of our own, so I didn't know just how much this might bother him.

Chapter Two

Trouble in Paradise Again

I did the Summer School and in September began the Bachelor of Education Degree Course at Nottingham University, which was in the main building of the same site at Clifton, just outside Nottingham City Centre. In the first year of the course, John, was very supportive and would bring, David, and, Jamie, into the department, if the need ever arose, or he would look after them on the days, that I would go to the library in order to complete an assignment on time. One day, David, who had been into the department with John, came home and innocently said to me, that he had seen, John, snogging behind the door of his office. John, had told, David, to stay in one office, but, David, had left it and gone to John's office to find him, and saw, John, who had hurriedly closed the door again, kissing, Cilla.

Cilla, and her husband, Laurie, were good friends of ours and we often visited each other for dinner. Cilla had a Degree in French, but was working in the department, as a secretary, which was beyond my comprehension. Laurie had a Degree in Botany, but was working in antiques, often going to the auctions to both buy, and sell items. I knew, David, was too young, at six and a half years old, to make up such a story and had just innocently told me, what he had seen. When I confronted, John, and later, Cilla, and, Laurie, with the story, it was simply laughed off and, although I made no more of it, a small doubt nevertheless remained in my mind. I successfully completed my first examinations and went on to do the second year of the three year course. That Christmas, John, was in one of his depressive moods and was just lying on the living room settee, not entering into the spirit of Christmas at all. As we had no telephone, I went to the public telephone box to telephone my father and wish the family Happy Christmas. My father soon detected, that all was not well between, John, and I, and I told him, that he was just lying depressed on the settee. When I spoke to, John, about the state of our relationship, he promised he would make an appointment with a psychologist at the hospital, as he still blamed his eye disfigurement for his mood swings. I often wondered, if he regretted the marriage and the responsibility of the two children, who were not his own natural children. He would often go up to Rodney's house in the park and return late. On one occasion, at 4am, I was sitting up in the bed waiting for him, when he quietly tried to sneak into the bedroom holding his socks and shoes. Surprised to find me awake, he began to make some feeble excuse, but I said angrily, that I didn't think four in the morning, was the appropriate time for any married man to be returning home and we argued. He asked, Laurie, if he would sell some things at the auction for us and gave him the gold watch that, Fernando, had bought for me in Spain. The bracelet was slightly damaged from moving furniture and, Laurie, said he could only get scrap value for it, which, John, said would be okay. He also gave him the picture, that, Jim, and, Carol, had given Fernando, and I, for Christmas. He later suggested that we sell the house in the park and buy another one in West Bridgford, which I thought strange, as it would mean down marketing and releasing the equity from the house. Couples usually looked to up market and we were already in the best area of Nottingham. To my reckoning, it wasn't as if we were experiencing any financial problems. John had all his salary to pay the mortgage, (which was small and at a low rate of interest) the car and the utility bills. I had my student grant, the child benefit and earnings from Summer School, to pay for all the household expenditure, food and clothes for myself; the boys and my travel expenses, to and from college. This arrangement suited me, as I felt I never had to ask, John, for any money for me or the children. John paid for a family holiday for us all to Menorca, getting a cheap deal for us all from one of the tutors from my college, who also ran a travel agency. Before moving to Nottingham, we had been involved in a minor car accident, in which I received a deep cut to the left hand side of my forehead, which needed stitching at the hospital. I also had bruising down the left hand side of my face; the other driver was at fault, as he had turned right at traffic lights without stopping, because he was looking at the street names. I was in the passenger seat and braced myself for the inevitable crash I could see was going to take place. Everything went into slow motion and my head hit the front windscreen of the car. I turned around to check that, David, and, Jamie, who were in the back, were okay, which they were, sat on either side of the laundry bag in the back of the car. The boys were taken into a nearby shop and given some sweets and, I was taken into the back of the shop to hold my bleeding forehead over the sink waiting for the ambulance to arrive. I remember being afraid to even touch my head, as numb from shock, I couldn't feel anything and was afraid of just what the exact damage to my head had been. When the ambulance men arrived, they said they couldn't feel a pulse, I said, that was probably because I was dead. They jokingly said, after I was stitched up at the hospital, that it was a good job, that I was already married, as I didn't look a pretty sight. John was worried, saying that my father was going to kill him. After we moved to Draycott the claim for the accident was settled with the driver's insurance company; as with all the other items of mine, that were sold, I never saw a penny and it all went to John. I always felt, rightly or wrongly, that, because the two boys weren't his, that I had to make sure, I was always paying our way. I began to feel very lonely in the marriage, because, to all intents and purposes, to all our friends and families, we were a married couple, yet there is nothing lonelier than lying next to someone in bed, who is not relating to you in any way whatsoever. I felt like I was sitting in a room, looking at four white walls, getting absolutely no stimulus or feedback whatsoever. I would often say to, John, that I thought it must be ice cold water, that flowed in his veins. It was becoming clear to friends and family, that all was not well in our marriage. His best friend, Martin Telfer, told me, during one visit, that he thought, I was the best thing, that had ever happened to John, because one day, when he had gone to see him while he was studying at Manchester University John, was living with an Aunt and Uncle in Manchester and not with the other students, which would be the norm the Uncle told, Martin, that he was glad, that he had come to see, John, and he was worried about him; because all he ever did was sit in his room polishing his shoes. An Australian friend of mine from college said, John, was draining me like a battery charger that he would forget to put back on charge. My father paid us a visit and I broke down in tears at the kitchen table and my father asked, John, what was it that he was going to work for? He didn't get a reply.

John had done my father's books for him, after he sold his corner shop with the flat above and moved to Berrylands, Surbiton with my mother, who was now the housemother, and employee of

Surrey County Council, in a small block of flats, providing sheltered housing for the elderly, who were living independently, but needed a house mother on the premises. My father, asked John, and I, to keep the equity from the sale for him, until they were settled. He gave me half the proceeds amounting to £4,000 and, John, the other half of £4,000. I put the money into my building society savings account and just forgot about it. Later in the year, my youngest sister, Angela, came to live with me, saying she wanted to study in Nottingham, and because she had met a handsome young minor called, Alvin, with whom she was badly smitten and wanted to be close to. She knew I would fall for the education card, and I did, (knowingly.) I got her onto a drama course in one of the local colleges and tried to get her an education grant, but was unsuccessful, as she was still only sixteen. Initially, my parents were offended, that I should want any financial support from them towards Angela's keep, but, as, Angela, smoked and wanted to go out to discos, I felt it was only fair, that the family, and not, John, and I, contribute to supporting Angela, financially. My father sent her a cheque by post containing a letter, saying to give Margaret x amount of pounds towards her keep and to keep the rest. I felt like a landlady in my own home. One Saturday morning, I told, David, to go up to Angela's room and waken her, as she had asked me to wake her in time to go to the building society to withdraw some money. After, David, had gone upstairs, I noticed a pair of men's shoes in the surround of the Thurland Range in the kitchen, that were far too small to be John's and suspected they were Alvin's. When David came back down, I saw his worried little face and asked him, if, Alvin, was up in the room with Angela. He said, that he was, and that, Angela had asked him not to say anything to me. I knew that, Angela had stopped taking the contraceptive pill and feared that, if she were to become pregnant, while in my care, that I would be held responsible by my parents for the rest of her life and the baby's life. When, Angela, came downstairs and I confronted her with the situation, her attitude was one of utter defiance, saying she was no different to any other sixteen year old. I told her, that she was different to many sixteen year olds I knew and I asked her, what she intended to do. Still defiant, she replied, that she supposed she would have to leave. I wouldn't back down, because of her attitude, and said, yes, she should. Angela went upstairs and packed her things and came down wearing a smart, black tailored suit, with a silver brooch her long, dark hair, having just been set with heated rollers, bouncing around. Still defiant, she left the house and got into a waiting taxi outside. I felt a sense of relief to be free of the responsibility of, Angela, and also, because there had been a constant battle of wits, between her, and John, about who would do the washing up, that there had never been between him and me. I always did the cooking, as he couldn't cook and he always did the washing up. I just assumed, that, Angela, had gone back down to Surbiton to live with my parents, until my mother, arrived on the doorstep. Angela had rung her to say, that she was depressed. She had gone to stay with, Alvin's, mother, and his sister, in their council house in St Anne's. Alvin's mother, found her a job at £25 per week, sewing ok, logos onto t-shirts. It is still a standing joke between, Angela, and me, how the girls would all say to each other, "I'm OK, are you OK?"

When I learned this from mother and, once again, feeling under pressure, I started to cry. My mother felt the top of my head and said that it was boiling. Angela did return to Nottingham and got a comfortable little bed-sit on the Lenton side of the park, where she could live independently, but still be close to me, and continue seeing Alvin. Just after, Angela, left, my sister, Maureen, came to visit, just ahead of a visit I was expecting from my father. We went into Bell's pub in the city centre and, Maureen, said she had something to tell me. I immediately reacted by saying, "You're not pregnant are you?"

She said that she was. Maureen had been going out with, Bill Nice, a friend of my brother, Peter, who worked as a British Telecommunications Engineer. His family lived in a big house in Kenley Road opposite Kingston Hospital, but Bill, chose to live in a squat with other friends. When my parents were living in the flat above the shop in Tolworth, my mother found the contraceptive pill in Maureen's, handbag and kicked her out. Ironically, Maureen was now pregnant, and I was relieved that it happened on my parents watch, rather than mine. I asked, Maureen, if she wanted me to tell my father, when he arrived and she said yes. I decided to tell him at the beginning of his week's stay, so that he had the whole week with us to get used to the idea.

My father could always pick the winner of the Grand National, which was the following Saturday. He told us the name of the horse he fancied, but I think he had a bad week on the horses that week and didn't put the bet on. Of course the horse won! On seeing the result, his face went bright red from raised blood pressure. After the incident with, Angela, my father, asked for his money back, that John, and I, had been keeping for him. I went to the building society and withdrew the money for him .John had used about £400 of his money, and asked me to make up some story about waiting for the interest to be paid in. I refused to do this and told, John, he would have to ring my father and speak to him himself. When my father arrived in Nottingham, he said that it was okay about the £400 and, John, could keep it for doing the books. John later said that he wanted to go back to London as he was applying for a position with various bookmakers in Risk Management. This didn't make any sense to me whatsoever, as he now had his permanent position, as a lecturer in Industrial Relations in Nottingham University. The renovations to the house had already been completed and I was nearing taking my second year examinations, and still had a third year to complete, before I could qualify as a teacher. John had told me in great detail, how his sessions with the counsellor at the hospital were going. He explained how a red shape had indicated, that he shied away from being the centre of attention, or drawing any attention to himself at all. He also said, that they were indicating, that I was resentful of his job, because it took his time and attention away from me. He added that all the sessions had been recorded onto a tape, which the counsellor kept. The moods continued, and I decided, without saying anything to, John, to make an appointment with the counsellor, to seek his advice, as to how best I could help John? I went to the hospital and explained the situation and said that I would like to make an appointment with John's counsellor. The receptionist in the department at the hospital checked through their records and told me that, John, had never been referred to a counsellor, and had never attended any counseling sessions. The whole story was a total fabrication on John's part and a very convincing one at that. I left the hospital distressed and in a state of total shock and disbelief. I rang my father and told him what I had just discovered. When I confronted, John, with this, there was no explanation he could offer for the deception. I told him I would move into the second bedroom and we could just get on with living our separate lives, as that was pretty much what we were already doing. As I was moving things into the other room, John became angry and aggressive and, David, who was helping me, began throwing shoes at him and stood by my side, defending me from him. On another occasion, I was standing at the cooker in the kitchen preparing the dinner and, John, was uttering a torrid of abuse, telling me that I was selfish and, that I cared about no one but myself. I carried on stirring the sauce for the spaghetti bolognaise, ignoring him, until little, David, who could stand it no longer, blurted out angrily, "No she isn't! You are!"

On another occasion, John, began smashing some of the plates, that were on the sink drainer onto the cemented kitchen floor, when I said, "Oh, you want to smash plates do you? Well, we can all smash plates!"

I proceeded to smash every cup, plate and saucer onto the floor; I then walked out. David, and, Jamie, was outside looking through the kitchen window unable to believe their eyes. I certainly found it therapeutic and a great stress buster. When I returned home, John had cleared up all the broken crockery. I had always taken the view, that in the event of any marriage break-up, the woman should remain in the marital home for the sake of the children, but, as things became worse between, John, and I, I knew he would never leave the house. One night out of sheer frustration, I threw a brick through the long glass front Victorian window and shouted that he could keep the house. Another evening when things became ugly, I had to go to my neighbours' house. I knew we couldn't continue as we were, so I went to see a solicitor on Maid Marion Way. He advised me to remain in the property and to let, John, move to London, if that was where he wanted to go. I found it increasingly difficult to continue to live in the atmosphere, that existed in our home and my exams were getting nearer and nearer. I made up my mind to leave and to take the two boys with me. That weekend, John, lay on the settee in the living room, neither of us speaking and I said to the two boys that I would take them ice skating. As soon as we made to go out, John got off the settee and blocked the door, refusing to let us out. It was only, if I ever made the effort to lift my own spirits, that, John, would decide he wanted to talk. I decided then, that I would not wait until Monday to leave, but quickly put the clothes in the laundry basket into the suitcase and picked up the box of books. John stood at the bottom of the stairs trying to block the front door, preventing us from leaving. When he saw the books in the cardboard box, he was almost apoplectic with disbelief and rage, saying, "You planned this, you planned this!"

David, Jamie, and I, eventually made it through the front door with, John, still trying to stop us. There were tears in David's eyes as we left, not only did they not get to go ice skating, but, David, was just five days away from having his ninth birthday. I learned later from my Australian friend, Vivienne, who had called round to the house that same afternoon that, John, told her, that I had gone out shopping with the two boys.

Chapter Three

Homeless

I booked two rooms for myself and the boys in the Hotel Antoinette, not far from where we had lived in Kings keep before moving to Nottingham, because I knew it was where homeless people were accommodated by the Local Authority. I went with the two boys to see my parents, to let them know, that I, had left John, and wasn't going back. On Monday, I went to the Housing Department to advise them, that I was now homeless with my two sons and in need of accommodation until my marriage was dissolved and I could find another place to live. They tried to persuade me to return to the marital home in Nottingham, but I was adamant, that I wouldn't be going back. The council moved us to the Bramley Guest House at Hook Road, which they used for homeless people. It was run by a father and his son. The boys attended, Our Lady Immaculate Primary School at Tolworth and I began to study for my second year examinations. My brother, Raymond, was over from Germany, where he had been working as a bricklayer, like my brother, Peter, who had also chosen this trade. He looked as though he was in need of a break and my mother was handing him his nourishing home cooked dinners. Both he and my mother made it very clear from their attitude to me and the boys that they thought I should go back up to Nottingham. Fortunately for me, I could always make my own homemade dinners, as well as everyone else's! I went back up to Nottingham by train and sat my second year examinations, which I passed. This allowed me to take a Diploma in Education, which

I could use towards another course, or as a qualification in its own right. John came down to Surbiton to see me and the boys and agreed to selling the house and giving me the equity, which I could put towards a flat for me and the boys, with a small mortgage of about £4,000. I asked the bank manager to let me have an overdraft facility until the house was sold and, although, Jim, and, Carol, both came with me to see the bank manager, in order to underpin the overdraft, the bank manager still contacted, John, at the University. As John, was joint owner of the property, they had to obtain his consent to the overdraft, which, John, gave. Using my Diploma, I applied for a place, and joined the CNAA course in a Teacher Training College on Kingston Hill, but left at the end of the first term. The course was similar to the first CNAA Generalist Course, that I had done in Nottingham and I knew, that I really wanted to train as a Secondary School Teacher of English. I decided to now use the time I had available to take driving lessons and achieve the other things I had always wanted to do in my life. Pass my driving test! The boys and I moved to half way accommodation in New Malden, which was an absolute disgrace; filthy and run down. The council certainly do not wish to make being homeless, attractive! I set about cleaning and painting the place with some help from my friend, Liz. I joined a Homeless Action Group, and, together with others, began campaigning to have empty houses in the borough used for the homeless. I joined other protests to try to stop the Council from cutting the 'Meals on Wheels,' service to the elderly. We all organized a protest outside the Guild Hall in Kingston-Upon-Thames, where the mayor's ball was being held at a cost of £5,000, displaying placards saying, "Cut the Mayor's Balls."

Norman Lamont, MP for Kingston, was at the time going into the hall, looking like, Dracula, in his long black cape. He stopped to angrily tell us to take our argument somewhere else. When he turned around again to go into the hall, one of the protestors did a big gob on his cape, which he failed to notice. Thames Television came to film the protest for the local television news, and later, they came to carry out an interview with me, in the half way house in New Malden, It did go out on television, but I never saw it. Tim Ewart, (now the reporter for ITV news) came with his television crew and they interviewed me and filmed, David, and, Jamie, playing with a football in the overgrown, neglected front garden. The electric plugs were turning black when I used them; this was due to faulty wiring, which the council refused to repair, as the house was condemned and due for demolition. I disconnected the black plugs and bought them into the Housing Department telling them, that I was going to take legal action against them for subjecting the lives of me, and my two children to the risk of fire. My mother and father were both working for Surrey County Council at that time, as I had asked, Mr. Waters, the head of the weekly paid staff, if he could give my dad an interview for a job there, after he sold his shop in Tolworth. Mr. Waters did interview my dad and gave him a job, which stopped him going around like a hen on a hot griddle. The manager of the Housing Department commented to my mother, that she had an intelligent daughter in me. The council offered me a two bedroomed flat in Brine Court, a small three storey block of flats in the same road I had lived in, when I lived in King's Keep. We were on the top floor and had no carpets. The neighbour below kept telephoning the council to complain about the noise. A young man, who lived in the block of flats, said he would accompany me in the old car I had bought, so that I could get a lot of miles under my belt before my driving test. Rather than taking a cancellation date, I kept the original test date, as I already had the car and could get more experience before the test. He also showed me how to park the car as driving instructors didn't teach parking back then and I needed a space big enough for a convoy of lorries, before I felt confident to park the car! On the day of the test, I kept going to the loo and decided to walk to the post office, in order to distract myself and take my mind off the forthcoming test. After the test, I couldn't believe it, when the examiner said, that I had passed first time. When I had been in the Bramley Guest House, my sister, Maureen, was also there; having had her baby, she was also going through the homeless route to get a council flat. She, and, Bill, had married and were having their reception in the Hotel Antoinette. My mother suggested, that a big marquis tent be erected in the garden of Bill's parents' house, and, that I do the catering. I told her that I had had two wedding receptions, had paid for both of them, and had never expected anyone who would be a guest at the wedding, to work at it! My mother was none too pleased, especially at how much this particular reception was going to cost her. I went with her to the hotel with, David, to discuss menus for the reception that was to be held there. My mother, David, and I sat on chairs outside the catering manageress' office, waiting for the catering manageress. David asked me what was wrong and I said nothing, to which he replied, "Then why are you keeping looking at your feet?" Exactly what I do when I'm tense, and uncomfortable.

We chose the menu for a sit down meal and on the day of the wedding, John, came down from Nottingham and attended the registry office service with myself and the two boys. During the reception, Carol, confided in me, that she couldn't get, Jim, to even lift his own lunch plates, let alone wash them, even though she was out at work all day as a doctor. Jim had finished his degree in Internal Relations at the London School of Economics and had his sights set on being an independent film director and producer. He was at home all day in their newly renovated house in Ealing, while, Carol, was out all day working. Carol told me, that she had told, Jim, he should take a stop gap job as a taxi driver to be working at something until his film work took off. However, to, Jim, image was everything and there was no way, he would take such a job, or even sign on as unemployed, even if it were only to get his National Insurance Stamps. I knew my brother, Jim, very well and I told, Carol, she had two choices. One, she could give up her career as a doctor and be the stay at home wife, doing the domestic work, that, Jim, saw as woman's work, or she could carry on being a doctor and use some of the salary she earned to pay a housekeeper to do that woman's work, because she hadn't a snowball's chance in hell, of ever getting, Jim, to do it. Carol took my advice and employed a housekeeper. We went to Bill's mother's and father's house in Kenley Road after the reception and the matter of Jim's low sperm count was all kept very hush hush, being very much a taboo subject, especially with my mother. In the evening, Jim, Carol, John, and I, went to an Indian restaurant and, Jim, was making noises, that marriage should be a time, when the man made a public declaration to the outside world, that his wife was the person, that he loved and cared about more than anyone else in the world. They were nice words, but too late for, John, and I. When, Maureen, and I were both in the Bramley Guest House, after, Maureen, had the baby, and, Bill, was away working in a good job in Tehran, Maureen, was clearly experiencing post natal depression. I took her and the baby in the pram around to my mothers', flat in Berrylands and said, that I thought, Maureen, should stay with her and my dad and not be left alone in the Bramley. Maureen was later given a maisonette in School Lane Council Estate in Tolworth, which she hated. When I got my council flat in Brine Court, my father came round and asked me to have Maureen, and the baby, as she was still suffering from post natal depression and Bill's parents were refusing to ask, Bill, to return from his good job In Tehran to be with her. Jim however, blocked this idea saying, that, (one of his golden rules)

"You shouldn't bring insecurity into insecurity."

He said that the baby, and, Maureen, should go and stay with Bill's parents in their big house in Kenley Road. Bill only had one brother, younger than him, who was mentally challenged. Jim said that he, and, Carol, would come with me, up to the house to Nottingham, to speak to, John, about the children and me, returning to live in the house and him leaving it. We made the journey up to the house in Nottingham and I was able to let myself in with my key. It was clear, that, John was no longer living in the house. He had moved into Halls of Residence as a Hall Tutor. The house was on the market with Dickens and Berry estate agents in Nottingham, but what was really shocking was that the pressure cooker I had been using on the day I left was still standing soaking and the water was totally covered in a thick green film of mould. The fridge had been turned off and the door closed, so that the whole of the inside was completely covered in black mould. What really angered, Jim, was finding my Diploma of Education which had been sent to the house, crumpled up in the dustbin in the kitchen. As the equity from the sale of the property would be coming to me, John had no interest in making the property look appealing to any prospective buyer and was actually thwarting any prospects of a quick sale. As an economist, he would have been well aware, that house prices in London were rising and my overdraft would also be rising, making it more difficult for me to afford to buy a property in London. Jim, said, that John's vacation of the property made things so much easier. We called a locksmith and had the locks changed. Jim went to see, John, at the University and told him, that I would be moving back into the house with the two boys and taking the house off the market. John said that he couldn't afford the mortgage and the bills. Jim asked him why he didn't claim benefits, as I had been forced to do. Jim summed John, up in the words, "Intelligence used as guile."

We returned to London and I prepared to move back to my home in Nottingham with the two boys. When I got back to Nottingham, John had removed a pane of glass from the kitchen window at the side of the house. He had then proceeded to have the electricity and gas supply turned off; he had then replaced the glass. I had to get all the utilities replaced urgently in my name, as it was winter and freezing cold. At Jim's insistence, I had a telephone installed for the first time now that I was living alone with the two boys. Jim, said that I, should put the two boys into boarding school, which I did, as I did not want their secondary education being disrupted by events taking place on the home front. I applied to Nottingham County Council, and the boys, David, in the first instance, in September 1982 were given places in Southwell Minister. It was a state school about half an hour away from Nottingham with boarding facilities at Hill House. This was a short distance from the school for the children of families in the Armed Forces. Peter Carlson was the Housemaster at Hill House and called to see me in Peveril Drive. It turned out, that he had been a teacher in Tiffen Boys' Grammar School in Kingston-Upon-Thames, before moving to Southwell Minster. Nottingham County Council agreed to sponsor the two boys at the school. I applied to Nottingham University to enter the third, and final, year of the Bachelor of Education Course, once again. I was advised that, because I only had the Diploma of Education, I would have to repeat the second year. I contested their decision on the grounds that I had had to pass the second year, in order to obtain the diploma in the first place and, therefore, should not have to repeat the second year of the same course. My appeal was upheld and I was advised that I could join the third year of the BEd, course again in order to complete my Degree and that my grant would be unaffected. I went to the same firm of solicitors on Maid Marion Way and started divorce proceedings. It was great being back in our old home again not having to worry if the boys jumped up and down, or were disturbing any of the neighbours below and I began to breathe more freely again. Maureen's post natal depression got worse, and, when I went down to Surbiton again, she was in Kenley Ward, the Psychiatric Ward of Kingston Hospital and the baby was in the baby ward of Kingston Hospital. Maureen would ask me for a glass of water and, when I would give it to her she would throw it on the floor. She would sit in the bed and ask me, if I wanted a puff. She was refusing to bond with the baby, who was also suffering some sort of withdrawal symptoms, and was unable to keep any food down. The nurses were taking, Maureen, over to see the baby every day in an attempt to get her to bond with him. As there was political trouble in, Iran at the time, foreigners had to leave the country and, Bill, returned to England. When, Maureen, got better, she, Bill, and the baby went to live in School Lane, Tolworth. Maureen had had a small red growth coming from a mole on her leg some years before and had asked, Carol, to have a look at it one day, when she was over visiting my mother and father. Carol took one look at the mole and rang a colleague doctor at the hospital and arranged an emergency appointment for Maureen, to see him. Maureen, who was also a manageress in a shoe shop in Kingston at the time, said she couldn't take the time off work, but, Carol, insisted she attend the appointment at the hospital. Maureen was diagnosed with malignant melanoma and was operated on immediately. Had, Maureen, not had the diagnosis and operation, she would have been dead within two months. She wore swimsuits afterwards and would go water skiing and sun bath on the beach determined not to let it prevent her from doing the things she wanted to. One day, however when they were still living above the shop in Tolworth, she confided in me, that, if it ever returned, she wouldn't let them cut any more holes in her. It had clearly affected her more than she cared to show. Jim had sat at her bedside crying after she had the operation. This was probably the reason why she didn't continue taking the contraceptive pill and became pregnant.

Chapter Four

The Lodgers

David, and Jamie, returned to St Mary's Primary School once again in September 1981 and I returned to Trent Polytechnic to begin the third year of my B'ED course. I decided to advertise some of the rooms in the house to let. As john, was now only paying the mortgage and the rates, this would bring in some extra money to help pay for the bills. Three female students from a course in Trent Polytechnic in the city answered the advertisement, and became my first paying lodgers. The size of the house made it ideal for taking in lodgers as no one was ever on top of each other. It was so big, that it was difficult to even tell, if anyone were even in the house at any one time. As Christmas approached, the girls asked if they could cook Christmas dinner for their boyfriends. I said no to the idea, saying, that it was a family home and, that I could not vacate the kitchen in order to accommodate their boyfriends. They said that it wouldn't cost me any more in gas, as they would only be putting a few more sprouts into the pot. They said that I cooked for my boyfriend, Brian, who would be travelling up from Windlesham, in Surrey, to Nottingham, so why couldn't they cook for their boyfriends. Taking exception to their attitude, I reminded them that I was the owner of the house, and the cost of cooking a few more sprouts wasn't the issue. Two of the girls gave me notice, and the third decided, that if they were leaving, so was she. I advertised the rooms once again, and a female student from the CNAA Generalist Course applied. She had been absent from the course for quite a while, due to glandular fever and was about to return. The second person to apply for the room was a bright, cheerful, young man from Liverpool, who was working as a lightning conductor engineer with Furze in Nottingham. The third person was a vet, who had just graduated from Liverpool University and was working at the PDSA just around the corner. I, was talking to the vet, when Julia, motioned from the kitchen door that she wanted to talk to me. I went out to her, and she said to me, all flushed and excited, "For God sake, have him."

These three lodgers were to become good friends, with whom I would socialize, and because of their great sense of decency, strong sense of humour and the moral support they gave me at all times, they saw me through one of the most difficult periods of my married life. The house had become a home that was full of laughter, humour, good company and amazing loyal friendship; a real circle of good friends. My suggestion, that we have a cleaning rota was met with a poem titled, SODS "Save Our Dust Society." My third year involved two lots of teaching practice in the local Nottinghamshire schools and then my final examinations in all my subjects at the end of the academic year. When the results came through, I had passed in everything, accept a minor option of Educational Technology. I couldn't believe, that I could possibly fail my whole degree on the basis of this one minor option, which I, had only chosen because I thought it would be useful to know how to work a slide projector! The course, however, had been more scientific than practical, involving how light and lens worked inside a camera and making a recording on a one to one reel of tape. I hadn't really taken the six week option course very seriously. Neither had my good friend, Peter Watts, who the lecturer called, "a half-baked coot."

Peter, and I, would often leave the lessons early and go and have a coffee, in the students' cafeteria. I now had a big wakeup call and needed to pass the option if I, were not to fail my whole degree. Fortunately, a large part of the option had been the Educational Technology theoretical, academic element of, the "Constraints Facing Teachers," which I revised, until I knew it inside out, as well as the other written elements and went to sit the retake, on the designated date. David was to be going to Southwell Minister, at Southwell in September 1982, and I was kept busy sewing on name tags to his clothes which were to be packed up in the trunk that he was to take to school with him. At the end of my final teaching practice, Johnnie, the vet, whose mother, father, and younger sister, lived on a farm in Chippenham, suggested that we have a party to celebrate. He had been nick-named, Slateloose at University, because all the other students said, that he had a slate loose! We bought two barrels of beer and, Johnnie washed lots of potatoes to bake to go with all the other food we had prepared. Lots of different alcohol was bought for those, who were not beer swilling students. I ended my relationship with, Brian, just before the party, because I could see, that there would be problems in the future with his ex-wife, who would use his only daughter as a pawn in our relationship, which I didn't think was fair to me, as I had never been involved in their marriage break up in the first place. I knew, that my feelings for, Johnnie, were becoming stronger and I think, that he would have reciprocated, but I was too afraid to get involved, as there were many similarities with my relationship with John, at the beginning. John had been four years younger than me and had just left university and was at the beginning of a career in management. Johnnie was eight years younger than me, single, just out of university and at the beginning of his career as a vet. Like John, he came from the West Country and had only one sister, who worked on his parents' farm. I suppose I was just too afraid of history repeating itself and felt, that, Johnnie, deserved to be a free, single, agent, at least for a while. My brother, Jim, came up for the party on his own. The teachers from the schools where I had done my teaching practice came, as did vet friends and a lecturer in Micro Biology from Liverpool University. It was a great party and one of the best I have ever been to, even if it was my own, mainly because of the great company at it. Just after the party, Johnnie, announced that he was taking a position in a private practice in Peterborough, and, Phil, his Welsh friend from Bangor, in Anglesey, would be replacing him at the PDSA and taking his room. Like Johnnie, though not as extrovert, Phil was the epitome of decency and we became firm friends too. Julia, who came from Brinkley in Cambridge, obtained a teaching position in East Stratford in the Borough of Newham. Phil, who worked as a lighting conductor engineer at Furze also moved on and his room was taken by a young girl, called Sandra. Sandra was studying French and Spanish and must have thought that she had come to live in an asylum! However, she soon fitted in well, and became one of the family also. On one of my visits down to Surbiton, I went to see my sister, Maureen, who was now living in her council house in School Lane Tolworth with her husband, Bill Nice. She was having problems with Bill, who had physically kicked her out of the house one day. Maureen told me, that she was going to leave him. I suggested to her, that she, and her young son, Georgie, come back up to Nottingham with me to give her a break. Maureen was writing, Bill, a note, right there and then, saying she was leaving him! I advised her against doing anything so dramatic and to give herself some time to think things over. I suggested, that she leave him a note saying that she, and Georgie were in Nottingham with me, having a break. They came up and we went on many social outings with the vets, and Julia, and, Maureen, couldn't believe the difference in her life. She said she had been out more in one week, than she had been with, Bill, in the whole of her marriage. She said she was definitely going to divorce him and wasn't going back. I advised her to speak with a solicitor in Nottingham in order to start the proceedings and to think about getting Council Housing in Nottingham. I told her to ask, Bill, to send her some money for her and Georige, which she did. She gave the money he sent to me, and I gave it back, so that she could buy what she needed and go out, keeping only the cost of food for her and Georgie. One day, Maureen, said, that she was going down to Surbiton, to see mum and dad, and she left Georgie, with me. When she returned she, said, that she had spoken with my dad and Jim. Maureen was going to hand, Georgie, back to, Bill, and go to stay with, Jim, and, Carol, and study for a Degree in Law. We put, Georgie, in his pram and I walked with her to Nottingham Railway Station. As we lifted the push chair, baby in it, I asked, Maureen, if she was sure about what she was doing. I had grave reservations, as it was something that I, could never have done. Apparently she was and her mind seemed pretty made up. When the summer holidays arrived, I planned to take, David, Jamie, and one of their friends who lived in the Park Estate, camping in Anglesey. I rang home to ask, Maureen, if she would like to come with us and spoke to my mother. A little while after ringing, Maureen, rang me back to say she would like to come with us. My father and, Jim, drove her up by car and dropped her off, quickly taking their leave of us. When, Maureen, walked into the kitchen, she was like a zombie. I went into shock and vomited up the tea I'd just drunk in the drain outside the kitchen door. I went into complete denial and blamed the milk in the tea for my reaction. I continued with the packing for the trip and asked, Maureen, to put the clothes that I had just ironed into the holdall bag. She just threw them in, without caring whether they got crumpled or not. I thought that the camping trip might lift the depression from which she was clearly suffering and just continued packing the tent into the car. The vets were astounded that I was considering taking, Maureen, with us, but I said, that the trip might do her good. We got to Anglesey and put up the tent, arranging everything else as we wanted it. I went with, Maureen, to one of the nearby restaurants to have a meal. We looked at the menu outside the restaurant and then went inside. It became obvious to me, that Maureen, could not make a decision and that her depression was so deep, that she really needed to be in a hospital receiving treatment for it; most certainly not roughing it, inside a tent, in Anglesey.

I decided to take, Maureen, back to London, and gave the boys the money to buy something to eat, until I got back. I asked the people in the tent next to ours who were scoutmasters, if they would keep an eye on the boys, as my sister, wasn't well and I was taking her back to my parents' in Surbiton. I rang my parents' home, but got no answer, so I rang, my friend, Liz, and asked, her if she would go round and tell my parents, that I was taking, Maureen, back to Surbiton and that she wasn't well and, needed to be in hospital. I told, Maureen, what I was doing, and, bless her; she began to fold the clothes neatly into the bag. She must have thought it was, because she had done something wrong and was trying to make amends. She was very quiet the whole way back in the car and, when we arrived at my parent's home, my mum, dad and, Jim, were there, like a reception committee. When we went into the living room, I said, that, Maureen wasn't well and needed to be in hospital, at which point, Maureen, began dramatically screaming, saying there was nothing wrong with her and she didn't need to be in hospital. I left immediately and went round to see my friend, Liz. Jim followed me round and sat in Liz's kitchen telling me about some big plan he had for moving to a big house in Ireland and he wanted me on board. By the time he left, Liz, and her sister, Sally, said I should stay overnight and get a good night's sleep, before returning in the morning. Angela came round to, Liz's, and asked, if she could come back with me, which I agreed to. We started out early the next morning and, when we arrived back in Anglesey, the man in the next tent said they had been about to call the police. The boys were starving, as they had spent their money on boat rides, thinking we'd be back the same day. They were happy to see, Angela, and we continued with the holiday, which went really well .When I got back to Nottingham, I telephoned home to ask how, Maureen, was. My mother, in her Mrs. Bouquet tone of voice, told me, that, Maureen was fine and there was nothing wrong with her.

After I dropped, David, off at boarding school in September, I went out one day with, Angela, to a fair in Nottingham when I was suddenly hit by a deep dark feeling of depression which just suddenly descended on me, totally unexpected, like a ton of bricks. I was exhausted and crying and put on black sunglasses to hide my red and swollen eyes. I went down to Surbiton to see my parents, thinking the break would do me good. When I arrived, I discovered that, Maureen was back in the Kenley Ward of Kingston Hospital. My father told me, that, the doctor had given her enough tranquilizers to knock out a horse, yet she was still running out of the hospital in her nightdress and bare feet. She was either going up to Bill's parents' home, banging on the door, demanding to have, Georgie, back, or making her way back to my parents' house. She had gone to stay at Jim, and Carols, to study for A' Levels, in order to study for a Law Degree, and had had her hair, which she always wore long, cut short. (She later confessed, that she thought this had traumatized her more than anything else.) Bill's parents called my dad, and Jim's 'bluff,' as they were only too pleased to have their first grandson to live with them as they had a big house in Kenley Road, (ironically just opposite the hospital ward of the same name, in which, Maureen, was fighting for her sanity, not all she would have to fight for in the future!) no financial problems with, Bill, having left home, and only one mentally challenged son living at home with them. There were marital problems between Bill's father, and mother, due to infidelity by both parties, but such is the hypocrisy of the suburban middle classes, who can still carry on living together and keep up appearances to the outside world. Jim and Carol's marriage was also in trouble. Jim was living in the house in Ealing and refusing to leave. They were experiencing some very personal and deep problems and, Jim had gone ballistic over one in particular and, Carol had stopped paying the mortgage. I suggested, that, Jim, sign on and claim for benefit, which would pay the mortgage interest for him, but it was against Jim's religion to ever sign on as unemployed; keeping up appearances was everything to Jim!

Jim had been sitting in the house depressed after, Carol, left and my mother and father had been going over to pick up his cups and plates and to see, that he was okay. Jim received a letter from the Head of Religious Programmes at the BBC, recommending him to the Head of Religious Programmes at RTE. I had gone to visit my parents' doctor at Tolworth and, on speaking to him, I, broke down in tears, saying to him that my son had gone to boarding school! The doctor, in a kindly voice, said, that they were hardly likely to beat him at boarding school and prescribed medication for anxiety and depression. My father was at his wits end with worry about, Maureen, who would turn up at their flat in her bare feet, which my mother said would be all cut and blistered and, Jim would try to persuade her to return to the hospital. My father suggested, that, Jim, my mother, and I go to Ireland, so that, Jim, could go to RTE in Dublin and leave my father to deal with, Maureen's situation. I wanted to take, Jamie, with me which, Jim was against, because, like, Fernando, he never had any patience, when it came to children. As, Jamie, was ten years old and absolutely no problem, whatsoever, I insisted that he should come with us. I had just been separated from one son and I wasn't going to be separated from the other. My mother wrote the cheque for the cost of the ferry and the rental of an Irish cottage close to Cork. We all drove in Jim's car to catch the ferry from Holyhead to Dublin. On the boat, Jim, and my mother bought a bottle of duty free whisky, so that they could have a little tipple in the evenings, when we were at the cottage. We were sitting having a cup of tea in a café, when, Jamie, asked me, if he could have ten pence to put in one of the machines to buy a bar of chocolate. Jim immediately smacked him across the face and told him not to ask for things. We arrived at the cottage, which had a coal fire and settled ourselves in. The next day, Jim, made the trip up to RTE in Dublin and, Jamie, and I remained in the cottage with my mother. My mood was still low and I certainly wasn't in holiday spirit, possibly due to the medication the doctor had given me. In the evening, I told my mother, that I missed, David, and my own home. I went to bed before, Jim, returned from Dublin late that evening. In the morning, Jim, asked me, in quite a curt voice, if I wanted to go home. I said, that I was missing, David, and would like to go back home. He brought a timetable of the ferries and asked me which one I would like to catch. There was an evening ferry, which I thought would be best, as it would allow us to sleep during the night. Jim then nastily said to me, that I was uncouth and I quickly retorted, "and you're so smart!" to which he punched me in the face with all the force that one man would use on another and continued laying into me, until I could only cower in the corner trying to fend off the blows. Jamie stood pale and trembling, watching him laying into me, saying, "Please don't hit her please don't hit her!"

When, Jim came at me with a shovel used for coal, my mother, got in the middle and told him to stop. When, Jim, looked at, Jamie, he gave him a nervous laugh and, Jim, said "Don't smile at me, if it's not sincere."

My mother and, Jim, went into town and I went in the opposite direction with, Jamie. I told, Jamie, that, even if, Jim, were to say anything to him, that he was not to answer him, as I knew, that, Jim, would use it, as an excuse to take his frustrations out on him. The beating was a unique form of shock treatment for depression, as I knew I had to keep my wits about me, in order to protect, Jamie. The lovely, friendly Irish woman, who was looking after the cottages, called to see how things were. Jim and my mother still hadn't returned and the woman must have wondered what had kicked off, when she looked at my black eye and bruised face. My mother returned and made sandwiches and a flask of coffee for the journey back, while she packed a small bag that she put in the back of the car. Neither, Jamie, nor I said a word to, Jim, or my mother, who carried on speaking to each, other as if nothing, had happened. We all eventually got in the car to make the journey back to catch the evening ferry. Jim, and my mother, sat in the front talking away, while, Jamie, and I sat in the back, saying nothing. Jim, some way into the journey, mentioned the sandwiches to my mother who turned around to get the bag from the back of the car. I made no move to hand her the bag and when she looked at the expression on my face, she knew better, than to ask me to reach for the bag. They stopped at a café in order to take a break. They went inside and, Jamie, and I stayed in the back of the car, until they came out again. When we arrived at the ferry and, Jim, parked the car on the lower level, I took note of where the car was and went up the stairs to the upper lounge, where I found a comfortable, vacant leather settee, where, Jamie, and I, could settle down and sleep for the night. When the ferry arrived at Holyhead in the morning Jamie, and I, made our way to the car and stood beside it, watching my mother, and, Jim, looking for where they had parked the car. Jamie and I got into the back and the four of us made the journey back to London. Jim stopped at Paddington Railway Station, in order to let, Jamie, and I, out to catch the train back to Nottingham. When I knew I was back in London, I got out of the car and banged on the front windscreen, calling them, "Two fuckers!"

I went across to a police station on the other side of the road and told the policeman, that I wanted to press charges against my brother, for the assault, that, he had carried out on me. The policeman asked me where I lived and, when I said, "Nottingham," he advised me to speak to the police there. I went to a nearby phone box and telephoned my father, to tell him what had gone on. He told me to shame them and to catch the train up to Surbiton Station, where he would meet me. When we arrived, my father was standing waiting for us. We went to a café, just across from the station and ordered two cups of tea and a soft drink for Jamie. As we sat on the bar stools of the café, tears were streaming down my father's face, when he saw what, Jim, had done. It was the first time in my life, that I had ever seen my father, cry. He told me to go back up to Nottingham and to just focus on my own two sons and that would keep me right. I learned later, that my father was back in the flat before, Jim, and mother, arrived. When they came in, my father said, "One day, you are going to do some real serious damage to someone in the family."

Jim, realizing that my father had seen for himself what he had done, suddenly lost it and pulled the chandelier light fitting right out of the ceiling. When I got back to my house in Nottingham, the lodgers were stunned, and shocked, at the state of my face, especially when they learned that it was, Jim, who had done it. I never did report the assault to the police in Nottingham, as I had no wish to bring legal proceedings against another family member, but I resolved that the next time, I felt low and exhausted I would simply have a week at home, until I was fully rested. I went to see my own GP, in Nottingham and told him, that my arms felt really light, as if they were ready to just explode. He said it was no wonder because of the medication I had been prescribed and to stop taking it! My GP in Nottingham would never prescribe tranquillizers, no matter how low, or anxious, I may have been feeling. He believed that it was better to acknowledge how you are feeling and to learn strategies for coping with them. If I'd ever gone to see them at the surgery, they would just send me away. I knew they were right, and were simply educating me on how to handle stress, rather than simply popping a pill. I asked the doctor, if I should pursue a career in teaching, as it was a very stressful profession and he replied, that, I should as it was one stress to beat another. He said the medical profession was also a stressful profession and to do what most doctors do, drink!

Every time I had a drink with friends after that, I would say, I was just following the doctor's orders! I passed my exams in Educational Technology and was awarded my Bachelor of Education Degree in December 1982 and could now think about applying for teaching posts. I still also had to pass a probationary year, in teaching before I could be awarded a DES (Department of Education and Science,) number, and become a fully qualified teacher. Margaret Thatcher was the Prime Minister at this time and cuts were taking place in education, (students weren't even paying tuition fees at this time!) When, Margaret Thatcher came to visit the Sherwood Rooms in Nottingham, David, and I, were among the other protestors outside, holding up the placards saying, "Stop The Cuts! Stop the Cuts."

It was difficult for English or Art teachers, to obtain a teaching position, but Maths and Science teachers only had to pass the breathing test. (The interviewer would hold a mirror up to the candidate's mouth and, if it clouded over, he would get the job.) I was able to get supply teaching for a term, while a teacher was off on long term sickness, or the school was advertising for a permanent teacher. The Education Department changed the rules and regulations to state, that any teacher doing a term's teaching at a school, should be offered the permanent position, if it were available. Most schools, however, were reluctant to lose a more senior grade position to a teacher on a lower grade, or a probationer, and got around this rule by offering a term's supply teaching on a day to day basis. Most teachers accepted this, because they needed the work, and the competition was fierce. My divorce nisi came through in April 1982, but the solicitor delayed applying for the absolute until the agreement for the financial arrangements, in respect of the property, had been reached. I went to see my bank manager, who advised me, that I would have to cut back on my spending, although he admitted, that he didn't see how I could, having two boys of his own. He advised me to get myself three rich young men and I told him I would be hard pressed to find even one rich young man. The overdraft had risen to the £4,000 limit and I considered the possibility of taking over the mortgage, which, John, wanted to be free off as he could not obtain another, while he had that one. Had the job market been more buoyant for English teachers, I might have been more confident about having the mortgage transferred into my sole name. However, I couldn't see how I could manage all the financial responsibilities on my own, even with the boys at boarding school, sponsored by Nottinghamshire County Council and the income from the lodgers, especially as there was the overdraft on top of everything else. I rang, Carol, to ask, if she could help with the overdraft, as she had underpinned it with, Jim.

Carol, very curtly, told me to ask, Jim, which was out of the question, so that, was that. I could have kept the joint mortgage with, John until, David, and, Jamie, were both eighteen, as it was our family home, but the solicitor advised me, that it was better to agree to sell, and have the clean break. I had to attend a Magistrate's Court in order to obtain a Court Judgment and the financial arrangements of the divorce. It was heard in a small room in the Family Division of the court in front of a magistrate. A barrister had come up by train from London and, still not completely decided, I attempted to ask his advice about whether or not selling the family home was the best course of action. He was very rushed, as he had tried to read his notes on the case on the train on the way up and taking my solicitor's advice, agreed that it was the best course of action. I sat on the end chair, of the four chairs at the back of the room, beside my solicitor. There was a gap between the other two chairs on which, John, sat with his solicitor. The two barristers representing us stood in front of us facing the magistrate whose table and chairs was raised higher than the others. John had contested the cost of my telephone in my list of expenses drawn up by my solicitor. The magistrate, peering over his rimless glasses, said in summing up, that he often had the sad duty of ruling on cases where neither party had any assets to be divided, and found it to be a rather sad state of affairs, when he was asked to rule whether or not, a woman, living alone with her two children, was entitled to have a telephone or not. (He looked disapprovingly at John's barrister as he said this.) John sat writing notes the whole time of the hearing without even looking at the magistrate and I saw my solicitor looking at him. John didn't work in a University Department right beside the Law Department and not pick up a few tips on how to handle these types of situations. It was agreed, that the house be sold and the proceeds go to me, in lieu of maintenance in order to buy another home for the children and myself. John was to continue to pay the mortgage and rates until the property was sold. He was also ordered to pay £25 per week for both of the children. The house was put on the market again with Nottingham Estate agents, Dickens and Berry at £35,000. House prices in London had almost doubled in the previous two years, while the prices in Nottingham stayed stagnant, putting the possibility of buying another home in London totally out of reach with the equity I would receive after the sale. There wasn't even one buyer, who ever came to look at the property, not everyone wanted such a big Victorian house, believing it would be too difficult to maintain. I received a phone call from, Dickens and Berry saying that, John wanted to buy the property, as he no longer wanted to live in Halls of Residence and could not get a mortgage while he had this one. This was bit rich, as he had given the reason to the court for wanting the house sold as his inability to afford the mortgage along with his other living expenses, which, as a tutor in Halls of Residence, with no children to support would have been minimal, while his salary, his earnings from tutoring students privately and the extra income he could earn from research Sponsorship from private companies outside the University, his income would have been at maximum level. I should have dismissed the whole idea immediately and even gone back to court, as he wasn't paying any of the child maintenance the court had ordered. However, as there had been the agreement to sell the property, and, pressed by the estate agent, who, said that the child maintenance, now a total of £1,300 would be paid on completion, I agreed to sell it to him at the bargain price of £33,000, as I couldn't now afford to buy in London.

I looked in the Wollaton area of Nottingham and found a three bedroom semi-detached house in Glade Avenue, a cul-de-sac at the end of one of the streets off the main Wollaton Road just opposite Wollaton Park. I exchanged on both properties and a date for completion was agreed. On the day of the completion, I hired a van, which I couldn't pick up, as I couldn't find my driving license. The solicitor was insisting that the keys were in the office by early afternoon, because of banking hours, and the need to have the completion done by a certain time, no excuses and no delays were acceptable. Phil, the vet, was still with me, and, Johnnie, who was visiting, Phil, as well as Peter Watts. We were eventually able to pick up the van and we bundled everything frantically into it, packed, and unpacked, in order to meet the deadline. I went round to the solicitors with the keys, and even thought the lump sum of maintenance agreed to me wasn't paid, the completion took place! The estate agent later tried to bill me for his commission, threatening me with legal action. I told him to collect his commission from Mr. Johnson, who was also a joint owner of the property and advised him, that, if he persisted with his threat of legal action, I would countersue him for conflict of interest, as he had acted solely for John's benefit in the sale of the property. He dropped his claim for the commission and, when I next contacted his office, I was advised, that he was in hospital. With everyone's help, I moved into Glade Avenue. That evening, there was a post Graduate Party in Lenton, being held by one of the vet's friends. We all went to the party at which there was a big punch bowl. I must have practically drunk the whole bowl by the end of the evening and, when, Johnnie, Phil, and I returned to Glade Avenue and I went to bed and the two vets went in the other room next door. They had to listen to the floodgates opening like a dam, that had suddenly burst and to the sobs which accompanied the sound of my heart finally breaking. They knew the reason and left me in peace. The next day, I had to pick both, David, and Jamie, up from the boarding house at Southwell Minister. During the journey I had to stop the car several times to be sick, and several times on the way back. When we got back I went to bed, and, Phil, and, Johnnie, took, David, and Jamie, out to play tennis. Later in the evening I got up and made some corned beef sandwiches for everyone. No one passed any comment, I had completely emptied my whole emotional system and was about to begin a new phase in my life.

Chapter Five

Time tells all Tales

David, and Jamie, went to visit their friends, who lived In the Park Estate. When they returned home, David said, that they had seen, John, come out of our old house with a blonde woman. They said there was a Bechstein piano in the window of the front living room and that leaflets had been put through the doors of their friends advertising piano lessons. When my friend, Peter, came to see me, I said this had to be Sylvia Bowden, (John's old flame, who had gone to the London School of Music.) If she was advertising piano lessons, then she would have to be in the phone book. We first looked under the name of Johnson, and didn't find anything, so we looked under the name of, Bowden, and there it was, Sylvia Bowden, at my old address with a new telephone number. In order to find out how much she was charging for the lessons, Peter rang to make enquiries about having lessons. Sylvia took the call and once she had ascertained, that, Peter, would be in the beginners' category, she told him it would be £9 per half hour and asked him, if he wanted to book a lesson, to which, Peter, said that he did.

She gave him a day, and a time, and then asked him, his name. Peter quickly chose a name from the open page of the telephone book and said, "Peter Bowles."

He later realized, that it was the name of the actor, who starred with, Penelope Keith, in the hit series, "To the Manor Born."

Peter and I laughed at the irony of the mistake, as, Penelope Keith, also played the part of Margo. It didn't matter, because, Peter, obviously had no intention of keeping the appointment for the lesson. We went out for a drink that evening and, when we returned, a small brown envelope had been posted by hand through the door. When I opened it, it was a hand written bill for one cancelled piano lesson, with a message underneath saying, "Please don't waste my time; it is valuable."

I immediately telephoned Peter' we laughed so loud, that I think, John, and, Sylvia, must have heard us in their house in the Park.

I hadn't felt that good in ages; the ice cold detached veneer, had finally cracked. As the lump sum children's maintenance had not been paid at the completion of the property and, John, was not making the £25 per week payments ordered by the court, I went back to the solicitor, told him, who, Sylvia Bowden, was and asked him, to take John, back to court to enforce the payments. Peter, and I went to Neale's Auction Rooms soon afterwards and I saw, John, in one corner of the room. I knew that Sylvia would be with him, so I stood in the doorway and waited knowing he had spotted, Peter, and me. Sure enough, this short blonde, haired young woman walked round to join him, wearing a long beige Mackintosh coat with a belt. She then walked to the door, where I was standing, and, if she didn't already know, who I was, as she came face to face with me, I think she was probably able to make a good calculated guess from the look of sheer hatred, that I flashed her way. I had never felt more like thumping someone right in the face, as I did then, but I controlled the urge. I noticed that her face had a real bad case of rough skin. She was short and frumpy looking in the blocked heel shoes she was wearing and I was incredulous, that I, and my two sons, had endured years of stress, turmoil and anxiety, not for the, Bo Derek image of, Sylvia Bowden, that I had conjured up in my mind from the description John's sister had given me of her, but for this short, dumpy young woman, with bad skin, standing in front of me. There is nothing like coming face to face with the reality of a situation to dispel the myths created by our own imagination.

Peter and I left the auction room and I admitted to him, that I felt a certain degree of smug satisfaction, now that I had actually seen the opposition. It never ever had occurred to me, that there could possibly be another woman, let alone, the ex, Sylvia Bowden. John had never seemed the womanizing kind and, of course I was only to ready to make all the other excuses of eye disfigurement, personality change, the responsibilities of two children, who were not of his own, which he cynically exploited over all of the years of our marriage. I could not believe anyone being capable of pulling off such a deception: Lies and cold, calculated, total disregard for the misery it was causing, on a daily basis, to those with whom he was living. Never any good at lateral thinking, I needed the last piece in the jigsaw puzzle to see the whole picture. It had suited him for me to think, that it was, "Cilla," who, David, had seen him snogging, because, now that I had seen, Sylvia, I could see how easily she could be mistaken for Cilla. It was also clear, that, Cilla, and, Laurie, and all our other friends in John's department would have known all about the affair, (in my case the wife was certainly the last to know.)

It explained all the trips down to London for interviews with Coral's Bookmakers and the suggestion of selling the house to buy a smaller one in West Bridgford, which would release the equity that had all come to me. I had dug the garden and, Sylvia, had just come along to pick the roses. I just wished, that, John, had remained with his ex, and, that they had worked out their own problems, instead of coming into the lives of me, and my children, and giving us the grief, that they did. John could have come clean and done the decent thing, but it was never about decency with him, it was all about the money. The two of them deserved each other, it's not evil spirits that move the Ouija board glass, it's the evil spirits, lacking in generosity of spirit, that have their fingers on the glass. My father came with me on the day of the court hearing regarding the children's maintenance and, John, was claiming, that, Sylvia, was merely the housekeeper. (How many housekeepers have their name in the telephone directory?) He may have been confusing her, with me! The barrister spoke to my dad and I and, as we stood in the small side room, John, and, Sylvia, walked past the open door to go into the court room. I wasn't required to appear and sat with my dad, until the barrister reappeared. He was jubilant and I still don't know, what transpired in the court room, but the children's maintenance was paid without fail until the exact day the children reached the age of eighteen. I can only surmise that, John was threatened with jail as I don't think courts like to be deceived any more than wives do!

Chapter Six

Talking of Ex's

I had had a few terms supply teaching in Nottingham, but it was proving difficult to obtain a permanent teaching position, so I accepted a term's work in Holyfield Girls' School in Surbiton, in the hope, that I would eventually obtain a permanent position and be able to move back down to the London area. I reasoned, that if I were having so much difficulty in obtaining employment, it would also be the same for the boys when they would eventually leave education. At the end of the summer holidays, David, was taken into hospital with appendicitis. After the operation, the doctor said, that the appendix had been gangrenous. Once, David got better, he would be able to return to the boarding house, where he would be in the care of the Matron, and I could start the position in Surbiton at the beginning of term. The day before, David, was due to leave hospital, he got an abscess on the wound, which would have to be drained. I explained to the doctor that I, had to start a new job, and he said, that, if I signed the necessary forms to have the abscess drained, they would carry on and a thirteen year old boy did not need his mother to be there. Phil and my other friends in Nottingham said they would go in to visit, David. I started the job and at the end of the week telephoned the hospital to see how, David, was. The nurse told me he had, a "bug," in the wound, so I, went up to Nottingham and, when I got there, David, was in intensive care, looking like someone, who had just walked out of Belsen. He had tubes in the wound, tubes in his wrist, and a tube in his chest. I could see immediately, that something was seriously wrong. When, David, stood up, he couldn't control his bowel movements. The nurse made to clean the floor, but I said that I would do it. She said she would call the doctor to come and have a word with me. The doctor explained, that, David had caught an infection, which, if it had spread to the 'babies' ward, they would have died like flies. For this reason, they had isolated David, and a boy, who had been next to him in the ward. She said they had stopped feeding him to try and get rid of the infection, but they had left it too long and, that, David, would now have to have another operation for the cohesion in his intestine. This involved cutting away a piece of the intestine and joining it together again, after which, David, would need long convalescence. Looking at him, I wondered if he would survive another operation, his arms were so thin, and his eyes were staring out of his head. I told, David, that I would be staying in Nottingham until he was better. I called the school to let them know how ill my son was and told them, that I couldn't return to the job, which they understood. I went home that evening and I cried all night, I prayed to God like I never had before that, David, would be alright. The following day, I went up to the hospital and the young male nurse, who was looking after, David, went to say something to me; I put my hand up, gesturing, that, if I were to say anything, I would just start crying again. He said, that, David was alright, because he had passed wind, indicating that his stomach, was working and that he wouldn't need another operation. The nurse said, that a happy boy is a healthy boy and, that a thirteen year old boy did need his mother. David recovered in hospital and was well enough to come home. He was a little fighter, who hobbled to go onto the hospital radio and who hobbled after the other boys, when he got home, who ran down the street, when they heard the sound of a fire engine. Not only was he a fighter, but he wasn't one to miss out on anything either. He eventually made a full recovery and returned to the boarding school. I was concerned, that, if anything ever happened to me, who would look after the boys. One day, while driving in the car, I tried to establish, who they would want to be with, if anything ever happened to me, to which, David, replied.

"If anything happens to you mum, it won't be your problem."

(Out of the mouths of babes and fools,) When my marriage to, John, broke up, I told the boys before they started secondary school, that, John, was not their natural father. I felt, that they were old enough to be told and, under the circumstances, it was the only right thing to do.

One day, while walking around the Water Sports Park at West Bridgeford with my Australian friend, Vivienne, I discussed the possibility of discovering where, Fernando, was, as I had decided, that, if anything did happen to me, the boys would be better off with their natural father. I knew nothing at all about him, and simply assumed that he had remarried and was probably working as a waiter, in Spain somewhere, with a family and kids. To my surprise, I received a telephone call one day and knew immediately from how he pronounced my name, that it was, Fernando. He simply said, "Margaret, can I take you out to dinner?"

I arranged to meet him in a pub in Maid Marion Way and felt a great deal of satisfaction, when I pulled up in my semi-automatic Citroen GS, that I had bought at a snip from an owner going abroad, who would have been forced to put it into an auction if I didn't buy it. We went into a pub to talk and I asked him, if he would like to see the boys and began crying, when I spoke of them. We went for dinner at Ben Bower's Restaurant in Canning Circus, at the top of Maid Marion Way and, Fernando, ordered fish, which they brought out, uncooked on a silver platter, to see, if it met with his approval. Fernando had always been fussy about his food and always like the best. He had asparagus in vinaigrette dressing as a starter and ordered a bottle of wine. During the meal, Fernando, said to me, "lady you drink like a fish."

To which I replied, "Yes I know." (The shackles were off.) I rang the boarding school and asked, if I could have the two boys home that weekend, as we had a family visitor, who wanted to meet them. I collected the boys and the four of us went for a meal, in one of the self service restaurants in Nottingham town centre. I explained to the boys, that, Fernando, was their natural father, and, David, said, that in the back of his mind, he always knew, that, John, wasn't his real dad. As, Fernando, sat in the back of the car with the two boys' he took out the boys original birth certificates and showed them to them I noticed, that his hands were trembling with emotion. We went by train to Lincoln and into one of the little tea chops there. When it came to paying the waitress, Fernando, brusquely handed over a twenty pound note, looking straight ahead and not at the waitress. I noticed, that both boys were embarrassed, by the arrogant manner in which he had treated the waitress. When looking at expensive trainers in a Sport's shop window, which the boys were talking about, Fernando, just went in and bought them. I should have seen the signs of what was to come, when we went to Nottingham Railway Station, so that, Fernando, could catch his train back to London. He handed, Jamie, a twenty pound note and told him not to tell me, that he'd given it to him. Jamie, with a puzzled look on his face, came up to me after, Fernando, had left on the train and showed me the money; he then told me what, Fernando, had said. I told him, that it was okay and, that he could keep it to buy himself something, that he wanted. At that time, the boys received 50 pence a week pocket money. Fernando told me, that, Jim had got my telephone number for him from my parents; he had told them, that a friend wanted to send her son to boarding school and needed some advice. It would have been nice to have been asked, before acting on my behalf, but, as I had been considering making contact with, Fernando, I just let it go. The next time, Fernando, came up to Nottingham, my two parents came up too. Fernando asked my mother, "Did you ever think you'd see me again?"

To which my mother, replied. "Oh yes, Fernando, I always knew I'd see you again."

The boys had a puncture on one of the tyres on their bicycle, so we took it to a garage to see if they would repair it. The man began to explain how much it would cost, to which, Fernando, replied very rudely, and abruptly, "Just fix it!"

Patience and politeness were never his strong points. He asked me, if I would like to come down to London, for a few days, after the boys returned to school, as he had business there. I agreed and drove down with him in the car, packing all my best clothes, as we would be staying in a hotel. I stupidly parked the car under the arches at Waterloo Station, right beside the homeless people sleeping there, and didn't even lock the car. When I returned to the car the following morning, the bag and the clothes were gone. They had at least gone to people, who needed them a lot more than I did. We stayed in the Inn in the Park, which charged £300 per night and didn't even include breakfast. Fernando's business colleague called at the hotel on the third morning. He was from one of the big brokers in London, JP Morgan's, now, in serious financial trouble for irregular financial dealings.

I sat in the lobby of the hotel with Fernando's colleague. While Fernando, got the bill, I could smell cheese cooking and resisted the urge to smell under my arm in case it was me! Fernando returned with his bill, a total of over £1,000, and showed it to me. Out of ear shot of, Fernando, his business colleague told me it would go on the expenses account. The meal, Fernando the boys and I, had cost £65 and probably also went on the expense account. I noted, that one meal in a restaurant came to double, that I spent in the supermarket on a week's shopping. When Fernando's business colleague left, Fernando, and I went round to Waterloo Station to have breakfast in one of the self service restaurants there and, Fernando, put sausages, eggs and baked beans onto his plate, which he'd have turned his nose up at, when we were married, but now said he missed.

"If you're eating steak and caviar every day, it makes a nice change." He said.

Fernando asked me, if I would like to go over to Spain for Christmas. I hated Christmas time in England and thought it would be a good opportunity for the boys to get to know their dad and his culture.

Chapter Seven

Missing Piece in the Jigsaw

David, Jamie and I travelled to London and called in to see my parents, before catching the plane from Heathrow, to travel to Madrid for Christmas. Before we left, my mother took me to one side and told me, that she had had to call the doctor out to my father in the night, as he had been suffering severe chest pains and was on his hands and knees on the bedroom floor. She was concerned, because the doctor had told him, that he had suffered a mild heartache, but he was still talking about returning to work (My father's answer to all things stressful, especially Christmas.) The doctor called in to see my father, while I was still there, and I asked him, if it were true, that he had suffered a mild heart attack and he said that he had. I then asked, if he would have a word with my father, as he was intending to return to work, and he said that he would. The boys and I caught the plane to Madrid and I promised to phone my father, to see how he was and to ask him to take it easy. Fernando had a two bedroom apartment, close to Retiro Park, where we stayed. We celebrated Christmas in traditional Spanish style with Fernando's Aunt Lola, her son, Fernando, (now a heart specialist), his wife, who was a nurse, their twin six year old daughters, Lollie, a school teacher, her husband, Miguel, and their two sons, Miguel and Fernando, who were about one year older than David, and Jamie. On Christmas Eve, we all sat around the long dining room table and had a clear chicken soup to start. The table was spread with various cold plates of prawns, parma ham, salad, and bread, to which everyone helped themselves and there were bottles of red and rose accompanying the meal. The following day, we all went by car to a restaurant in the mountains to have lunch. Although it was Christmas Day for us, it was a normal day in Spain. The boys bored, with all the adult company, wanted to go outside to play, but were told, that it was too cold. I went with them to the door of the restaurant, intending to go outside with them, but sleet like, cold snow was falling and the wind was bitterly cold. I persuaded them, that it was most certainly too dangerous to venture outside, so we all stayed inside. Sitting inside the restaurant, after the meal, Fernando's Aunt Lola, (with Fernando, translating) told me, that she thought not all young people in life were capable of accepting responsibility. (She was preaching to the converted).

She also said, "You see the gentleman, Fernando, is today, I sweated blood to make him so."

This I could believe and replied, "Yes, I know, I had it much easier with the two children."

Fernando had to go into the office and had arranged, that the boys and I would go to the apartment to another aunt who lived in a nearby block of flats, to have the main meal of the day, at the traditional time of two o'clock. Again, the long table was beautifully laid and we all sat down to lunch; to dinners of thin fillet steaks, fried eggs and potatas fritos. Fernando's aunt was working as an agent from home, selling properties most of the time. She came out with me shopping one day to buy something new for a New Year's Eve dinner, which proved quite difficult given the smaller sized and different styles of fashion. As we rushed around one particular shop, she took a red print silk dress off one of the rails and quickly passed it to the shop assistant to keep it for her. I was surprised at how expensive the dress was and that she didn't even bother to try it on.

In the end, I bought a woollen, dark red and black, tunic-style top, which I could match with black trousers. Fernando's cousin, Mayte, and her sister were delegated the task of entertaining me, and the boys, while, Fernando, was at work. They took us to the Prada Museum to show us the famous oil paintings, which included the Nightwatch. Mayte pointed out, that, when one stood right up close to an oil painting, it just looked like a lot of dots, but, when one stood back and looked at it from a distance, one could see the whole picture. I sometimes think life's a bit like that! The cousins were horrified, when, one day, I asked them to take me to a shop where I could buy some pots and pans, as, Fernando, only had one little copper pot in which he boiled water to make his Camomile tea. They said, Fernando would kill them, but I reassured them, that I would take full responsibility and, that he wouldn't. Fernando had taken me into a small room in his apartment that he used as an office. He opened a deep bottom right hand drawer in the desk that contained cash right to the top and told me to take whatever I wanted from it. He went on to tell me, that he had bonds and other investments worth x amount of pounds; in other words, he was extremely rich. On the book shelf were books that were all the same colour, style, and size, that were a façade, entirely intended for show, as, Fernando, only ever read paperback cowboy books.

I took just enough money from the drawer to go shopping in the local supermarket, so that I could cook quick, easy evening meals for myself and the boys, not wanting to eat in restaurants every day. I did, however, treat myself to some expensive chocolate liqueurs, it was Christmas after all. In the rush to go to the airport I had left my jacket in my parents' flat and, Fernando, took the boys and me to El Corte Ingles. He suggested buying me a fur coat, which I immediately declined, because, like his mother's beautiful white shawl, I would not have had any place to wear it; it just wouldn't have fitted into my current life style. I tried on a blue suede coat with a fur lining and, as I looked at myself in the full length mirror, I could see, that I was blushing, red with embarrassment, and the two boys could see it too. We bought the coat, as it was cold and I had to have something to wear. One day, as I was sitting in Fernando's car, waiting for him, outside a block of apartments, he came along, got in the car and said to me, "See that woman there in the fur coat, (I looked at the woman in the wing mirror of the car) I had an affair with her. She is married with three children to the security man for the block of flats. When I told my aunt she took a knife to me and said that I was to stop the affair immediately."

He also told me, that, when we were married, he had had an affair with the manicurist in Bentalls' when he was working there, as a men's hairdresser, which explained, why he would find an excuse to come home, find something wrong and walk out again, four days in a row, and just two weeks before, David, was born. It also explained, why he left the job after, David, was born. He also told me, that he had a thing, with my cousin, Philomena, (on my mother's side) who came to stay with us with her two year old daughter, in King's Keep, after she left her husband, because he was leaving her a cricket widow. He then said that both of the affairs were my fault! (Of course they were, nothing was ever, Fernando's, fault and there had to be someone to blame.) Fernando told me he had to travel north with his boss and would be gone for a few days. While he was away, a Spanish woman with a deep voice telephoned to ask to speak to him. I told her, in my limited knowledge of Spanish that he wasn't at home and was in the north of Spain with his boss. I was so bored, that I drank quite a lot from his cocktail cabinet, which must also have been for show or entertainment purposes, because, Fernando, didn't drink. When Fernando, returned I was suffering from a hangover; thinking that I wasn't well, he called his cousin, Fernando, to come and have a look at me.

Fernando came, and said that it wasn't anything serious; he did, however, recommend an anaemia, which, having never had one in my entire life, I refused. There most certainly wasn't going to be a first time on this particular occasion. A Spanish woman would come in and put Fernando's clothes in the washing machine; the rest went to the dry cleaners. Fernando told me, that he didn't need a woman for anything. He didn't need someone, who was going to tell him, he had to be at such and such a place, whatsoever, and back home by a certain time. He said it was better to use prostitutes, who would just come to his flat at an agreed time, give him a massage, be paid and leave, making no demands on him whatsoever. Well, I suppose that's one kind of relationship, but it would certainly never be one that I could find fulfilling or satisfying. In spite of all these attitudes to women, Fernando, fully expected me to go back with him and confirmed, that all his family thought that I would go back with him too. I told, Fernando, I couldn't move to Spain, because I didn't want to disrupt the boys' secondary education. He arranged for the two of us to have dinner one evening, in a really expensive restaurant, with a couple who were friends of his, and worked in banking too. They had moved from Argentina with their two sons and were now settled in Madrid. Fernando wanted the friends to convince me, that the boys' education wouldn't suffer, if we all moved over to Spain, as there were good private British schools they could attend, and, should I want to work, as a teacher, I would have no problem obtaining a position in one of the British Schools, teaching English. However, back in Fernando's apartment, I knew, that, should I agree to move to Spain, that I would be just like a bird in a gilded cage. Fernando had always done just what he wanted and now had everything he wanted and believed that he just needed me and the two boys to complete the picture. I knew that it wouldn't be long, before the boys would be off living their own lives and I would be left living mine with, Fernando. I knew that I could be civil and on good terms with, Fernando, for the sake of the boys but only as the father of my two sons and never as a husband again. We celebrated the New Year in the traditional Spanish way, buying boxes of handmade chocolates to take as presents to relatives and then trying to push twelve grapes into our mouths before the last stroke of twelve, which brought in the New Year. We stayed until after 6th January, The Feast of The Three Kings, when the children in Spain received their presents. We then travelled in Fernando's car to catch the flight back to England, Fernando had to stop the car, get out and be sick. Unlike me, he wouldn't have been suffering from a hangover and I suspected it was because he knew, in spite of all his efforts, and all his money, there wasn't going to be any reconciliation. Fernando had booked our tickets on Iberian airlines. After checking in, we went to the boarding lounge to wait with all the other passengers. The announcements were being made in Spanish and, Jamie, wanted to go to the toilet, so I told him to go, but, David, was getting anxious, in case we missed our flight. On the journey from the UK, we had simply walked along the passageway straight onto the plane and I thought it would be the same on the way back. However, when we returned from where the toilets were, all the passengers had already left the departure lounge and caught the bus that would take them to the plane. Fortunately, one other Spanish woman had also missed the bus and was running along the passageway in a panic and began speaking to one of the ground staff, who radioed the plane. A bus came and collected the four of us and took us out to the waiting plane. The door of the pilot's cockpit was open and all the passengers were already seated waiting for departure. There was a big cheer as the remaining four passengers entered the plane, one who looked very embarrassed, to say the least. David has never let me forget that incident to this day, saying, "No, Jamie, it's alright, you can go to the toilet."

My father, fortunately, made a good recovery and returned to work. I returned to our home in Glade Avenue and the two boys returned to boarding school. Phil, the vet obtained a position in the PDSA in Coventry, but kept in touch with me when he came to visit his friend, Peter Speakman, who lived in one of the streets off Lenton Boulevard. Peter Watt's friend, Graham, took over the rental of Phil's room for a while until he bought a place of his own. I didn't like living in the suburban cul-de-sac, as it was like living in a gold fish bowl. I bought a refurbished flat in the middle of the Park Estate, which I'd been led to believe would be two bedroomed, while the refurbishment was being carried out, but turned out to be one bedroomed. As completion was due to take place, I nevertheless, proceeded with the purchase, as, with the boys at boarding school, I felt, that it would still be sufficient, as they could share the bedroom, and I could use the large Victorian living room, when they were home. Fernando gave me £5,000 to buy new furniture for the flat! I bought an expensive gold and cream striped three seater settee, a two seater settee and a large armchair, which complimented the gold velvet curtains and the chandelier, that were already included in the refurbishment. I bought a beautiful antique circular mahogany Victorian table from Neale's Auction Rooms and a gold, thick piled Chinese rug from a couple, who had brought the rug back with them from Hong Kong. Mr. Carlson, the housemaster, at the boarding house, had taken, David, under his wing and would often play rounds of golf with him. David also took riding lessons at the local stables and could have free lessons in return for mucking out the stables. Mr. Carlson also taught, David, Religious Education and it was one of his best subjects. Although Southwell Minister was a Church of England School, David was free to attend Mass on Sunday, at the Catholic chapel, if he so wished; he also joined a karate club, as part of his extra curriculum interests. He was required to attend a supervised home-work period of study after school and discipline was very strict. The boys were required to make their own beds and had designated tasks in the dining room, which encouraged independent living. Mr. Carlson told me, that, David, was one of the top six boys in the school and he would look at him with a will of iron. He had cause to discipline him on more than one occasion. As for, Jamie, he said he had superstar status in the student common room, not surprising with his George Clooney lookalike good looks, and naturally extrovert personality. The fourth year girl students would visit the students' common room to see him; other girl students would ride to the boarding house on horseback to see him, when he was just in the first year. Jamie was naturally talented in football, golf, fishing and cricket. He knew just about every sport there was, including how to play bowls on a bowling green. One day, another boy who was late for class, told the teacher, that the reason he was late was, because he was being bullied by another boy, while walking across sites to class. The teacher asked the boy, who it was and the boy said, that it had been Jamie. Jamie was summoned by the teacher and asked about the incident, which, Jamie denied. The teacher kept pressuring, Jamie, to admit, that he had bullied the boy and, Jamie, kept denying it, saying he hadn't done it and couldn't admit to something, that he hadn't done. Upset and distressed, Jamie, ran out of school and was making his way home on foot to Nottingham. Mr. Carlson picked him up in his car before he reached home and brought him back to school. He later, on questioning the other boy about the incident again, discovered that the boy had made the whole incident up, as an excuse for being late and, when asked for a name, had simply said it was Jamie. Jamie wasn't happy at the boarding school and Mr. Carlson asked me, if I would consent to him seeing a counsellor, which I refused. With hindsight and a lot of teaching experience under my belt, I often wonder, if I should have agreed to the counselling, as I never really considered, at the time, the emotional impact of meeting their natural father, for the first time, and Jim's vicious assault on me, may have had on them at such a crucial stage in their young lives, and before beginning boarding school. Jamie grew increasingly unhappy and kept asking me to take him out of the school. In the end I agreed and he came to live with me in the flat in the Park and attended a state school in West Bridgford. It became more and more difficult to obtain teaching work and I was forced to claim unemployment benefit, as English teaching positions, were practically non-existent and due to the change in the rules and regulations, even supply teaching work was drying up. When my mother reached sixty, she was in a position to retire and my parents took the option of buying one of two, large, spacious flats above Surbiton library and, when my father reached sixty five, he retired from his job in County Hall. After retirement, my mother continued to work, as a carer, with a private agency, and went to work for a lovely, genteel, elderly lady, who lived in a large Victorian house, full of character, just around the corner from where, Carol, had bought a second home, close to Hampstead Heath, having already purchased a flat in Dolphin Square, after, she, and, Jim, separated. When my father, reached retirement age my parents went to live in a rented house in the village of Piltown, close to Watford, leaving my sister, Angela, and her partner, Gerry, to live in their flat, thereby helping to cover the mortgage payments. Not working, being on benefits and suffering from social isolation, I began to become more and more depressed, until I reached a point, where I felt I just couldn't cope anymore. I phoned my father, in Piltown, and told him how I was feeling and he rang, Jim, and asked him to go up to Nottingham to see me. Jim and my sister, Maureen, arrived with a bunch of flowers and took me out to the pub. Jim gave me some money and told me to go to the bar and order some drinks, while he went to the toilet. We returned to my flat and, Jim rang my father, telling him my head was full of spaghetti, as I kept talking about Peveril Drive and John Johnson. My father said, that he would have, Jamie, over in Piltown to give me a bit of a break. Jim and Maureen had to return to London the same day, as, Jim, was now in a new relationship with a girl called, Sophie, who was a friend of my sister, Angela, and ten years his junior. Jim was perhaps hopeful, that the age difference would increase his chances of having children. They were moving to a large character flat, just off Hammersmith Bridge, close to Wood Lane and BBC TV Centre. Jim looked at the lovely, tasteful furniture in my flat and said that he could use it in his new flat and could come with a van to collect it, in case I was burgled, while I was away in Ireland. I was depressed, but not that depressed, that I didn't know, that the only burglar I was likely to have, was the brother, who was standing right in front of me! Maureen had recovered from her nervous breakdown and had been re-housed in the Bonnerhill Road area of Kingston-upon-Thames, opposite the cemetery, and met her new partner, Robert, through his sister, who lived in the flat below. Robert was a handsome, young man, who worked as a civil servant in Kingston. He was calm and responsible and supported Maureen, in her efforts to regain custody of her son, Georgie. After regaining custody of her son, Robert and Maureen married and bought a two bedroomed flat in a block of flats, surrounded by gardens, just off St Marks Hill, Surbiton, a stone's throw from King's Keep and a five minute walk from my parents flat above the library. Maureen also had to rush back to be with, Robert, as they were also moving that day. I went to give the bunch of flowers to Maureen, saying they'd only die, when I went to Ireland, so she should have them, whereupon, Jim, impatiently pushed them back into my arms saying, they were for me and to keep them. So Jim, and, Maureen, returned to their respective new partners, their new homes and their new lives on the same day they'd arrived. My brother, Peter, came up from Banbury, and, though he had more family commitments than any of us at that time, we still went out to the Water Sport's Park at West Bridgford and he stayed with me, and, Jamie, until we caught the flight over to Ireland, to my parents' home in Piltown. My father arranged for, Jamie, to attend the local school there, and I'm sure he was glad to have his company, as he and, Jamie, were always very close.

I contacted, Fernando, and asked him to pay the money for the school books, Jamie, would need and the money for his keep, which he did. I arranged to meet with, Fernando, in the Inn on the Park Hotel, once again, and my friend, Peter Watts, came with me. When he arrived, Fernando, offered, Peter, a bottle of Coca Cola from the mini bar in the hotel room and had to do his favourite trick of opening it with his teeth, as there was no bottle opener. This amused, Peter, greatly, that a hotel room costing £300 a night didn't even have a bottle opener. Peter took his leave of us, and Fernando and I went out to a bar to talk about David and Jamie. I could see the black looks Fernando was giving to the man in the group standing next to us, because he was looking at me; he was still jealous and possessive, even though we weren't together. I told him, that I needed to get back down to London, if I were to have any hope of getting work. I said that, if I were to buy a place in London, he could put it in the boys' names as an investment for their future. He said he wouldn't do that, as the boys would just grow up and put their mother out on the street, (I think this idea was based on his experience of Spanish wills, in which the wife, on the death of her husband, is only entitled to a third of the estate, and the second third goes to the eldest son; the remaining third can be disposed of as he wishes.) He agreed to give me the money to buy a property in London, so I went back to Nottingham and put the flat on the market. I took a volunteer's job in Keffolds, in Haslemere, Surrey, a big house for refugee Vietnamese boat people, so that I could have free accommodation and food, while I looked around for a suitable property. The flat sold very quickly and I found a three bed, semi-detached house in Ewell, ten minutes away from Surbiton and close to Epsom, but £10,000 cheaper than the same property in Surbiton, which was on the commuter belt to London. I went over to Ireland, to collect, Jamie, and when I arrived, the tension between my parents was palpable. Normally, they could rise to the occasion whenever they had a visitor, but it was a long time, before the veil broke and they would even speak to each other. Jamie had made friends with other boys in the village and was popular with everyone. One family had given him a job flattening all the empty coal sacks ready for filling to deliver again, and Jamie would come home totally covered in black coal dust. My dad told me how he had gone down to the school to meet Jamie, and had seen him smoking, before, Jamie, saw him. My dad and I brought, Jamie, and a friend to a nearby seaside town and left them at the amusements, saying we'd return at a certain time. When we returned, the two boys were standing smoking. Jamie's friend, seeing us first, tried to hide his cigarette quickly behind his back, but, Jamie, blissfully unaware, that we were there, carried on smoking, until he turned around and saw us. While I was there, the children played a game, full of mischief and innocence; they would tie a piece of string to an old handbag and place the bag in the middle of the road and then hide behind a wall. When a car came along and stopped to pick up the handbag, they would all jump up, laughing and pointing their fingers at the driver, saying "pike, you're a pike."

They thought this was great fun. They would go fishing in the river, with only a stick with a piece of string attached to the end and a piece of cheese to use as bait. It worked and they managed to catch a few fish. When we returned to Nottingham, Phil, the vet's friend, Peter Speakman, and, Jamie, helped me move the furniture to the new house in Ewell. I promised to give, Jamie, five pounds, if he could give up smoking and, Peter, said he would too. By the time we reached the new house, Jamie said he needed to have a cigarette. I respected his honesty, as he could have had a smoke without telling us, and collected the ten pounds. Instead, he put his hands up to a lack of will power.

PART FOUR

Chapter One

Everyone Has Their Price

Fernando transferred £60,000 pounds towards the cost of the new house that cost a total of £68,000 from which £2,000 commission was deducted; I used the proceeds of the flat to cover these costs. Fernando said he would give me a further £8,000 so that he had paid the purchase cost of the property (less the 2,000, because of the commission, that had been deducted. The additional £10,000 plus the costs required to complete the purchase of the property). Jamie, and I, went to Brighton for a day and, when I asked him, if he would like to go into a restaurant for lunch, he declined, preferring to spend the day in true British seaside style. We bought fish and chips and mushy peas, which we ate from the paper sitting on a seaside wall looking out to sea. I took photographs of him, which captured the whole atmosphere of the day that we both really enjoyed. I enrolled, Jamie, at the local Secondary High School, which he would attend in September and, David, came down from Nottingham, when Southwell Minister broke up for the summer holidays. Fernando came over to see the new house and my mother, and father, (on a visit from Ireland), my brother, Peter, too came to see the house and we all went over to the pub across the road for a good old get together drink. As Fernando was going to the bar to get the drinks, I asked him, if he had enough money and, offended by the question, he showed me a thick wad of notes he had in his pocket. I jokingly said to him, "go and do your duty then," as this had always been one of his lines to me, "it's your duty," but he wasn't joking. He told us that he was having a big villa built on a golf course outside Madrid and I suggested that he give the work to, Peter, which he simply scoffed at. Phil, the vet, called in, while Fernando was there and we were all sitting in the front room of the living room of the new house, which had cost double the price of Peveril Drive, in Nottingham, and was a lot more than half the size, when, Fernando, said, "everyone has their price."

It was always about the money with Fernando. I saw Phil glance across at me to see how I had taken the remark, but my face remained passive. If he'd have read my mind, however, he'd have heard my thoughts, "and there's a price to pay for everything, we just have to make sure the price we to have pay isn't too high!" Fernando said, that he would take the boys shopping in Kingston and, Phil, and I stood outside on the pavement watching, Fernando, with David, and, Jamie, either side of him; Fernando, put his arms around both their shoulders and they walked down the road like three children going for a day out.

Julia, who had been one of the lodgers and had become another good friend, started her teaching job in East Stratford and came to visit me, and I would go to see her. On one of her visits, she told me, that, Johnnie, the vet, was getting married and, that I was invited to the wedding, but, even though she was going, I said that I wouldn't go. Even though I knew entirely, that it was the right thing to do for his life, as a single man without children, at the beginning of a professional career, it would have been too painful seeing, Johnnie, marry another woman. I had learned something from my doomed marriage to John Johnson. Peter Speakman and, Phil, came down from Nottingham to go to Michael Jackson's concert at Wembley and I went with them. It was a great evening and I was really impressed at what a great showman Michael Jackson really was. Not only did he sing magnificently, but put the work and effort into the dancing and choreography, that accompanied every song he sang. At the end of the evening poor, Phil, found, that his car had been clamped. I began a part time teaching position in Merton Further Education College teaching Social Studies, to students training to become nursery assistants, on NNEB courses, which I enjoyed. I also taught Communication Skills to students on other vocational courses, such as catering and motor cycle maintenance courses, which I didn't enjoy. As much of the summer holidays had been taken up with the move from Nottingham and the beginning of my new job, which was hourly paid and didn't come with a contract, I decided to take the two boys to Lanzarote for Christmas to avoid all the extra work it would involve, and to give us all a much needed break. The boys were not keen on the idea, complaining that they would miss out on all the parties their friends would be having, but all to no avail, I booked, and paid for the holiday for the three of us. Fernando came over to see the boys just before Christmas, saying, that he would bring the other £8,000 he had promised for the sale of the house. There was always a heightened state of tension that surrounded a visit from Fernando. My father came up from Surbiton, to say my parents had decided to move back into their flat above the library there, which meant my sister, and her partner, Jerry, moving out again. I had had a call from, Fernando, saying that, Angela had phoned him to ask him for a £1,000, which she needed for a deposit and first month's rent on another flat. Indignant, that this had been done without my knowledge or consent, I went with, Jamie, down to my parents flat. My father, came down the stairs to the door and I said to him, "why are you ringing, Fernando, to ask him for money?"

I knew from my father's distressed reaction, that he knew nothing about it! I went up the stairs and confronted, Angela, asking her why she had rung my ex-husband to ask him for money. My mother came out of the kitchen and interjected in a nasty tone of voice, "No wonder he's your ex!" She then turned to, Jamie, and said sarcastically, "Look at your mother, aren't you proud of her?"

To which, Jamie replied in a firm voice, "Yes, I am very proud of her!"

I told, Angela, that she should have spoken to me first, to which my father agreed. Angela later telephoned me to apologize, saying that she realized what she had done had been wrong. I knew from my mother's guilty, angry reaction to the situation that Angela wasn't the only person, who should be apologizing, but I didn't hold my breath!

The boys brought a little brown and white pup home after one of their friend's dog had had a litter; a cross between a Labrador and some other breed. My father, Fernando, and I had gone across the road to the pub for a drink. When we returned, Jamie came in and was obviously upset about something and went upstairs. He was crying and heartbroken, because his current girlfriend had dumped him. I sat talking to him for a while, before going downstairs again. Fernando was chasing the little dog up and down the front room and the dog was getting over excited. Feeling uptight, I told, Fernando, to stop, saying, that I would have been better off with a dog, instead of a husband, in the first place and clearly offended the over sensitive, Fernando, in the process. I had taken the two boys into Epsom to buy some Christmas presents for, Fernando, before he arrived, because I wanted them to know, that in spite of how wealthy he was, Christmas was about giving, and not just receiving. We bought a beautiful red and grey silk pattered scarf with gold fringes, suitable for a businessman and a comical book on golf, by Ronnie Corbett. I had popped them into Fernando's briefcase, before we went out to the pub, as I wanted them to be a surprise for him, when he got back to Madrid the next day. The following morning, Fernando was due to catch his flight back to Madrid. As there was obvious tension between us, I said that I didn't feel like driving to the airport and said, that I would order a taxi to take him there. David was upstairs and picking up on the vibes between us, and fearing, that his father was walking out of his life once again, he began to argue with me and pushed me down the stairs, something he would never have done before in the whole of his life. The taxi arrived and, Fernando, left taking the £8,000 cash he had in his briefcase for the house with him. After he left, the two boys told me he had given them £50 each, as the spending money he had promised for their holiday in Lanzarote. I put the £50 notes, in front of the boys, into an envelope and wrote Fernando's address on the front of it saying, "fifty pounds didn't rear you."

I took, Jamie, with me to the post office to witness, that the money had indeed been posted back to Spain. While I was at the post office with, Jamie, Fernando telephoned the house; he had found the Christmas presents in his brief case and was presumably ringing to thank us for them. David took the call and told him that I had taken the two fifty pound notes from them and was down at the post office with, Jamie, posting them back to him. When I returned from the post office, David, told me that, Fernando, had telephoned and, when he had told him, that I was posting the money back, he had said, "but that money was for you," and that I, shouldn't have done it.

I resolved, that, Fernando, could keep his money and I would keep my two sons, in both senses of the word, and time would tell, which was more important. David, Jamie, and I went on our self-catering holiday in Puerta Del Carmen. We all paired up with a football coach from Esher and his friend, that the boys had got talking to, and did a sightseeing tour of the island with them. Although it was a very small volcanic island with black sand, was diverse and interesting, with many places of interest. In the evenings, we all went to a little bar in Puerta Del Carmen, which had a good atmosphere and many social events that we all enjoyed together. One of the two men we had made friends with gave us all a lift from Gatwick airport back home. It was most gratifying to listen to a conversation between, David, and his friend, Andy Horton, that took place in our living room. Andy was saying to, David, that he could never go abroad for Christmas, to which, David, replied, that going away at Christmas was great. I re-mortgaged the house for £11,000 with the bank: had I known that Fernando would not pay all the money for the house purchase, I would have held back on my own money and taken out a mortgage for the difference to relieve some of the financial pressure, until I'd settled into a permanent teaching position. Fernando had instilled in David's mind that he had bought the house for him and, Jamie, but I also told, David, that we couldn't eat the grass in the garden, burn it to create heating and lighting or make clothes out of it. My father told me, that, Fernando wasn't worth just one million pounds, but several million pounds, so I reckoned that £58,000 to have his sons reared for fifteen years was a pretty good deal, even if he wasn't legally obliged to pay anything. In the eyes of the impressionable fifteen year old, David, however, his father had bought a house for him, and I was depriving them of both a father, and a lifestyle, that all the money could provide. In my eyes, I was now pleased, that the boys knew who their natural father was, and that it was good, that he wasn't a bus driver, living in a dingy bed-sit, trying to pay child maintenance on top of his rent, who we might all have to worry about too.

With only three years to go, until David reached eighteen, it wasn't his decision to make, it was mine! Fernando, had already planted the seeds in, David's, mind to change his name from Johnson, to Olias and one day, in the car, David angrily protested, that his future depended on it! I knew that no legally adopted child could legally change their name until they were eighteen, in order to prevent an identity crisis taking place. As I tried, to tell, David, this, I could hear the words of Mr. Munsy, the solicitor all those years ago, echoing in the back of my mind, "Well, what do you want me to do, you let him back in didn't you?"

The answer still would have been the same, that he was their natural father, and, that I thought it was right for the boys. I had had so much grief and emotional turmoil with, John Johnson that I had forgotten the grief and turmoil I'd had with, Fernando, in the first place. Fernando had now reappeared, like a knight in shining armour, coming to rescue me from the woes of being a single parent, suffering the indignities of claiming benefits, necessary for the health and welfare of her children, but still so little, when the process she was forced to go through was eventually completed, ensuring, that they were only ever going to experiencee a life below the poverty line, in a poverty trap, hard to break free off. Certainly not a life style of fancy hotels and fancy over-priced restaurants!

Before the end of the academic year, I was once again suffering with stress. When the college, saw "stress" on the doctor's certificate, they advised me, that they had filled the position and, that I didn't need to return. My sister, Maureen, sent me up a blank note book with a very pretty embossed cover. Inside, on the front page, she sent her best wishes, saying the pages were blank and, that I should use them to write down all of my thoughts. It was a lovely gesture from someone, who had suffered so much depression herself and was able to empathize with me. I never did write in the book, as I was too pragmatic and needed to be earning money. I decided to take a break from teaching, which was proving to be as unsatisfying as marriage and I thought, "What else do I enjoy?"

The answer was driving, so I applied for a job in a taxi firm in Mitcham and was the first, and only, lady cab driver they had ever had. I reasoned, that, if university students weren't too proud to work as bin men during their vacations, then I wasn't too proud either to work, as a cab driver, seeing it as gap year or a kind of sabbatical. The other taxi drivers were great, funny and supportive and would carry out repairs to my car, if I ever needed them. I saw an advertisement for lady drivers in the local paper for a new taxi firm, which was starting up in Tolworth which was closer to where I lived, and only took bookings for lady passengers. I applied and met with the Jewish lady owner, Bea, (short for Beatrice) and her partner, Jane, an art teacher, who lived in Richmond and who had two children; a boy and a girl about David's age from her first marriage, and three younger children from her second marriage.

They both wanted the concern to be very up market, so the drivers had to wear uniforms, that made them look like BA air hostesses. The business cards were in the same printing style as Harrods to give a subliminal, up market message to the ladies using the service. The Jewish partner was a hard-nosed, demanding business woman, but, Jane was the real brains behind the business, as she had been to a public school and spoke with the posh plumb in the mouth piece, one associated with public schools. She was hard working, organized and did the interviews on radio promoting the business, as well as interviews with local journalists, giving coverage in the local papers. I became good friends with, Jane, who really was being put upon, by her Jewish partner. As the partner started to be demanding and unreasonable with the drivers also, I told her I was leaving, refusing to accept a job into London, which would have meant, that I had worked two shifts from early morning, to late at night. Jane, and I, decided to start our own ladies, mini cab firm, working out of my home in Ewell. After finishing his G.C.S.E examinations at Southwell Minster, I received a letter from the school, saying that, David, was being excluded, because of bullying and smoking. David was clearly stunned and upset by the letter, as he claimed the allegations had been exaggerated, if not contrived. The headmaster suggested a meeting to discuss the situation. However, I was also of the opinion, that it had been contrived. In the summer, I had asked the school to replace a broken cricket bat, that visiting Polytechnic students had used and broken, while visiting the boarding house. The school then asked me to pay for the repairs to a cupboard door, that they said, David, had broken. The school objected to their authority being challenged, especially by the mother of a son, whose father was obviously a very wealthy man, but who was being sponsored by Nottingham County Council. I felt, that, if that was the attitude of educationists towards a pupil they had had in their school for four years, then it was probably better, that he didn't return and take his A' Levels there. I wrote a letter to say, that a meeting wouldn't be necessary, as David would be returning home to live with me. As a rebellious reaction to the letter from the school, David, unaware that I had made an appointment at Ewell High School, for him to attend sixth form there, got two tram lines put into his hair and when he came home, the roof nearly came of the house! We attended the interview anyway, but, David wasn't offered a place at the school; it may have been because of the tram lines in his hair, or it may have been because of the report the school received from Southwell Minister; or a combination of both.

David, enrolled at North East Surrey College of Technology to take three A' levels in law, Economics and Business Studies, which his father had advised him to take. Had I not lost the influence I previously had over David, I would have told him to choose the subjects he was both good at and interested in. When, David, came to live at home with me, he made friends with the local boys, who were all pursuing training in the trades their fathers already had. Socially, David was now a round peg trying to fit into a square hole. He had to adjust to an educational environment that was very different to what he had been used to. NESCOT offered a lot more freedom, as it took the view, that students were there, because they wanted to be, whereas Southwell Minister had been very tightly structured. Both boys were teased mercilessly for their Nottingham accents by their friends and they soon found, that they had different interests to their friends as well, such as golf, fishing, football and cricket. Their friends were less into outdoor activities and more into technology games and watching TV. At the age of sixteen, David, immediately passed his test for a motor cycle and bought a 50cc motor bike. For years, I had tried to put both boys off motor bikes, but I might have been more successful, if I had encouraged it and said, "When you get to sixteen, you should get your licence and buy a motorbike."

Once I saw how determined, David, was, I insisted, that he pass his test, buy all the correct protective clothing and get insurance cover. I learned to let go and not lie awake at night, worrying about him out on the bike. I was secretly relieved, when it would be off the road and, David, was tending to this bit or the other bit, all the technical names he would explain to me, but I've since forgotten. David and his friend, David Redman, who was also into motor bikes, decided to spray a bigger 125cc, or perhaps it was a 250cc, motor bike, David, had bought. They sprayed it the same green colour as a can of 7 UP, the soft drink, and sprayed the petrol cap to look just like the pull ring on a can of 7 UP. It was an excellent, professional job. They took a photograph of the bike and sent it off to 7 UP to see, if they would use it for advertising their product, but they never did. I would pass, David, in the car close to Tolworth roundabout, standing on the pavement beside his distinctive green bike, two policemen checking his documents, happy in the knowledge, that he was legal; at least, that was one piece of advice he did take. However, I did get a late night call once to collect him from Redhill Hospital, when he came off the bike at a roundabout. Thankfully, there was very little wrong with him, or the bike, and I think the look on my face hurt more than the minor injuries he had sustained. David, Jamie, and their friends, were all great when it came to helping Jane, and I, set up the mini cab business, which we called, Elle Cars, partly because of the elegance of the name, and partly, because I had a cat called

Ellie. Ellie was one belonging to a litter from a girl passenger that I immediately fell in love with and kept. The boys delivered the thousands of leaflets to homes in the area and, if, Jane, and I, were out on jobs at the same time, David would take the calls for the bookings when he was there. We got a school run over to Gunnersbury Avenue on the North Circular, which provided regular work and gradually built up a small regular clientele in the area. On my fortieth birthday, my next door neighbour gave me a cake with Elle Cars written on it and put streamers all over my car. I removed the streamers in order to go on the school run, only to discover, when I returned, that I had missed the one on the bumper, that said, "I am 40 today."

My brother, Raymond, his German wife, Ellen, and their two children, Sean and, Emily who I was meeting for the first time, came over from Germany for a holiday and stayed with me. My father had taken Raymond, out of Hampton Grammar School, because they wanted to have him wear some kind of army uniform. My father was always adamant, that no son of his would ever join an army and he wasn't having him attend any school that was encouraging it in any way whatsoever. Raymond had been so bright he had been moved up a year, but left school with no qualifications, as he never got to sit any examinations. Jim, had taken Raymond, who, like, Peter, had gone on to train as a bricklayer, and working alongside, Peter, before going to Germany, to stay working in his house in Ealing, while he was married to, Carol, and made him study for his A' Levels, that were to be his entry qualifications into the London School of Economics to do a degree course. Raymond made friends at the university, but Jim, was unfriendly and unwelcoming, when, Raymond's friends would call to the house. In spite of Jim's interest in furthering Raymond's education, his rigid, inflexible attitude to the other aspects of Raymond's life provoked a somewhat resentful attitude towards him. This attitude remained long after, Raymond left England to return to work in Germany. Both, Raymond, and, Ellen, were both high maintenance people used to living the good life. It was obvious the children, aged five, and seven, had been brought up in a different culture. The younger boy, Sean, would say, "Why don't you make me some chips?"

It was a rhetorical question and he would tell me, that Jamie should be drinking apple juice instead of Coca Cola. However, he was prepared to swallow his principles now and again, if I offered him a glass of Coca Cola. Emily was more like, Raymond, in both looks and temperament. In the supermarket, she would dash to grab whatever it was, that we were buying, failing to notice an old lady in the way in her rush to get the item. Ellen had long blonde hair and the classic good looks of a German woman.

She was older than Raymond, cool, and measured, but neurotic and obsessive, when it came to cleanliness and style. Raymond made a return trip on his own and wanted to hire a car to get around. I called a company offering good deals on second hand cars, and the agent brought the car to the house. I noticed that Raymond was a nervous wreck, as he made to sign the agreement forms. Raymond told me he found the authoritarian mentality of the Germans very stressful, as well as their rigid mentality of adhering to every rule. He said a child in the street would not hesitate to tell any adult, in no uncertain terms, if they were parking in a place they shouldn't be parking. He was looking to move back to England with the family and wanted to meet up with his university pal, Gary Blackburn, who was running an employment agency in London. Raymond was anxious being away from, Ellen, because he said, that, when he was away, she would go on a shopping therapy spree. The pressure on my shower was low, because the tank in the loft needed to be raised up. Raymond said he would fix it for me and then proceeded to say he would tile the whole bathroom, replacing the small pink tiles with large white Italian ones. True to his word, he removed every tile in the bathroom back to the bare plaster wall and we went to buy the Italian tiles he'd suggested. Raymond, then proceeded to attend to the pipes and left, David's, friend, Andy Horton, who was training to be a plumber with British gas, instructions as to what needed to be done and went off to dinner with Gary Blackburn. The upshot was that, Raymond went out with his friends, and the bathroom was left unfinished. He then returned to Germany. As I had no bath, the shower and the hand basin in the bathroom were our only means of washing ourselves and the walls remained totally stripped back. My brother, Peter, came down form Banbury and finished the bathroom. He knew I was quite happy with my small pink tiles, especially when they were attached to the wall, but he put up the Italian white tiles for me and I had a new, flash bathroom. Meanwhile, my sister Angela, had parted from her Scottish partner, Gerry, and they had sold the flat they had at Hook, (close to Surbiton) and, Angela, now working in a good job in a computer company, bought a small two bed house in a street, just off the main road, close to Hook roundabout. She met an accountant friend of a neighbour, who lived in the house opposite, who came from Grenada In the West Indies. Darrell wanted to return to Grenada, to set up his own printing business and wanted, Angela, to go with him and get married out there. I told her, that I would definitely visit her in Grenada, and, Raymond, and, Ellen, agreed to rent her little house and continue to pay the mortgage for her, which would have been cheaper than paying rent. My brother, Peter, separated from his partner, Caroline, with whom he had three children. Although they'd never married, he re-mortgaged his house and gave, Caroline, the money to buy the council house in which she was living. One day, Raymond, came over to me, and said, that, Fernando, had rung him to say, that he was staying in the Strand Hotel and to ask the boys to go down to the hotel to see him. I told the boys, that if they went to see, Fernando, in the Strand Hotel, that they could pack their things and leave home. I asked, Raymond, what they all took me for; I could just sit in a corner and go out and earn a living for myself and the boys and, Fernando, could just walk in and out of our lives, whenever he liked, causing havoc, and walking out again. I told Raymond, that, Fernando didn't have the guts to come back in the front door, so he was using him to get in the back door. Raymond got the point and apologized, saying that if Fernando, didn't get in by the back door he would come up the drainpipe. I trusted the boys, when they told me they were going to a friend's house, but, when I rang the friend's house later, to see, if they were coming home, their friend told me, they weren't there and hadn't been all day. I didn't want to be walked over by them and Fernando or lose credibility, so when they returned I told them to go upstairs and pack their things. David was pleased and, where David led, pleased or not, Jamie followed. David made a telephone call and I heard him saying to someone on the other end, that he would see them in an hour. I took this to mean an hour to get back to the Strand Hotel in London and automatically assumed, as I am sure the boys did, that Fernando would take responsibility for them. I later learned that Fernando told them to get a house and he would pay for it.

David aged seventeen, and, Jamie, aged sixteen, soon found they were standing on the pavement, with nowhere to live, while their friends were all in their own nice comfortable suburban homes. They spent their first night sleeping in a friend's car. The next day they went down to my parents' flat, David, and Jamie, had difficulty in obtaining passports to go to Spain to visit, Fernando, because of the full adoption, birth certificates and needed the shortened ones from me. I received a potted plant and a card, advising me, that they were there and asking for their birth certificates. I went down to the flat and posted the plant and card, torn in bits, through the letter box. I took a week's holiday in Crete, and on my return I posted the two birth certificates through my parents' letter box which brought a wry smile to David's face, realizing, that I was free to travel abroad, but he wasn't.

My mother came up and said to let them get their own place, that Fernando would pay for and have the whole burden lifted from me. She didn't understand that my two sons were never a burden to me. I had always had the attitude, that I had had my two sons and was responsible for them, and, if anyone else didn't want the responsibility, that was fine too; I would just carry on without them! Sixteen was too young to leave home and these were not the right circumstances, in which any young person should leave home. There was a right way and a wrong way of doing things and Fernando was not doing things the right way. But, as Fernando, had never been a present hands on parent, he wasn't capable of thinking like any other responsible parent would. I argued with my father for taking them in and further undermining my authority, and he replied, that he couldn't do anything else. Did I expect them to live under a bridge in a cardboard box? I asked him, why should they live in a cardboard box, when they had a millionaire father? Being young and honest, David failed to take Fernando's words at face value and should have chosen a house to buy, but, instead, he went to the student accommodation office at Nescot, and found a house in Epsom to rent. The two boys, all excited at having their own place to live, called to see me, to see, if they could have their duvets. I said that they could take anything they needed and that I would bring it around to their new place in the car. They showed me round their new place, which was owned by a Chinese man. It was a good place; I knew where they were and, at least, they were only two miles away from home cooking. David worked out an exact budget of what they would need to live, keeping it to the very minimum and not even adding anything on for sundries. They did their own shopping, cooking, washing and cleaning, boarding school had, in its own way, already prepared them for independent living.

Chapter Two

The Car Accident

With, David, and, Jamie, now living out of home financially supported by, Fernando, Raymond, Ellen, Peter, and I discussed buying a larger house, in which we would all live together. We viewed several properties, one of which was at Thames Ditton and was on three floors; the most distinctive, memorable feature, being black and white floor tiles throughout. My brother, Peter, my college friend, Peter Watts and I arranged a holiday in Grenada to go and visit, Angela. My friend, Peter, sold his car in order to pay for his holiday. When we arrived, Angela had already rented a large wooden house on an exclusive, secured complex, as well as a four wheel drive jeep, which was essential for getting around. On the first evening of our arrival, I sat up with Angela, listening to the problems she was having with, Darrell, who was spending most of his time setting up his private business. They were both living at Darrell's mother's house, but, as his mother was a zealous, church going Christian, she would not allow them to live together, until they were married, and insisted, that, Angela, sleep in the basement flat and, Darrell, in her part of the house. Angela was resting in bed most of the day, as she was becoming more and more depressed, because of the boredom she was experiencing every day, "Another lovely day in paradise." I think she was also feeling very home sick once the initial euphoria of living on a paradise island had worn off. I advised, Angela, to find herself something to do and suggested that she go into the printing factory and help, Darrell, in the business, even if it was only to sweep the floors. The next day she had perked up and said that she would act on my suggestion.

So that we didn't have to pay separately for food and drinks, when we were out, the two Peters and I decided on having a kitty and pooling our money. We all put £100 each into the kitty and brother, Peter, and, Angela went to the local store to buy food and drink to have available in the house. They then went off together in the jeep, leaving Peter, and I, together in the house. There was no TV or any other form of entertainment in the house, so, with hours to kill, before, Peter, and, Angela, returned after dark, which took place around 6pm every evening, Peter, and I, made our way through a good lot of the booze they had bought. We went around the island with a young, black Grenadan youth, who attended the gardens, but was jeered at by the other young lads, "for sucking up to the whites."

My brother became really friendly with the lad and they went cray fishing in the rivers together. Darrell joined us for a meal at a Chinese restaurant, but said he had to dash off immediately afterwards, "as they break things," if he is not there. They certainly didn't suffer from a British work ethic and, if faced with a bad attitude from an employer, would just walk out, saying there were bread fruit on the trees and fish in the sea and the employer could stuff his job! The four of us went for a meal around the harbour, where they served sword fish and fresh tuna, deep fried and served in a basket. We went one night to see the, Mike Tyson and, Frank Bruno, fight, which was being shown on the satellite TV in a big hall, with a large coloured, rotating ballroom light, as the hall was generally used for dancing. We soon discovered that we were the only ones rooting for, Frank Bruno, which helped to remind us, where we were. Angela assured us, that it would be livelier at the weekend, as, that was when everyone came out dancing. Unfortunately, it rained a little on Friday night and everyone remained indoors. Darrell had a friend with a small yacht and arranged for us all to go fishing; he came along with us. As we headed out to sea, they attached fishing lines from the back of the boat, which would trail along behind and, hopefully, catch a few fish. I was fine, as the boat sped across the water like a motor boat, but, when they stopped it further out and the boat began to undulate in the sea, which was really smooth and calm like a warm bath, I began to feel sea sick and vomited over the side of the boat. We weren't far out from the shore and I asked them to bring me back, so as not to spoil the rest of the day for them. When we got to the shore and they had gone out again, I was approached by a local man, asking me, if I wanted any dope. He had asked the wrong person; I didn't even smoke cigarettes, never mind dope, and had always tried to deter, David, and, Jamie, from ever smoking it, telling them, "Only a dope, smokes dope."

The great chat up line was, "would you like to go to Grand Anse Beach?" I politely refused both offers, and found a taxi to take me back to the house, where I spent the rest of the day lying down. There was one funny incident, as we were driving around the island; we were driving up one rough road, when a group of school children, dressed in red and white check uniforms, tried to stop us continuing along the road. We carried on, but then the road came to a sudden end and there was no more. We had no choice, but to turn around and go back the way we had come, only to be greeted by the same group of laughing children, wagging their fingers at us in a "told you so manner." When I took a photograph of two children on another occasion, the mother came over to ask for money, which I gave her. Peter Watts' forehead caught the sun, as we drove around the island and we were somewhat concerned, when it swelled up and he began to look like the elephant man. Fortunately, the swelling went down and there was no real cause for concern. I also caught the sun, as we lay on the beach one day. I was face down on the sand, when an American tourist came by and began chatting to the others. She had a real OTT American accent, that went gushingly on and on about the sights on the island. Not wishing to be brought into the conversation, I remained face down in the sand, where I stayed until she had gone, only to discover, that my back had really caught the sun in the meantime. Grenada is known as the Spice Island and it was interesting to see cocoa beans, grapefruit, oranges and spices, growing in their natural environment. The young Grenadian lad would climb up the coconut trees outside the house and cut some of them down, which he then slashed with a machete allowing us to drink the milk inside. The interior of the island was green, dense, still and quiet; it reminded me of scenes described in Earnest Hemmingway's stories. With eight days to go of our three week holiday, the atmosphere grew a little fraught, as, Peter and Angela went off more and more in the jeep, leaving Peter Watts' and I alone in the house. What with it getting dark at six and with no transport, it was difficult to do anything or go anywhere, as there were only little shack like shops close to the complex and it would not have been safe to go too far outside the complex on foot. Peter, and I, decided that it would be better, if we just returned home early. It cost an extra £80 to change the tickets, but we calculated that we would spend this in the remaining time anyway and it would be better to go home. Angela was angry at the decision. I told her, that we didn't want to spend another eight days in the house bored out of our skulls, while she and Peter went off with the only available transport every day. Angela brought to my attention that, Peter, and I, had drunk most of the booze. Angela had asked me to pay our share of the house and jeep into her bank account once we were back in England.

While Peter, and I, sat at the airport waiting for our flight home, my brother, Peter, arrived and asked us for the money for the jeep and the house. We both immediately signed travellers' cheques made payable to, Angela, and gave them to Peter. Peter was apologetic and said that he didn't want to get involved in buying the bigger house with, Raymond, Ellen and me. As things turned out, it was a wise decision on his part. When I returned to England, I told, Raymond, and, Ellen, what had happened in Grenada and, that, Peter, wouldn't be going ahead with our plan to buy the house. While we had been away, Raymond, and, Ellen, had looked at other houses and found a much better property in Villiers Avenue, Surbiton and said we should still go ahead with the plan without, Peter. Although I was aware of what had happened between my parents and my Aunt Bernadette, all those years ago, I had two golden rules of my own.

1. Don't live with family

2. Don't go into business with family

I reasoned that we were living in different times and, that history wouldn't repeat itself. I decided that everything was to be done legally, through a solicitor, and, that, although I would be financing the arrangement, that it would be a 50-50 agreement between, Raymond, Ellen and me. Raymond was delighted, that I didn't expect any leverage from the capital that I, was investing in the property and, Ellen was even more delighted, that she would finally get the big house she wanted. Ellen, had been constantly complaining, that Angela's house was too small. I spoke with a mortgage adviser and he told me, that I could mortgage up to 75% of the property in Ewell. He told me, I could put a 25% deposit down on the purchase of three flats but I said, I wanted to do a joint purchase of the house in Villiers Avenue, with, Raymond, and, Ellen. The mortgage adviser referred me to a solicitor in Guildford to act for us in the purchase of the property and the drawing up of the agreement between us. He told me, that I would have to put the mortgage into, Raymond, and, Ellens names, as I already had a mortgage, (where had I heard that before) and have a Trust Deed drawn up to protect my interest in the property. The property cost £235,000, so the 25% deposit and the costs that I paid amounted to £62,500. Raymond, and, Ellen, paid £139 to have a full, structural survey carried out on the property. A 50-50 spilt meant, I would pay one third of the mortgage, and, Raymond, and, Ellen, would pay two thirds. The agreement would be for two years, after which time, either party could buy the other one out, or sell the property and split the equity, (no thought of losses or negative equity came into the equation, as it had been unheard of in the property market before.)

Raymond had a job working with his friend, Gary Blackburn, and I, gave, Ellen, half of the school run and other work, that fitted around the children's school times. Ellen wanted the children to attend the private German School in Ham, just past Kingston. At Easter time the boys were on their way to a fair, being held in Horton Park. David was the front passenger in one of his friend's cars. Someone suggested, that, Jamie, travel in the back of the car, but, Jamie, said that he would go in the jeep of the friend, who was following behind them. As they drove down the road to where the fair was, the car in front of them stopped, as the lady, who was driving the car was looking for the entrance to the fair, signalling at the very last minute. James Dear, tried to avoid hitting the car by going on the inside, but there was a high double curb and the car turned over, hitting a tall concrete lamp post and carried on going along the road. David was not wearing a seat belt, which on this occasion was probably a good thing. David was catapulted through the front windscreen, which had come out of the car in one piece, and landed on the grass verge at the side of the road. One of their other friends, driving past the scene of the accident, commented, when he saw the car, "whoever was in that car can't have survived," not realizing, who had been in the car. I received a telephone call from one of the boys' friends, saying, that, David was in hospital, but he was alright. Raymond, and I, went to Epsom Hospital. David was lying unconscious on the hospital trolley bed with a collar around his neck. On seeing him, I burst into tears and turned to, Raymond, who put his arms around me. I then began talking to, David, in my school teacher voice, saying it was his mum and he was going to be alright. He began responding and was panicking and I kept saying to him, "take deep breaths, you're in hospital and you're going to be alright."

He answered me saying, "Yes miss, yes miss."

David had suffered head injuries and had two fractured vertebrae in his spine. He was put on a special bed face down, which allowed the nurses to turn him. There was a delay in attending to his spine, as the hospital was unable to get the specialist required to do it, and in the end, they stood him up and applied the plaster to his spine. Jim Dear, was in intensive care with head injuries and internal bleeding and looked so ill, that we feared he might not survive. However, he eventually left hospital, before David, as he hadn't suffered any kind of fractures. David spent his 18th birthday, 15th May 1989, in hospital. I bought a large birthday cake and my mum and dad came up to visit him in the hospital. The boys were facing eviction from their house, which David was challenging, because neighbours were complaining about the motorbikes and the noise they were making when all of their friends came round to visit them. The landlord wouldn't allow a telephone in the house, so, unable to telephone, the friends had to come round instead. The landlord moved his young daughter into the property, (probably on the advice of his solicitor, as they could then argue it was someone in the family's first home.) The landlord came to see me and told me about the neighbours' complaints and said, that the friends would use bad language to him. I wasn't having, David, experience any more stress, whatever the rights and wrongs of the eviction action. I told the Chinese man, that he could have his house back, as, David would be coming back home to live with me. I did not want the money I had from the remortgage dwindling away for any reason in Villiers Avenue, which I knew the boys couldn't feel was their family home, so I decided to buy a flat for them, as a future investment, rather than having them at the mercy of the landlords and paying rent, that was going down the drain. Ellen and I went looking for a flat for the two boys and we found a large three bed maisonette above a bookmaker's. It was ideal, as it was at the end of a parade of shops, free of neighbours either side. I wanted the mortgage to be in the boys' names, but was advised, that, because of their age, it would have to go into my name. I left Ellen, and Raymond, to deal with the completion details of Villiers Avenue. In the meantime, I sorted the purchase of the boys' flat, and the renting out of the house I had remortgaged. The seller of Villiers Avenue was pushing for a quick completion and, Raymond and, Ellen, moved in, while I settled the boys into the new flat, and dealt with renting out the other house. Before completion had taken place, Ellen, had already allocated all the rooms to her, Raymond, and the two children, leaving the large studio area at the top of the house for me. My friend, Jane, advised me to insist on having a bedroom of my own on the first floor, as well as the studio area. I moved into Villiers Avenue on the third week in June and it was immediately clear, that, Ellen, now considered the property to be her family home and me, to be the unwelcome family relative, who would share it with them. My mother came down to see the place and, when, Ellen, showed her the studio, which was to be my living space in the house, my mother asked her, "Is our Margaret depressed?"

Chapter Three

History Repeats Itself

Before the exchange and completion on Villiers Avenue, I was driving, Raymond, to the airport, as he was catching a flight to Berlin. On the way, he began talking about a business that he was intending to start. Knowing that, Raymond, and, Ellen, hadn't any capital of their own, (that I was aware of) and, that we were already committed to the mortgage repayments on the house, not to mention the private school fees, Raymond, had to pay, I telephoned, Ellen, when I got back. I asked her, if, Raymond was intending to use the equity in the house to start up this new business, to which she meekly replied, "I think so."

All the alarm bells started to ring in my head, (I have learned, to my cost, to really listen, as well as heed such alarm bells.) At this stage I could have pulled out, but, on his return from Berlin, Raymond, persuaded me, that he would never use the equity in the house for his business. It was becoming more and more clear that now, Ellen, had her big family house, she would have preferred that I wasn't living in it with them. One day, as I passed her bedroom, I saw her hiding a large brown envelope under their mattress. I later went in to see what it was, that she was hiding and found it be quotations from a removal firm, for a move from London to Berlin. I knew she was putting pressure on, Raymond, and not, wanting him to come home one day and find her and the kids gone, I told him about the letter under the mattress. The draft form of the Trust Deed, that had been agreed, came through in the post. In the rush to finalize completion, and with me preoccupied with, David's accident, it had been left until after the completion had taken place. I knew that there was very little chance of, Raymond, and, Ellen, now signing the Trust Deed, because their names were on the mortgage deeds, now making them the legal owners of the property. I spoke with both of them about the situation, and asked, Ellen, who was an only child, if her parents would give her the money to buy me out and she calmly replied, that they couldn't. I always had my house keys, car keys and clothes, in readiness for going out on a job in the evenings. I was in bed one night, when, Raymond arrived home totally drunk. I could hear him shouting and walking about downstairs saying, "I'm between two women! I'm going to axe someone."

Ellen appeared from a bedroom, that wasn't the marital one, wrapped in a duvet. (Conjugal rights had obviously been withdrawn.) I quickly and quietly got dressed, grabbed my keys and bag, headed straight down the stairs and out of the front door. Raymond followed me into the street and proceeded to pour the bottle of mineral water he was drinking over my head, making all sorts of threats. I got in the car and went up to the boys' flat and told them what had happened. They were immediately concerned and said, that I should stay there that night. I contacted the solicitor Mr. Humphreys, in Guildford High Street and told him what had happened and asked his advice on the matter. He asked if, the house could be divided into two separate flats, but I knew, that I wasn't going to get a reasonable agreement to settle the matter from, Raymond, and Ellen. The solicitor suggested that I take out a second mortgage and buy them out. I went back to the Mortgage Advice Centre and completed mortgage application forms, which came to nothing. Raymond, and Ellen, were asking for £25,000 more than we had paid for the property in a market that was already going down. My father went down to see, Raymond, and told him to protect his sister's money, (but he wasn't the one who was married to Ellen, or was the father of Raymond's, two children.) My father told me, that, if I had spoken to him first, he would have advised me against it. I told him, that because of all the problems, I had had, I was just trying to help, Raymond and his family, to which my father replied,

"Sometimes people just have to have their problems."

I added another golden rule to my list, "Don't get involved with married couples, especially if you're related to them." I went to see a different solicitor and he advised me to take legal action to have the property sold. As I was no longer living in the property, I stopped paying my third of the mortgage. I telephoned, Raymond, to say that I wanted to collect some of my things from the house, and found that they had changed the locks. He arranged a time for me to come down and I arrived with one of the boys' friends. All my belongings had been put outside including the furniture, in a covered area at the bottom of the garden, and the side gate had been left open for me to collect it. The washing machine, I had bought, and with which, Ellen, was totally obsessed, hadn't been put outside with the other things. Raymond, Ellen, and the children, were conveniently not around, so the boys,' friend and I gained access through the side kitchen window, by removing the handle of the window, disconnected the washing machine, and loaded it into the car. We then replaced the handle on the kitchen window, closed the kitchen door and collected all the remaining belongings from the bottom of the garden. I wrote a letter to Raymond's bank manager advising him, that I was a beneficial owner in the property, that legal proceedings were being taken to have the property sold and the equity should not be used as collateral by Raymond, or Ellen, towards any business venture. As the property was on a main road, I asked the solicitor to write to Raymond, and Ellen, to instruct the agent selling the property to erect a "For Sale" board right outside it. David was uncomfortable with me living in their flat. Firstly, because they no longer had their own freedom and independence, and, secondly, because it was their father's money, that was paying the mortgage and, David, was anxious in case I would answer the phone, if he rang and would want to know what I was doing there. David said he wanted to leave and find another place to live. My father told me to go over and see, Fernando, to clear the decks. I rang, Fernando, and said I wanted to come and see him to discuss the boys. He agreed to the meeting and I gave him the details of the flight. He met me at Madrid airport and we went to a restaurant inside the airport to talk things over. I explained everything to him, including my concerns for the two boys and he asked me, what I, wanted him to do. I told him I wanted him to tell the boys, that, if they left the flat, he would stop their money; this he agreed to. He then proceeded to tell me, that he was married again, from one year ago, to a good Catholic woman, who only put God, before him, to which I replied, "I'm surprised that you stand for that."

I asked him, if he were going to have any more children, to which he said no, it had been a condition of the marriage and he'd had enough of that. When I divorced, Fernando, he told me, that he wanted an annulment of the marriage to marry a good, Catholic woman, whose family were insisting, that she marry in a Catholic church. At that time, divorce was illegal in Catholic Spain, as it was in Catholic Ireland. The debate on a referendum on divorce was taking place in Ireland, at the time, and the arguments against it were, that it would make any children from the marriage illegitimate; deny them their legitimate right to inherit; and would mean selling farms, that had passed from generation to generation to divide the proceeds between the two parties. I refused to agree to an annulment, as there were no grounds for it, and I would not make any children of mine illegitimate. When Fernando, had discussed the annulment with my father, he said, that he could use insanity, as the grounds for the annulment, (referring to my post natal depression). My father told him if he were ever to do that, he would punch him right in the nose.

When Jim and Carol's marriage ended in divorce, Jim, told, Carol, that he wanted an annulment of their marriage on the grounds, that she had been married before and hadn't declared it and therefore, had no right to marry again in a Catholic church. Carol raised no objections to this and calmly and coolly agreed, saying it was no problem. After all, she, and, Jim, had no children in the marriage to consider, (Carol's conversion to Catholicism would, in all probability, have allowed her to marry in a Catholic Church, as the Catholic Church would not have recognized her first marriage). Fernando, spoke with a Catholic priest at the time, who telephoned me to say he was concerned for my mortal soul and I told him, that at that precise moment in time, "I was only concerned with the health and welfare of my two children and my mortal soul would just have to take care of itself."

I asked, Fernando, why he hadn't told, David, and, Jamie, he had got married, (David thought that his father, wasn't ringing him, because I was in the flat), and why he hadn't invited them to his wedding and he said he didn't think it would be right. Right for whom I wondered? He said he thought it was better to marry someone you liked, rather than someone you loved. I disagreed with him saying I'd prefer to like the person I loved. I never could accept the idea of amicable divorces and staying friends, because, if I'd just had a friend in the person I'd married, I would never have wanted to divorce them in the first place. You can be sure, that, when you finally find the last piece in the jigsaw puzzle, more often than not, it will have another woman's face on it. Worse than the infidelity, lying and deception, is the lack of moral courage to just be straight and honest with the other person and to do the right thing, by one's children. As far as I am concerned, the other party is welcome to them, and all the money, that comes with them, in lieu of the children, "the good Catholic woman agreed not to have!"

One is a hypocrite, as is the other, and they deserve each other. I returned to Surbiton and told my father how things had gone with, Fernando, and I cried, as I told him he had married again; not for myself, but for my two sons who were to be put through the pains of divorce, that they had been spared the first time round. I went to the flat and told the two boys, that their father and I had both agreed, that they were to remain in the flat or their money would stop, and broke the news to them, that he'd lacked the moral courage to tell them himself, that he had married the year before. It was, Jamie, who surprisingly reacted angrily, saying I'd been going over there telling him tales about them, and calling Fernando's new wife his floosy. (He was wrong. She wasn't new she had been writing to him from Spain, when we were first married. Another ex, who had let me dig the garden and come in and picked the roses.) Raymond, and Ellen, handed back the keys to the mortgage company, and I gained access to Villiers Avenue, in order to try and protect my rights, as a beneficial owner in the property, and changed the locks. I told the estate agent to remove the "For Sale" sign, until the matter was legally settled. When I entered the house again, I found advertisements in German newspapers, offering accommodation to rent in the property, which would undoubtedly cover more than my third share of the mortgage. The boys had their flat to themselves, and my father, mother, my friend, Liz's, sister, Sally, and the two boys spent Christmas in the house in Villiers Avenue. I obtained a position, as a home tutor with Surrey County Council and the Head of the Home and Hospital Teaching Service applied to the Department of Education and Science, to obtain my DES number based on all the terms supply teaching I had already done in Nottingham, so that I was now a qualified teacher and did not have to complete a probationary year. I rented the top studio to a young Italian girl and her partner and had no mortgage to pay, as I wasn't the mortgage holder. Before, Raymond, and Ellen, handed back the keys to the mortgage company, the two boys wanted their independence and freedom of living out of home that Fernando's money was financing. I spoke with, Fernando, and told him, that I would look for a rented flat for them through an estate agent. I asked him to be the guarantor for them and he agreed. We found another flat that was for rental, with a six month tenancy agreement above a parade of shops on Stoneleigh Broadway. The boys bought white paint, and painted the walls of the flat to brighten it up and stamp their own mark on it. After his car accident I advised David, to sit his A' Level examinations, hoping it would give him focus once again. I said that, as he had lost his valuable revision time due to the accident, he couldn't be expected to pass them, but it would be good examination practice for when he came to retake them. Still in his plaster, David, sat his A' Levels and said it had been difficult as his head was thudding the whole time, making it difficult to concentrate. He didn't pass the examinations the first time, but retook them in November and applied for a HND, Business Studies Course at Guildford College of Technology. Jamie was doing a Hospitality Course at NESCOT although his main interest was always in sport. They received a letter from the estate agent reminding them, that the six month rental agreement was reaching its completion date. David, mistakenly thought, that it was an eviction letter, when it was in fact only a letter advising them, that the rental agreement should be renewed at the end of the first six months. Three friends of theirs were renting another flat above a shop, just across the road from them, and two of the boys were going back home to live, so the boys agreed to move into the other flat. One of their friends was an estate agent, who was going on a skiing holiday with another friend, when the boys moved in and, Jamie, was going on a field trip to Wales with the college for a week, leaving, David, alone In the flat. The radiator in the flat was leaking and the landlord was on to David, about it who, had just moved in. I received a phone call from, David, saying he couldn't even get it together to go to the shops to buy a pen for his final examinations that were coming up. I went up to the flat, which was dark and dingy, and suggested to, David, that he come down to Villiers Avenue, to stay with me until the others came back, but he refused. I later got a call from another friend to say, that I should go and see, David, because he had flipped. I went with my friend Liz's sister, Sally, only to find, David, with the word "YO" on the back of his head and obviously on a high. I once again asked him to come back with me, but he refused. An older girl, Sarah, the sister of Jamie's ex-girlfriend, Laura, managed to take,

David, up to hospital and brought him to me in Villiers Avenue, with a letter from the hospital to his GP. I opened the letter to see what it said and discovered, that the hospital was advising the GP, that, David had been a heavy cannabis smoker for the last four years. I rang the GP and was totally freaked out, as I spoke to her, saying I knew nothing about it. The GP made an urgent appointment for, David, to be seen at West Park Psychiatric Hospital. David was agitated and asked the doctor for a cigarette, which the doctor gave him, but made him wait for the light for it, going out of the room and leaving us together. It was at this point, that, David came over to me and put his arms around me, and I held him in my arms. David was referred to a drugs counsellor attached to Epsom Hospital, and after running the streets, throwing away cheque books and being totally manic just as, Maureen had been, he was given an injection in the bottom to sedate him. He spent one night in the unit, and came very close to being sectioned. The following day, David was refusing to stay in the unit and the doctor released him into my care, with medication, that he was to take to stop the shakes and a drug support councillor calling to the house. The councellor, at first, suggested family councelling, to which I agreed, but then changed it to a one on one session with, David. My mother called down to the house and I cried on her shoulder for the first time in my life. I asked her how my father was and she made a face, suggesting that he wasn't alright. I just put my head in my hands and cried. Shortly afterwards, my father, who by that time must have steeled himself, came into the house with a quarter bottle of whisky and gave it to me, a drink to settle my nerves. He said to me firmly, "hush, huh, you're just a broken stick no-one can lean on you."

I knew his words would give me the strength to see, David, through this really dark period. David was hallucinating, threatening to jump off the roof of the house at the back and kept ringing lots of numbers on the telephone and saying into the phone, "Don't put the phone down on me, dad."

Fortunately the Italian lady lodger was sympathetic and understanding, saying the same thing had happened to her, and her mother had seen her through it. When David wouldn't settle down in the bed one night, I swore at him, angrily, telling him to lie down in the bed and stay in it! He turned round and gave me a devilish little grin, but lay down just the same. When he began to stabilize on the medication, he was really weak and said that anyone could knock him down, if they just blew on him. He came shopping to Sainsbury's in Surbiton with me, and to the cinema to see, "Silence of the Lambs," which was less scary, than what I had just been through. I was still seeing the solicitor and would take, David, with me, as he grew stronger. It was during this time, that I got a telephone call from my neighbour complaining about the noise the students renting the house were making. I went up to the house and told the students, that my son was very ill and I didn't need complaints about their loud music right now. The music was turned off and the party ended right there and then. When the students vacated the property, Jamie, and his two friends moved into the house for a short time. However, it was now the time of boom and bust, interest rates were doubling to over 15%, twice what anyone expected to pay for just one mortgage. I had the mortgage repayments on a separate budget account to ensure, that it was always paid. Without advising me the bank transferred a £3,000 overdraft from the current account to the budget account and one mortgage payment was missed. The mortgage company removed the deferred payment discount, and said that it now also had to be paid as a payment had been missed. They refused to listen to my excuse, that the bank had been the cause of the missed payment. The rent would never cover the already high interest payments plus the deferred discount, and it wasn't long, before the mortgage company, the same mortgage company, that had granted the 75% mortgage for Villiers Avenue, issued repossession proceedings. For the first time in history, house prices in the London area were falling into negative equity. I hadn't the strength, or the will power to fight the mortgage company, so I handed back the keys as so many other home owners and businesses were being forced to do. Fortunately, the flat I had bought for the boys was with a different mortgage company and the deferred discount remained. As the flat was in my name, I could control the situation, although it, too, was now in negative equity. Tragically, young Sarah, who had brought, David, up to the hospital, was later murdered by her boyfriend, who lived in Shepherd's Bush. Mentally ill from drug use, he heard voices in his head, telling him to kill her. Epsom and Ewell was voted the best place in the country to live, but, in spite of it being an affluent, middle class, suburban area, drug use among the young was prolific in my day, parents worried about their teenage children getting drunk or pregnant, but drugs were now the greatest social evil confronting the young, and their parents, in modern society, making parenting more difficult than it had ever been before. Fernando heard about the boys' drug use on the family grapevine and stopped the boys' money. In his drug crazed state, David, said to my father, and me, that Jamie was a drug dealer and, Fernando, a drug baron. I said to my father, that it was a preposterous idea, but my father said, that there was possibly a hint of truth somewhere in the notion. When David was well again, I went to see, Fernando, in Madrid, without announcing in advance, that I was going. I booked a three day ticket, as I had no intention of having a brief meeting at the airport like before and taking a flight back the same day. Fernando's wife's mother had suffered a stroke and I thought, that we could all sit down as adults and discuss the situation with the boys and I could get to meet Carmen, (his wife) and her me. I took a taxi from the airport to his office in the CIMD bank in Madrid, where he was now one of four partners who owned the bank. When I was shown to his office, I introduced myself as David, and Jamie's, mother, to his secretary, who was really warm and friendly, telling me, that she had met, David and Jamie, when they were over, showing me the two large photographs of them, that Fernando kept of them on his office cabinet. She said, Fernando wasn't in the office, I asked her, if she would telephone his home and ask for the address and I would take a taxi out there. She spoke to someone on the other end of the phone; she was clearly worried and uncomfortable. She said, that she had spoken to the housekeeper, (another one posing as the housekeeper) who told her, that Fernando wasn't at home and Carmen was out in the garden, (probably now tending to her own roses.) I told her, that I had come over from London specially, to speak to, Fernando, about the boys and, that I wouldn't be leaving until I had spoken to him .One of Fernando's partners came to speak with me and said he would put me up in a local hotel, but I knew, that, if I moved from the office to the street, Fernando would not put in an appearance. I told his partner that I wasn't leaving until Fernando came to speak with me and I asked him, if he had any children of his own. I told him about David's illness, as I knew, that everyone would be given the impression that I was only after his money. The partner said, that he had to close the office and even made a point of saying that all Spanish people are not like, Fernando, by way of an apology. I said I wouldn't leave until Fernando came to speak with me about his two sons. The partner went out and came back in again, saying, that he had called, Fernando, who had told him to call the police to have me removed from the building. I told him, that he had better go and call them, because I wasn't leaving. The partner showed me into the boardroom and offered me the seat at the top of the table. He had the secretary bring me in some tea and biscuits. He returned to say that Fernando, was on his way. Fernando arrived straight from the golf course by the look of the yucky, lime green golfing pullover he was wearing. He was in an agitated state, as he rushed into the room saying, "what gives you the right to come into other people's lives disrupting them?"

That was a bit rich coming from him, who had come back into my life and his two sons' lives, with no legal rights, whatsoever, and had used my brothers Jim, and, Raymond, to get what he wanted, instead of respecting my rights and position in the situation. Now that the shoe was on the other foot, and he was in his new marriage, with his "good, Catholic woman," (I wonder if she had a few conditions of her own, in respect of his first family) it didn't sit too comfortable with him! The partner stood around outside for a few minutes, in case things should turn nasty, but, as I began to speak to, Fernando calmly, but firmly, he went off and left us to it. I told, Fernando, that he was the one, who had told the boys to get a place of their own and he would pay for it. I also told him, that I knew he'd told, David, that, "he didn't want his mother to have the benefit of his money, but, David had always had the benefit of a mother which was far more important than his money!" I said what I had to say to him, and he asked me what I wanted. I told him, he was now responsible for the situation and he was not going to stop their money, but he was going to pay it directly to me, because David was not well enough to bear the responsibility of it all and it should never have been put on him in the first place. In true banker's (as opposed to father's) style, Fernando had already calculated in his own mind, what he was going to concede financially to get me out of the building. He agreed to give me, directly, the money for the remaining two years, in a lump sum, until their education was completed. The one thing I did know about, Fernando, was, that, when he said he would do something, he would do it. I told him, that my ticket was for three days, so he brought me to a hotel in Madrid and left his American Express Card at the reception and told them to put my bill for everything on his card. I telephoned, David, in Villiers Avenue and told him, that I had sorted everything out with his dad, that his money was being reinstated and paid straight to me. Fernando came on the last day and paid the bill, complaining, that the phone bill was more than the cost of the room. I told him, that his son needed a lot of reassurance right now and I had called him every day.

We got a taxi and went to a restaurant for a meal and were able to talk freely and comfortably, after which I went to the airport with him to catch my flight home. I never did get to meet Carmen, or see their new home on the golf course. I had to meet with Counsel in Gray's Inn in London and drove down with my solicitor, Teresa Nicols, from Russell Cook Potter and Chapman in Kingston-Upon-Thames. The councel advised me, that I had to first sue Raymond and Ellen under the terms of the Trust Deed and show them to be people of straw. He advised, that in view of the amount of money involved, I would then have to sue Mr.

Humphreys, of Humphrey's and Co Solicitors for professional negligence and failure of Duty of Care to his client, in order to be awarded the money I had lost. Through the family grapevine, I learned that, Raymond, and Ellen, had rented a house in Hampton, near Hampton Court Station. I bought my nephew, one of Peter's sons, in the car to show me, where the house was, as he had been there before. We drove to the house and I got out to get the door number. A light came on in the house, as the car door closed, but I just went closer to get the number and then drove away again. I heard that another guy who Raymond was going into business with, was also chasing him, as he was also suing him for some tape, or other, that he had taken. Raymond had also received £10,000 from the Criminal Injuries Board, because he'd said something offensive to a guy in a pub, and the guy glassed him in the face with a bottle. Knowing that I had the new address, Raymond, and Ellen, left the property and returned to Germany. I brought, David to a solicitor's in Surbiton, to make a claim for his injuries with the Motor Insurance Bureau, as, Jim Dear, had no insurance. David would also have to sue, Jim Dear, and prove that he was a person of straw, before he could receive compensation from the MIB. David came under a lot of pressures from his friends, but I insisted he proceed with the claim, which would be very much reduced, because it was through the MIB and not the insurance company. When the claim was eventually settled, David was awarded £15,000. When David was well enough, the two boys moved into the flat I'd bought for them, and I continued to live in Villiers Avenue until the situation was settled. The mortgage company issued repossession proceedings and Counsel advised me, that he couldn't represent me in court, as legally the mortgage company had first claim on the property and, that, if the hearing went against me, I could be bankrupted, if the mortgage company claimed their costs. I said I would represent myself in court, hoping, that I could ask the mortgage company to transfer the mortgage into my name, as they already had £57,000 of my money in the property and I was a Beneficial Owner in the property.

Sally came to court with me for the hearing. The barrister for the mortgage company was there with the woman from Lloyds Estate Agents, in Surbiton, who was clearly nervous, as she smoked one cigarette after the other outside the court room and couldn't sit down, but kept pacing up and down instead. When we went in because I wasn't legally represented, the judge had to make his decision based on the papers in front of him. I did stand up and speak, saying that I was a Beneficial Owner in the property and I stood to lose a total of £62,500. The barrister presented his case and said, that the estate agents had a buyer for the property at the price of £219,000 when we bought the property, it had cost £235,000 with the £57,000 25% deposit the mortgage was for £177,000, (but of course all the mortgage arrears would have been added to the original mortgage.)

The judge asked me, if I had anything to say, but I was taken unaware, not expecting the other side to say they had a buyer, so I said I didn't. The judge said, that he wasn't supposed to offer legal advice, but, as I wasn't represented he went on to say, that I could bring a case for Duty of Care at some stage in the future, so he would put aside the mortgage company's request for costs which they could pursue, if my case in the future awarded me compensation. He was a fair judge and administered justice, in as far as he was able to, in law, ensuring, that I wasn't made bankrupt. It later transpired that the property sold for £158,000. There was probably no buyer at £219,000, and the estate agent had good reason to be nervous, as she probably knew she was going into a court room to tell a deliberate lie. The first house I had bought was remortgaged by my next door neighbour, after it was repossessed, for £80,000, so that her daughter, and her partner, could live next door to her. I had always wanted to go abroad to do VSO, but could not do it, while I had any dependents. David, and Jamie, now had their respective partners and were twenty, and twenty one, when I applied for and was accepted by VSO in 1992. It was for a two year contract in Egypt. I got the money up front for the mortgage from, Fernando, to ensure the mortgage was paid, while I was abroad for the two years and the boys had a secure place of their own to live. I left Power of Attorney and my address in Egypt with the solicitors, who were to bring the case against Humphrey's and Co Solicitors. When I returned from Egypt and contacted the solicitors, Teresa Nichols, who was acting for me had left the company and I spoke with another lady solicitor, who said she would obtain Counsel's advice for me. This was when I learned, that Villiers Avenue was sold for £158,000. When I received Counsel's Advice, I went round to see my sister, Maureen, who was now divorced from Robert, because of an affair he'd had, and who was now seeing one of the law lecturers from the London, School of Economics, where she was studying for a Degree in Law. Her partner, Richard, was there at the time and looked over the counsel's advice, and told me, that the case was time barred, but I now had a case against Russell Cooke, Potter and Chapman for allowing it to become time barred. I went for a walk along the Thames, where they had their offices and came face to face with Teresa Nichols, who had just come out of their offices. I put in a complaint to the office for the Supervision of Solicitors. Maureen had helped me sort all the relevant documents to send with the complaint and said she'd send it from work.

Russell Cooke Potter and Chapman had told me Humphey's and Co had gone out of business. I went abroad again and when I returned and rang the OSS regarding my complaint, they said they hadn't received it. They did say they had had a fire in the basement, which had destroyed some of their files, but did, Maureen, ever post the complaint: she was, and still is, on close terms with Raymond and Ellen, The OSS also told me, that Humphrey's and Co were still in business. (Solicitors closing ranks) I was advised, that the only way I could bring another case was to find another Counsel, who would go against the Counsels Advice obtained by Russell Cooke Potter and Chapman. I went to Kuwait for one year and had saved some money. I thought about obtaining another Counsels Advice, with which the judge had also concurred, and to have closure once and for all. I spoke with a London solicitor charging £135 per hour, who obtained Counsel's Advice at £500 and obtained a further advice that indicated I didn't have a case, (more closing of ranks) but I had closure. I lost £62,500 plus, but I also lost my relationship with my brother, Raymond, who was prepared to do the dirty on his family. I accepted my share of the blame for the loss, for breaking my own golden rules in the first place and believing, that we were living in different times and that history wouldn't repeat itself. Raymond smoked a lot of pot, when he returned to Germany and suffered a nervous breakdown. Ellen laid down the law once again, and, Raymond, with a reference from Gary Blackburn, obtained a good position, as the manager of Finance and Administration for Europe with the Australian Trade Commission and the Australian Consulate General in Frankfurt.

David completed his HND course and went to train as a trader in the City, earning a good salary and driving a flashy, company car. He was in a serious relationship with a girl he'd met at college and one day told me, that he'd be better buying a place of his own, than continuing to pay a mortgage, that was in my name. Although the flat had been purchased for the two boys the circumstances had changed drastically and I was not in a position to transfer the property into his name, now that the other two properties had been repossessed, and all my efforts to recover the monies I had invested in Villiers Avenue had come to nothing. I told him he would be better buying a place of his own, as the flat was now in negative equity too. David bought a top floor flat in Wimbledon in order to be able to commute to London. He was able to take advantage of the fall in the property market and bought a repossession property at auction and had his first home of his own. Jamie had a baby with his partner, at the age of nineteen, and went on to buy a flat of his own, with some help from, Fernando, in Raynes Park, also close to the railway station to commute into London. He later started working as a manager with Ladbrokes just across the road from where he was living. My mother and father sold their flat above the library and moved over to Ireland. Jim's marriage, to Sophie, ended in divorce and he also, moved to Ireland, as Southern Ireland was giving tax breaks to artists. He sold his flat at Hammersmith and rented a wing in a large house belonging to a Church of Ireland minister. Angela, who had returned to England to marry, Darrell at his mother's insistence, returned once again to Grenada. A woman from up country called to see Darrell, to ask for maintenance for a child she had had with him. When, Angela, married Darrell, Jerry said, that she might be marrying him, but that she'd come back to him, which is what she did. She had a baby girl called, Heather with whom she'd been pregnant, when she left Grenada. She had a baby boy with, Jerry, called Henry. On learning, that Angela had a baby girl, Darrell refused to pay maintenance, saying she was in England which had a social security system. He refused to see the child and said she could come and see him when she was eighteen.

In 1985, I returned from Tanzania, where I had worked in a Teacher Training college. I married a Tanzanian pharmacist I met there, and we later separated and divorced by agreement. Maureen married, Richard and moved to Birmingham, where he worked, as a lecturer in law and later moved to Edinburgh, where she obtained a position as Head of Macmillan Nurses in Edinburgh. Jamie returned to live in Nottingham. I returned to work as a Home Tutor again with Surrey County Council, living in the flat, that I had bought for the boys, which I rented out when I was abroad. My parents moved to Armagh, my mother's home town in the North of Ireland. After moving over to Ireland, Jim met his third wife, Nula, who is from Dublin. They were on good terms with my parents and had good social gatherings. Carol, his first wife, remained on good terms with Jim, and would visit him, Nula, and my parents, if she were ever attending a conference in the South of Ireland where they lived, and, if, Nula were ever over in England, she would visit Carol.

Chapter Four

The Family Reunion

In 2012, David married his present wife, Mel, whom he met in the Bank of America. Ironically, they booked the wedding venue in the Mitre Hotel, where Fernando had been a waiter all those years, before David had even been born. I bought my wedding outfit for the occasion, paying more than I'd ever paid for any outfit in my life before, even for my own three weddings. During a telephone conversation with, David, he casually mentioned the top table and the vision of it sent me into a panic, as I hadn't had time to think of such details, especially as David and Mel were such good organizers, needing no advice or help from me. It suddenly dawned on me, that, Fernando and Carmen, who I still had never met, although the boys, their partners and Jamie's eldest son were now frequent visitors to his new home would be there. I was annoyed at the way I had been treated in order to protect Carmen's, sensitivities, but here she was, attending my son's wedding, (the same son, who'd never been invited to her wedding, because they didn't think it would be right!) I mulled it over and telephoned, David, to say I thought it would be better, if I didn't go to the wedding and to just let Fernando and Carmen, represent me. David's reaction was one of rage and anger and he slammed the phone down on me. Mel later phoned to ask, if there was anything she could do to persuade me to attend the wedding, as David really wanted me to be there. I explained that I was really happy for them both and, with Fernando and Carmen attending, that they could just agree to let me off the hook. Knowing that I didn't object to Fernando being there, as David's father, she said she would speak to Fernando, to see, if he would agree to attend alone.

As my back was beginning to play up, I booked a week's holiday in Crete, where I bought a gold necklace, as a wedding present for Mel. I spent the week taking it easy and feeling suitably restored to face the situation, I telephoned Mel when I got back, and, without even asking what Fernando had said to her about attending the wedding alone, I told her I would be coming to the wedding. On hearing that I wouldn't be going to the wedding, my parents said they wouldn't be going either, (bless them.) I rang them, and told them that I would now be going, and they said they would come over for it too.

I collected my parents at Heathrow airport and bought them to the Mitre Hotel on the way home to show them the venue and we had a drink together in the bar, before going home. On the morning of the wedding, I called a taxi to take the three of us to the Mitre. It had rained in the morning, but, fortunately, it cleared up and the sun was out in time for the wedding service. My parents and I went into the lounge bar of the hotel. Suddenly, someone came bounding up to me and kissed me on the cheek. It was Fernando. He greeted my father, calling him his friend: he certainly was, and his sons' friend too! He then introduced me to Carmen, who was no Penelope Cruz or bore any resemblance to Bizet's, Carmen; my father's favourite opera. She was a short, plain, middle aged woman. When Fernando introduced her to me, I greeted her in Spanish. She proceeded to speak to me, in Spanish, saying how happy she and Fernando were, as if she, somehow, needed my blessing and turned to Fernando, as if she needed him to reaffirm what she was saying. I was holding some flowers, that were being distributed to the relatives of the groom and proceeded to pin one on the lapel of Carmen's blouse and I told them, that this was David's day. Seeing that the ice had been broken, Jamie, who was the best man at the wedding, came over and my brother, Peter, and his three grown up children, of whom I am very fond also came over. I had insisted, that I not be placed next to, Fernando, at the top of the table, so my eldest grandson, Luca, Jamie's son, aged ten, sat at the end of the top table beside Jamie, to fill the space. Fernando and Carmen had been placed on the circular table in front of the top table, with Luca's, mother, Anna and other friends of, Jamie, and their children. Maureen's son, Georige, who hadn't initially been invited to the wedding, had telephoned, David, and asked to be there. He sat at the table with my mother, father, Peter, and his three children at the far end of the room. It was a lovely day, which was filmed by Mel's father's friend, Paul, a fellow Greek Cypriot, who, like Mel's father, had settled and married in England many years before. This was the last social occasion, when all (or nearly all; Jim, Raymond, and Maureen were absent) our family came together to celebrate a really happy occasion and it didn't disappoint. Fernando and Carmen had booked into the Mitre Hotel, as had Mel's family, the day before, in order to meet each other and avoid travelling over from Spain and Kent, respectively, on the big day. Jamie and Anna, and their friends, mainly entertained Fernando and Carmen, and my family kept together enjoying our own opportunity to come together. There is nothing like Christmas, weddings, and funerals to expose the cracks that exist in the fractured, modern, blended families of today. In January 2004, I received a phone call from my mother's home help, saying, that my father had been hit by a car and he was in the Royal Victoria Hospital in Belfast. His leg had been broken and he had to have a pin in his knee. He had a fractured shoulder, which was being left to heal by itself and a grazed forehead. I spoke to him on the hospital's telephone for patients, telling him where he was and what had happened and, that I'd be over just as soon as I could. I telephoned my Aunt Philomena's family, who have hearts of gold, just like her, and asked, if they could go and visit my dad until I could get over. My mother was travelling down to Belfast from Armagh. Although my mother could have stayed with my cousins to avoid the travelling, she didn't want to impose on them, as my cousin, Bernadette, had just given birth to a Downs Syndrome baby. My father was moved closer to Armagh, to Craigavon Hospital, in Portadown, until a bed became available in the rehabilitation hospital of Mullinure, a ten minute walk from where they both lived in Armagh. My dad suffered with macular degeneration, which made things difficult for him at times, but he remained independent and had his own little coping strategies for dealing with his condition. At 82 years old he was very lucky to survive the accident at all, as the shock of it could have killed someone of that age. When I arrived at Craigavon Hospital, my father was complaining that he had nothing, no money at all or the keys to get into his bungalow at home. I gave him some money to put in his drawer and went with my mother to buy him a little personal radio with head phones, that he could listen to in order to alleviate the boredom and distract him, from what was going on around him. I bought him a container for his false teeth, as he had been putting these into his glass of drinking water. I had brought him over a Christmas cake bar from Marks and Spencer's, along with some other goodies. On the way to visit him with my mother, one day, I bought him some lovely grapes from the hospital shop and, when we arrived in the ward, my mother sat at the side of the bed eating the grapes. I told her, that they were for dad, and that we'd buy some more for her on the way out, if she wanted. She would poke around in the hospital dinner that they brought him, and, far from giving him the reassurance that he needed from her, she would just increase his already high stress levels. At this time, my mother and father were practically living their own separate lives. They had their own bedrooms, their own bank accounts and often went their own ways, which was now difficult for my father, who had given up driving, because of his macular degeneration and my mother had never learned to drive. As my mother had a free travel pass, she would just travel wherever she wanted and often left my dad alone. My dad was eventually transferred to Mullinure for convalescence, when a bed became available. I received a call from, Alice, again saying that my mother was now in hospital in Craigavon. I telephoned my father in hospital to let him know, in case he wondered why my mother, wasn't going to visit him. When he heard the news, he became really distressed and upset, so, to reassure him, I said, that I was coming over again. I rang my sister, Angela, to ask her, if she knew, that my mother was in hospital, and she immediately said, "She's a bad bitch!"

She told me, that my mother had phoned her to ask her, if she would come over, just after I left. My sister said, that she couldn't leave her two children, who were attending school, and the dog, so my mother, effectively downed tools. When I arrived at the airport, the home help's son, who was training to be a nurse in a hospital in Belfast, met me at the airport and bought me to Armagh. I asked him, if he would show me, where Mullinure hospital was, and he drove me there, literally a five minute drive from where my parents lived. I went in to see my dad and said, that there was nothing seriously wrong with my mother, and that she had a chest infection and had been prescribed antibiotics for this. My father was due to go to the Royal Victoria Hospital the next day to have his knee checked and they wanted someone to go in the ambulance with him, so I told them I would go. When I went into their bungalow, the Christmas cake I brought over was in the bread bin with some mouldy bread. All the personal items, I bought for my dad, (his radio and bits) were in the drawer of his bed side cabinet, and his clothes for bringing to the hospital were laid out over his bed in readiness for whoever was taking over from mother. My mother had a chest infection and had seen the doctor, who prescribed antibiotics for her to take at home. Alice, her home help, called in every day and was the link between home and family. She was like a family member and would run my mother here, there and everywhere, in her car, if it were ever necessary. My mother had an emergency call link to another neighbour, just across the road, whose son worked in the hospital and would often call in to see, if she needed a lift up to see my dad, when he was going in. The support services and the community around my mother were second to none, but my mother rang the emergency services in the night and insisted that they admit her into hospital. The next morning I went to sit with my dad. While I waited for the ambulance, that was taking him to the Royal Victoria Hospital in Belfast, the nurse came and told me, that I couldn't go, because the ambulance had other pickups to do and there was no spare room. She said a nurse would accompany my dad instead. I decided to go and see my mother, in Craigavon Hospital, and found her lying on the top of the bed reading a magazine, with her pink dressing gown I'd bought her from Marks and Spencer's over the back of the chair, lots of juices beside her and her bag and keys at hand next to her. It had most definitely been a well- planned, and well thought out emergency. Some poor soul with a real emergency was being denied the bed she was occupying. As I approached her bed, I said, "Ah, Butlins is it?"

The nurse asked me, if I was over on holiday and I replied, "Yes a two-centre holiday between Craigavon Hospital and Mullinure Hospital."

There was a man in the bed opposite my dad, who had had his two legs amputated and his wife, using a walking stick, would come to visit him. There was also a big lounge, where relatives could sit with the patients, giving them moral support and company. The atmosphere was relaxed and friendly, and my mother, as well as my father, could have benefitted, if my mother, had had the will, to give my father the support he needed. When I went through his clothes that my mother had brought into Mullinure, I saw an old pair of calf length leather lace up boots, that my father, never would have bought let alone worn, and were totally inappropriate and unsuitable for an elderly man, who was recovering from a broken leg with a pin in his knee. The jacket on the back of the chair was old and shabby. I went through all the clothes, packed them and took them home, where I sorted out suitable ones to take back to the hospital. The impression being given to the outside world was that my father was some sort of pauper, which he certainly wasn't. Neither was he ever one for putting on the style. He enjoyed simple pleasures in life, a day at the races, a small accumulator bet in the bookies, a pint with friends, (preferably those he could talk horses, trainers and breeders with) classical music, good books, good art, politics and going for a walk in order to keep fit, or to get out of the house.

Unlike my mother, he could hold an intelligent conversation with anyone on most subjects, and he took an interest in everything his grown up children were doing, especially, Jim, with whom he would play chess and talk about whatever TV work he was engaged in at any given time. He would have shied away from the limelight of the leading roles, but would never fail to play the supporting role, whenever it was required, especially when it came to his family. He once told me that he had always tried to be a presence, that, he most certainly was and a whole lot more: a rock, an anchor, a calming and reassuring presence, a tolerant, wise and caring father, and husband. While there, I received a phone call from, Nula, Jim's third wife, whom I had never met. She had a deep, rasping, old voice and spoke with an Irish Dublin accent. Although I had never met her, or spoken to her before, I found it easy to have a long conversation with her, mainly about the family. I instinctively knew this would be followed by a visit up to Armagh to see me, now that mum and dad were both in hospital. Sure enough, the next day, my brother arrived at the door, wearing a small black and white check jacket, his hair now totally white. He walked through the door, smiling his usual charming smile, and said, "Hello Margaret, I'm sorry I did that to you. I never should have done it."

And that was it, like twenty two years hadn't passed between the incident he was referring to and the present. Jim had an easy Irish charm and no more needed to be said. He suggested we go out for dinner and a drink, before which we went to see my father, in Mulliure. My father, looked at the two of us at the bottom of the bed, a brother and sister reunited, and I could see, that he was pleased. He said to me, "I think you and Fernando, only needed five more minutes."

To which I replied, "Fernando didn't have five minutes."

Jim and I went to the Charlemont Hotel in Armagh and had dinner and drinks in the bar. It had a warm, friendly atmosphere was popular with the locals and served good home cooked food. Jim and I sat talking and just enjoying each other's company. My mother's week in hospital was up and she was being discharged the following day. I had already packed my mother's clothes for coming out of hospital, being careful to pack the shoes and clothes I'd seen her wearing on my first visit over, in order to avoid any issues, when she was leaving. When I arrived at the ward with the bag of clothes, she, predictably, began to be difficult, before she'd even looked in the bag to see what I'd packed. I immediately responded with a very firm, "don't you start," which brought an end to the proceedings.

Alice, her home help, was going up to the hospital on the day she was to be discharged and offered to collect her from the ward after she had had her lunch and been seen by the doctor doing his rounds. My mother was for calling a taxi in the morning, but was compelled to wait until the doctors had signed her discharge papers. Jim, and I, went out to have lunch in the Triad Centre in Armagh, an arts and culture centre, which also serves good food, at reasonable prices, in a pleasant, congenial environment. After lunch we were heading back home to await my mother's arrival with Alice. As we passed the bakery, I wondered, if we should buy some cakes for mother's arrival, when, Jim said, "shall we buy some cakes for when mother gets home?"

We went into the bakery to buy something nice, and, Jim was pointing to the fruit pies, but I put him off buying these, as I knew the complaint would be, that I hadn't made them myself. I suggested a large sponge cake with lemon and white icing, knowing how colour always appeals to the elderly, and, because it looked quite special, so we bought the cake instead of the fruit pie. We weren't long home, when my mother, and Alice, arrived. Alice refused to stay for a cup of tea and cake, making excuses that she had to be somewhere else. We put the kettle on and made the tea and I cut the cake and put it on to the plates. My mother took a bite out of her cake and said, "That cake's crap!"

Jim immediately launched into an apologetic explanation of how he had wanted to buy the fruit pies, but we thought the cake looked nicer, and I thought how absurd it was, that a son of his age was still standing and answering to his mother. It should have been the thought that counted. Instead, it was just another opportunity for my mother to be difficult. After we'd all had our tea, and crap cake, Jim suggested he drive us up to see my convalescing father, who was still convalescing in Mullinure Hospital, but my mother said she didn't want to go. After some persuasion, she finally agreed to come with the both of us to see my father. We later went to the Charlemont Hotel for dinner, and then returned home. Jim was keen to show me the video of his interview with Noel Browne, the author of, "Against the tides," the book he had hoped to make into a film. He saw a video they also had of me, chairing a debate, while I was working, as a volunteer, with VSO in Egypt. I was aware, that, although it was twenty two years since I had fallen out with Jim, he had instinctively fallen into the role, of a protective big brother, who thought I needed to be defended from my own mother. The day, however, ended on a happy note, as I shared my father's bedroom, which had two single beds, with my mother, while, Jim slept in the bed in my mother's bedroom.

We all went to sleep laughing and I said, that I hoped dad, wouldn't be coming home tonight as we had no beds either.

Jim was returning to Rathdrum, in Co Wicklow, where he was now living with Nula, although Nula, also spent a lot of time in Dublin, where she had her business. As, Jim, prepared to take his leave of my mother and me, he took the large black and white photograph of me, that his friend, Stuart, had taken of me when I was nineteen. My mother and father had had the photograph freshly mounted and framed and it had pride of place in the hall of their bungalow. Jim also took the photo of him in Confirmation (another Catholic ceremony older children attend after their First Holy Communion) together with me in my First Holy Communion dress and veil, saying he'd get copies of them made and let my mother have them back. He took the video of me in Egypt and the video of him with Noel Browne. I went alone to Mullinure, after Jim left, to see my father. I was sitting at the side of his bed, and I could hear someone asking questions from behind the drawn curtains of one of the opposite beds.

"Which town are you in?" Wishing to be helpful, I shouted across to the person behind the curtains, "Armagh."

My father, then, to my surprise, went on to ask the next question, before the person asking the question had even asked it. My father had been a progress chaser in Short Bros and Harland, in Belfast, and had trained his memory to remember the numbers of parts. He was also an intelligent man, who would have still been testing and training his own mind following a car accident. The elderly man behind the curtain, who was being assessed for dementia, which, unlike me, my father was fully aware of and was ensuring, that his own mind was going to remain clear and active.

With my mother now at home, the way was clear for my father to also return home, once he had clearance from the doctors. The physiotherapists were due to make a call to my parents' bungalow, the day after I returned to England, in order to assess the home for potential risks to my father, and to put additional support workers in place. Shortly after my father, returned home, I received a telephone call from Nula, saying, that she was worried about, Jim, and she'd taken him to see a professional friend of hers in the West of Ireland, who had advised her to have him assessed, as she didn't think, that Jim was well and she had seen the same symptoms in other patients, that had been brought on by trauma. Nula continued to tell me, that she had contacted, Carol, who had set up some appointments for Jim, to be assessed privately, and, that she, Nula, was going to Los Angeles, to have a full health check carried out on herself and Carol, and she, thought it would be too far to take Jim. The first appointment was to be in Harley Street which Nula would attend with Jim. The other appointments all of which followed each other were at the Royal Free Hospital in Hampstead I agreed to attend with Jim. On the day of the appointment with the Harley Street Specialist Consultant, I received a phone call from, Nula, who had taken a taxi from Harley Street, asking for directions, to give to the taxi driver, as to how to get to my house. I gave the directions and told her to tell the driver to stop on the opposite side, as it was a dual carriageway, and I would come across to meet them. This was my first meeting ever with Jim's third and present wife, Nula. They came across the dual carriageway into my home, for the very first time, and told me, that the Harley Street Consultant had advised them, that Jim was in the last stages of dementia, and had approximately one year to live. Nula handed me some hand written notes listing Jim's symptoms, together with a newspaper article outlining the effects of long term unemployment on one's mental health. Jim was extremely calm, saying, that he was going to paradise in an almost carefree, resigned tone of voice. Nula was distressed and in tears. I made us all a cup of tea, which was all Nula, had time for as she was due to catch a plane back to Dublin, in order to catch her plane to Los Angeles the next day. She left me all the names of the professors there and their telephone numbers should I, or the consultants, need to contact them. I drove, Nula, with Jim, to Heathrow Airport to catch her plane back to Dublin. The next day Jim, and I, went to the Royal Free Hospital in Hampstead, where, Carol was Head of Rheumatology at the time. I parked my car in Richmond Park, and we took the train from Richmond, in order to avoid the traffic. Jim was happy and relaxed and chatted the whole way to the hospital. He was to have an MRI scan, which he called a CAT scan.

As we sat on the chairs waiting to have his scan, he sat telling me about a programme he had made for television about brain scans and how they could slice the X-ray in order to see the different parts of the brain. After the scan, the radiographer told me, that the X-rays would be sent to, Carol. The following day, we had an appointment to see a Consultant Neurologist at the Royal Free Hospital. When we went into his consultant's room, he was unable to find Jim's X-ray on the system and asked his receptionist to try to locate it, (I'd forgotten the Radiographer had told me it was to be sent to Carol first.) While we waited for Jim's X-ray the consultant carried out some physical tests on Jim. He asked me, if I'd noticed any changes in, Jim and I said, honestly, that, Jim, and I had been estranged for twenty two years, so I wouldn't really have been in a position to notice any changes. I said, that I had met up with him again, at the time of my dad's car accident, and noticing tears in his eyes on one occasion, (when he was speaking of Father Laverty's kindness all those years before, in allowing him to take the children's First Holy Communion photographs with his first pentax camera,) and knowing, that he hadn't been working, I said I thought, that he may have been a little depressed. There was also one other occasion, when my mother, Jim, and I had gone into the Triad to have a pot of tea and scones, when I noticed, that Jim was attempting to separate my mother and me, by calling and gesturing for me to come and see something in the centre. We went down one floor from the restaurant to where he showed me a figure of St Patrick, in a large glass case. He was bent over and kept pointing to it in a way that reminded me of a scene from the Mozart film, in which Mozart is behaving in a child- like imbecilic way. (Jim was totally obsessed with Mozart) and it was the one, and only time, that I thought he was, "out of his tree." The consultant arranged for Jim, to have some blood samples taken to be sent off, and we joked with the nurse telling her to take enough blood to cover the cost of the consultant's fees. The consultant told us he would telephone us, when he had a chance to look at the X-ray. Jim said something to the consultant about "the wealthies," (one of his favourite rants at the time) and I responded to it by saying, "Even the wealthies get sick."

He was separating people into the "goodies" and the "baddies." Jim still had enough of his faculties to be aware, that the consultant was, "a goodie," and I'm pleased to say, he also considered me to be a "goodie." The following day, we received a telephone call from the consultant saying, that, Jim wasn't suffering from Dementia after all. I immediately telephoned, Nula, on the telephone number I had for her, and it was joy and jubilant all around. Nula's daughter, Sian, was saying we should sue the Harley Street Consultant, who had given the first diagnosis. I was just happy to receive good news, but it was short lived. The next day, I received a call from a Consultant Neurologist in Hammersmith Hospital, who was also affiliated to the Royal Free Hospital, as a private consultant. He told me, that he had been asked to provide a second opinion on Jim's X-ray, as they thought something had been overlooked by the first consultant, when he had examined the first X-ray. He continued to say, that he thought, Nula, as Jim's wife, and immediate next of kin, should be present also at the appointment he had made for, Jim, and I to attend at Hammersmith Hospital. Jim, and I went to meet, Nula at Heathrow, on the day of the appointment and we drove straight to Hammersmith Hospital together. As we waited to see the consultant, the receptionist asked, Nula, to complete some forms, whereupon Nula dashed off in tears to the bathroom. I followed her and told her she had to hold it together for Jim's sake; she composed herself and we returned to where we'd left, Jim, sitting in the reception area and the three of us went in to see the consultant together. Jim and Nula sat at the front of his desk, and I sat a slight distance away from the desk to the side. Nula sat with a notepad in her hand writing notes, as the consultant spoke, (reminding me of, John Johnson, in the divorce court.) The consultant showed, Jim, a picture and asked him, what was happening in the picture. (a simple reasoning test,) Jim was totally lost and couldn't explain what was happening. Another consultant, a Linguistic Specialist, came into the room and asked, Jim, to describe what a worm was, which Jim, did. She then asked him to explain the concept of fraud (court connection) and, Jim was blank, unable to attempt any explanation. She then asked him to explain the concept of Cathedral (the church) and, once again, Jim, was totally blank and unable to even attempt a definition. The consultant then took us to look at Jim's X-ray and showed us the temporal lobe, on the left hand side of Jim's brain, (just behind the frontal lobe,) which was clearly thinning, degenerating in comparison with the temporal lobe on the right hand side of his brain.

He took, Nula, and I into his office and told us that Jim, was suffering with temporal lobe variant dementia, which effects the higher cognitive reasoning skills of the brain, and it had been creeping in for about five years. It would have started when Jim was fifty five years old in January 2000. He continued to say, that, if Jim had worked as a bricklayer, (like my brother, Peter,) or an artist even, (like Nula,) he could have carried on working, but, as Jim's work as a freelance director involved the use of the higher cognitive skills, it would affect his ability to continue in this line of work. Jim had been working on turning the book, "Against the Tides," by Noel Browne, into a film script and was carrying the manuscript he had typed around in a battered old briefcase, along with an old medical dictionary, which gave the definition of Dementia as, "insanity." The consultant, on being told about the script, said, that Jim was a director, not a writer, and he'd very much like to see the content of the script, casting some doubt on its rating as a film script. Nula asked the consultant, if the court case, around the time of the onset of Jim's illness, could have triggered his illness, to which the consultant would only reply, "It wouldn't have been helpful."

I asked the consultant other questions, I believed to be relevant, and was told, that Jim wouldn't be put on medication yet, because of the side effects; and that he should not continue to drive.

Ronald Reagan had suffered for fifteen years with dementia and it would be obvious, when the time arrived, that Jim would need to be institutionalized. When we left the hospital, Nula appeared extremely calm and normal, as she sat on the back seat of the car with, Jim, on the way to catch the flight back home to Dublin. (A burden shared perhaps.) I was in a state of shock, gripping the steering wheel hard in a bid to get us all safely to the airport, before returning home to make the telephone call to my anxious parents' back in Armagh and tell them the devastating news. I was worried about my father surviving the news, so soon after his car accident. I arrived home and made the call I had to make: my father answered and I relayed the diagnosis details and facts to him and asked him to pass them on to my mother. He said he would do so, and would give her the abbreviated version.

Chapter Five

The Court Case

I went to Tanzania with VSO in February 1997, to teach in a Teacher Training College in Nachingwea, Lindi, and made a surprise visit back to the UK, in May, at the end of the academic year. My younger son was then staying with my sister, Angela, in Surbiton when I called to see them. I learned, that, Angela, and her two children, were on a week's holiday over in Ireland. Jim, and Nula, had gone down to Dublin and my mother and father had gone down to their home outside Clonmel, where they were living, in order to look after their dogs and house while they were away. My mother and father had suggested, that, Angela, and her two children, join them there, in order to give her a break, and so that they could all have a small family get together. Jim, concerned about keeping up appearances, as always, wasn't keen on the idea, as he feared that they would all end up in the local pub having a sing song, although Nula didn't have a problem with it. While Jim, and Nula, travelled back from Dublin, my father, took a telephone call saying, that Noel Browne had died. Jim, on hearing the news, reacted typically under pressure, and told, Angela, to tell my parents to, "fuck off back to Armagh!"

Angela, sensing a difficult and stressful situation was about to unfold, said to my parents, "Get me out of here!"

My dad had put a ten thousand pound bond in the bank, to cover Jim's overdraft, until a dispute between Noel Browne's relatives and him, as to who would be the director and producer of the film, (in other words, who would have control of the budget) had been resolved. Angry at Jim's reaction, my father went back to the bank to attempt to have his £10,000 bond refunded, but was advised, that it wasn't possible. When I called down to see my sister, Maureen, who lived close to, Angela, in Surbiton at that time, she was on the telephone to Jim, who was clearly pouring his heart out on the other end of the phone, while, Maureen, was telling him, that he should pay my mother and father their money back. Usually, I would have gone to visit my parents, but on this occasion, I thought It was best not to get involved in what was a messy family situation. I telephoned my friend, Peter Watts, in Nottingham, and asked him, if I could stay with him until it was time to return to Tanzania again. He said it was okay and I went up to Nottingham, where I received an angry phone call from my father, saying that he thought me, and my big brother, resented the other four younger ones. I said I certainly didn't, if anything, it was the other way round. I said, "Goodbye dad," and put the phone down. I went back to Tanzania without going to see my parents' in Armagh.

It would be several years later, before I learned how the argument between, Jim, and my parents, had played out. My father telephoned, Jim, in an attempt to get his money back and said angrily to Jim, "what have you ever done for this family?"

Jim's equally angry response was to write the "twenty seven pages," as if he were writing a film script. The twenty seven pages were a scathing attack on my parents, but mainly of my mother who he referred to, as brass necked, shrill voiced, (this was mainly when my mother was in her Mrs. Bouquet Bucket role,) and how she had embarrassed and humiliated him by working in a domestic capacity for the Christian Brothers, who taught him, and, which he felt, adversely affected their attitude to him. He went to my parents' home in Armagh and made them give him the addresses of everyone in the family and sent a copy of, "the twenty seven pages," to each of them.

(I never received mine, as I was in Tanzania at the time, but he gave me a copy from his computer, when he came over for his diagnosis, at The Royal Free Hospital approximately five years later.) Although "the twenty seven pages," were factually correct, my attitude to the facts was different to Jim's, as I was more understanding of the circumstances at the time, and I was less concerned with appearances and more concerned with the practicalities facing families in certain circumstances. The first I heard of the court case, that followed the argument between my father and, Jim, (which was more to do with my father, rushing to my mother's defence, than it was about the money, because he told me later, "I did it for her,") was, when my mother came on holiday with me to Portugal. She told me, that the judge hearing the case had commented on how unusual it was for a father to take his son to court and (with tears in her eyes) she said, how Jim was sitting absolutely white faced, saying nothing. I felt myself go cold all over and was covered in goose bumps, even though it was a hot afternoon in Portugal. After Jim's diagnosis and prognosis, Nula arranged a week's holiday in Waterville, with the express intention of meeting my brother, Peter, whom she had never met before. Peter was devastated, when he had called in to see Jim, during the week he had stayed with me. He said, that he was going to take his dog out for a walk, and, when he returned, I could tell from looking at his face, that he had been crying and, that walking the dog had just been a convenient excuse to release his emotions. This was the first time Peter had seen, Jim, in the twenty two years following the beating I had taken from him, in front of my ten year old son, Jamie, of which he had strongly disapproved. Peter dropped out of the arranged week in Waterville at the last minute, so I went alone. Nula had booked us into 'The Smugglers Inn Hotel' in Waterville, right on the beach. It was a small, friendly, family run hotel with views out to sea, where it was possible to spot a dolphin in the bay. Behind the hotel was a golf course, where private helicopters would land to drop off the golfers staying at its hotel. Nula had planned a week of fishing for, Jim, who was already familiar with the area and she reminded me of my mother, who had also accompanied, Jim, on many fishing holidays and had run around after him, catering for his every need. Unlike my mother, however, Nula was now the main bread winner, trying to maintain a certain lifestyle, (as well as Jim's pride and dignity,) and cope with a terminally ill husband, who was already showing signs of being difficult at times. During this week, I heard Nula's version of the events that had taken place at the time of the court case. On the day of the hearing, Jim's solicitor had wanted to settle the matter outside the court and my father had been willing to comply with the solicitor's suggestions, (his anger probably having subsided by this time.) However, my mother had received a telephone call from someone in England, (probably my sister, Maureen,) telling her, that she must go into the hearing and obtain the county court judgment. So, at my mother's insistence, my father went into the court and obtained the CCJ against Jim. Nula also told me, that Jim was unable to speak a word and that his hair had turned totally white afterwards. She told me, that she received phone calls from Maureen, saying, that if they didn't pay the money back, she would write to all the Irish newspapers, and, Nula would never work in Ireland again. Nula said, she was less affected by the court case than, Jim, as it wasn't her family. She knew Maureen's threat would not affect her ability to work, and she did, in fact, carry on working. Jim, however, who had in the meantime resolved the legal issue with Noel Browne's family, (Nula bought the rights to the book and a small piece of land on the west coast of Ireland) was unable to begin work on the film, once the grant from the Irish Arts Council came through, because of the case against him, by my parents which was still pending. To avoid the shame of it all, in a small place like Clonmel, Jim, and Nula, moved to a remote place in Wicklow, and Nula travelled up to her place of work in Dublin, or, more often than not, had to go abroad, to places like Paris, in order to work, leaving, Jim, alone in the place in Wicklow. Nula told me they experienced really hard times after the court case and they had debts in the bank that were rising by the minute, at that time, because of the interest that was being added on, the debts were already at around £68,000. In the first instance, Nula's family supported her by taking care of Jim, while she worked, but they also had their own lives and families to take care of. Jim was also totally ostracized from all his own family, following the court case. The bank settled a case my father was bringing against them, for allowing Jim to run up the overdraft, after he had been in to see them, and they paid him £2,500, (my father, was down £7,500.) I asked, Nula, if she and Jim had legally married, as at times she spoke, as if she was separate from, Jim, rather than one of a married couple and she said they had. Perhaps, it was their business and private lives that were separate. Sometime after the court case, and before Jim's diagnosis, my parent's went down to Wicklow to visit, Jim, when Nula was away. They discovered, that there was no food in the house and, Jim was sitting in front of the computer writing the film script, 'Against the Tides.'

My father said, he just kept going on and on about, "the glory days."

After his divorce from, Carol, Jim's career, as a freelance film director did take off and he made many serious documentaries for QED and London Scientific films, shown on BBC Television, as well as many documentaries for Granada Television. Did the court case trigger his Dementia? Unable to begin work on, "Against the Tides," and with no family, or children, of his own to motivate him, it certainly wouldn't have helped. His work was everything to him, he had come a long way from taking First Holy Communion photographs, had achieved his dream, only to find his path blocked by those, who had always shared his dreams and reflected in the glory of, "his glory days."

It was his sixtieth birthday on 24th January, 2005, so I thought I'd go over to Dublin that weekend, to see, Jim, and Nula, and spend the week of the half term, in February with, Jim, to give, Nula, a break away. I booked the plane tickets, in case I'd lose them, by the time Nula got back to me, thinking this wouldn't be a problem. However, as she took a long time to get back to me on her mobile, I telephoned her home phone number, and, Jim spoke to me. He ranted on, saying it wasn't convenient, as they were in the process of moving. Recognizing that this was part of his illness, and realizing, that both he and, Nula, were still coming to terms with it all, I said, that it was no problem, whatsoever, and left them to carry on with their own lives, as best they could, and for as long as they could. I changed the two tickets, to fly to Spain, in the half-term, to look around for a retirement home, and to Barce-

Iona, for the Easter holiday. If ever my mother wanted to go to Dublin, to see, Jim, I would receive a panic stricken text from, Nula, saying it wasn't convenient, as she was either moving offices or going to visit friends on the west coast of Ireland. I think she found it difficult to cope with Jim's family coming to visit, on top of coping with, Jim, her work and her own feelings and emotions, which was hardly surprising under the circumstances.

Chapter Six

I Move to Spain

'Tis all a chequer-board of Nights and Days
Where destiny with Men for pieces plays:
Hither and thither moves, and mates, and slays
And one by one back in the closet lays.

Rubáiyát of Omar Khayyám

At the end of November, 2005, I moved to Spain, with a view to giving myself a few years to get settled, prior to retirement. Looking to the future, I told, Nula, that she could always use my home in Spain, as a bolt hole, should she ever feel the need for a break away, and, that I would always be there for her, should the need arise. She said she would come over and help me get set up, but she never did. I expect Jim, and work, kept her very busy. It was with some surprise, to say the least, that I read the following letter from, Carol.

Dear Maureen, Margaret

I am writing to you both because you are the only family addresses I have. I have, as you know, been helping, Jim and Nula medically in the last 3-4 years as his illness became more apparent and he went downhill. He has Pick's disease, a form of early Dementia, with a dreadful prognosis. I suspect he has had it for many years. Nula has borne the caring load alone with paid help, but obviously must work in order to pay for it. My reasons for writing are. If any member of the family wishes to see, Jim, before it is too late to converse sensibly, I suggest they contact, Nula. If, between you, you might have, Jim for a weekend, or visit in Dublin and take the load off, Nula-this would be most welcome. She would be cross with me for suggesting this but the load is terrible. I enclose enough copies for you to send to other family members.

Kindest regards

Carol.

I replied immediately to the letter, which I thought was both patronizing and arrogant and intrusive on my family's lives, who were already fully aware of, Jim's diagnosis and terrible prognosis, and were all perfectly capable of responding to the situation without any nudging from, Carol. After Jim's diagnosis, my father spoke on the telephone to Nula, and asked her, if she needed any money, which, to her credit, she declined, as she only wanted to make his family aware of the situation and to have, Jim, back in their lives once again, knowing how much his family meant to him. In my reply to, Carol's letter I told her, that I would be sending a copy of Carol's letter to, Nula, and a copy of my letter to her. As a medical professional, I would have expected, Carol, to be the first to appreciate the necessity for openness and honesty, when dealing with the relatives of a terminally ill, and vulnerable patient, and to have sought Nula's permission, before sending the letter. The letter also suggested, Carol, and Nula, already knew the diagnosis and prognosis of Jim's illness, before, Nula brought him over to England for the appointments Carol, had arranged and had taken the opportunity of my father's car accident for, Nula, to make contact with me, reunite me with Jim, and then use me to have him assessed in England, so that the family would, subsequently, also get the diagnosis and prognosis that they already knew.

Perhaps they both thought that the end justified the means; perhaps they did, but no-one, not even a relative suffering with dementia, likes to think, that they have been so cynically manipulated. I asked, Nula, if she had no qualms about involving Jim's ex-wife in their lives and she said, that Carol wasn't a problem for her, as she was his first wife, but Sophie, as the second, most recent wife, would have been. It was an interesting answer, which gave me much food for thought, and still does. Following Jim's diagnosis, my mother went into Pontius Pilot mode, as the onset of Jim's dementia coincided with the time of the court case. Nula had already told me, that her professor friend in the West of Ireland had said, that she believed, that, what Jim was suffering from had been brought on, as a result of the trauma and she asked the consultant, if the court case had caused it? The Consultant Specialist in Linguistics had chosen the words, "Cathedral, fraud and worm," with good reason. On a visit to my parents, after the diagnosis, my mother was saying venomously, "Oh yes, I'll fix him," which, no doubt, was my father's immediate response to reading Jim's twenty seven pages, in which he was totally scathing about my mother. However, I do believe, that when my father said, "that he did it for her," he was telling the truth, because that's the kind of man he was; typically, old school. His loyalty to her, however, would not be returned, as she would have had me believe, that she was an innocent party in it all and had not insisted on going into the court and obtaining the CCJ, when my father would have been willing to settle it outside the court. When the solicitor advised my father, that they could send in the bailiffs to recover some of their debt, my father totally rejected the suggestion. My mother did not need to embark upon a blame shifting exercise, as my father already probably blamed himself, but he was now elderly, suffering with macular degeneration and just recovering from a car accident he was extremely lucky to survive. For the first time in their sixty years of marriage, my mother had the upper hand and she took full advantage of it. Instead of supporting him, when he needed her the most, she abandoned him on many occasions and went on holiday to Italy with, Maureen and Richard. The day I went to see my father, in the Retreat in Armagh sitting in a wheel chair in the corridor, with all the air of an abandoned person, who has no family, was the day I ended my relationship with my mother! My father's room was stark, not an item of homeliness in sight, and he was wearing an old brown pair of leather shoes, with holes in the toes of them. My father had worn a black pair of leather shoes to my son, David's, wedding, which were a little bit down on the heel, so I bought him a new pair of Clarke's shoes for his birthday, six weeks later, and posted them to him. My mother had only brought up a packet of Jaffa cakes and a bottle of orange cordial, because she knew I was coming over to see him. My father told me, my mother and sister, Maureen, were planning to abandon him leaving him destitute. I never saw any evidence to the contrary. I never went near my mother on what would have been my last ever visit, but returned to England, leaving my father, in the care of the nurses and staff in the care home; people who were capable of showing him more care and kindness, than his own wife of sixty years.

Two days after returning to England, I received a telephone call from the manager of the care home, asking me, if I wanted to be involved in my father's care. I told him, that yes, I certainly did, (I always had been,) but I didn't want to be involved with my mother, ever again. I learned from the care home manager, that my father had already been in two other homes in order to give my mother some respite, so that she could go and look after Jim, (my mother was in Italy with Maureen, and Richard) and to the best of my knowledge, never looked after Jim, because, Nula, never wanted her there.) I had been told nothing of this by my mother, (for obvious reasons.) My mother had my father, back home on his birthday, although I had been told, that he would be staying in the Retreat for good. When I spoke to my father on the phone in the Retreat, I asked him, if he was pleased to be going home, and he said, with a heartfelt sigh of relief, "Oh yes," so I left it, knowing that there were good support services in place. I later received a registered envelope with £1,000 cash in it, a church pamphlet on Love and Forgiveness and a letter from my mother, inside. I began to read the indecipherable letter from my mother and stopped after the first sentence. I returned the letter, cash and pamphlet straight away by registered post. As, Maureen's marriage guidance counsellor told her, after Robert had his affair, "Some sins are unforgivable," and I agree.

My father went back into the Retreat the following year, and the nurse I spoke to in the home said he was not the same man, who had left them in November. They were totally shocked at how much he had deteriorated, to such an extent, that he had to be put on a special bed, and had to receive around the clock care. I kept up my contact with my father, at the Retreat, by telephone, and made a point of ringing him every Sunday afternoon to try to support and reassure him. He was always so beautifully spoken and I know that we both benefitted from these brief conversations. My cousins in Belfast and my sister, Angela, went to see him and told me, he was suffering with a chest infection. When I telephoned, on his birthday, I was told that he was in Craigavon Hospital and was expected back in a week. I telephoned Craigavon Hospital and was told, that he had taken a turn for the worse and, that I should think about coming over to see him. I telephoned my brother, Peter, in Banbury, and we arranged to meet up at the International Airport and go on to the hospital together. When we arrived, my mother and, Maureen, were standing by the bed. I asked the nurse, if I could leave my bag somewhere and she showed me a place in the room, where they kept the sheets. I then suggested to, Peter, that we go to the hospital restaurant, (with which, by this time, I was really familiar) and have something to eat, until such time, that my mother, and Maureen, had used up their visiting time. My father was on his second lot of intravenous antibiotics. Peter, could only stay two days, I stayed a week, sleeping in the small room set aside for family. We knew my father was dying, and my father knew it too. I treasured the last of the time I got to spend with him and the precious little moments that we were able to share together. My brother, Raymond, arrived from Germany the day, Peter, left. My mother and Maureen were trying to persuade, Peter to stay on, because, Raymond was arriving, but, Peter said he couldn't. He told me later, that he wasn't staying around for any shindigs. I never spoke a word to my mother, or Maureen, and when, Raymond arrived, he passed me on the corridor outside the ward, and said, "Hello Margaret," to which I replied, "I have nothing to say to you, Raymond."

It was true I, had nothing to say to any of them. He seemed taken aback and said, "Oh well, hello anyway." Knowing, that I would not be staying to support my mother, Maureen, extended her ticket back to Edinburgh and remained with my mother. I took my flight back to Spain, and asked the nursing staff, if they would telephone me and let me know when my father, passed away. They said the next of kin usually did this. I asked them if they would make an exception and ring me in Spain, and they said they would. Jim and Nula didn't come to see my dad, saying it was better, if everyone came to see him, when he was dead. This was following a phone call to him, from my mother, complaining about my initial thought to stay with my cousins in Belfast. I didn't blame, Jim, for this particular rant either, as I knew he was ill and never should have been troubled, in the first place, by my totally insensitive mother. My cousins were blocked from coming to see my father, before he died, by my mother, and Maureen, even though they had known him all their lives and were really fond of him. I would have thought it would be better to see someone, before they died: you can't give them much comfort or support, or say what you want to say to them, once they're dead.

My dad's next of kin were not like other people's next of kin, that much was becoming increasingly obvious. The family of the man, who was dying in the next bed to my father's, were absolutely wonderful people, as were all the nurses and care staff, who were looking after, not only their patients, who were dying, but their relatives as well. It was easier to unite with people, who, until that week, were total strangers, than it was with a family I'd known all my life. All the people I met in Armagh were good, decent people, deserving the highest of accolades that it was possible to bestow upon those, who care for the sick and the vulnerable. It is a sad indictment of my family, that the same can't be said for them. My father sadly passed away, on 6th December 2006. My mother, Maureen, and Richard, Raymond, and Ellen, my sister, Angela, and my, son David, attended the funeral along with mourners wishing to pay their last respects. It was out of respect for my father, that I didn't go to the funeral.

My mother telephoned me, after my father's funeral, to say that she was grieving and I told her, that we were all

grieving. She tried to engage me in conversation, as to what would go on my father's headstone, but, on noting my resolve, her tears quickly changed to anger: frustrated, that she was not getting her own way this time, she slammed the phone down. She moved to Edinburgh, close to, Maureen, and Richard, after my father's funeral, where she was, once again, well supported.

My Mother and Father

In memory of my beloved father.
(10th November 1919) (6th December 2006)

You were my rock, my anchor
My guiding light through life
It was your time to leave
All of life's trouble and strife.
People speak of grieving
Of a loss so hard to bear
That follows a loved one's leaving
Because they're no longer there:
That person loved so dearly
Who stilled all my fears
The one who was right beside me
Throughout all of my years
How much I loved you
This you always knew
How much you loved me
This I knew too
It's this love I will remember
Throughout my remaining years
Your lovely face and your gentle voice
Will be there through my tears

Rest in peace my dear father

Chapter Seven

The Edinburgh Fiasco

The following year, I received a telephone call from, Nula, saying, that my mother had made the journey from Edinburgh to Dublin, by ferry and train, totally unannounced, to see Jim. Once again, Nula was in panic mode, saying, that she was moving offices, and, that it was all too much for her. My mother had booked into a hotel for three days, so I suggested, that, Nula ask my mother to have, Jim, there, in order to spend some time together and have dinner. My mother and Jim were not happy with this suggestion, so Nula put the dinner in the oven, while, Jim and my mother went out together. When they returned, Jim went into one of his rants, (probably provoked by my mother.) I advised, Nula, to stay calm and cool, until the time was up for my mother to leave, which she did. Shortly after this, Nula telephoned to ask what I thought about her sending, Jim to Edinburgh for five weeks, as, Richard, an academic, had the long summer holidays free and could look after him. I advised her against it, as I knew from past experience Richard and Maureen's attitude and she would be ill advised to take such a step. Nula failed to hear my advice, and on the pretext, that, Maureen was having, Jim, for the weekend, Jim flew to Edinburgh, with his notes and copies of the recent assessments, that had been carried out by his GP. Richard was absolutely furious and told, Nula, that he was putting, Jim, into a home on the Monday and would have his own assessments carried out on him. He told her, they would have her marriage annulled, and, that she would never see him again. He also threatened to sue,

Carol, who had orchestrated the visit in the first place. Richard telephoned Jim's GP, to tell him, in no uncertain terms, what he thought of both, Carol and Nula. Carol, in an attempt to back pedal, said, that she would fly up to Edinburgh, with a social worker, and collect him. At first Richard agreed to this, but, later, went back on the agreement. I received a distressed phone call from, Nula, saying, Jim wasn't ready for going into care, as there was still a 'window of knowing,' and he would be terrified, because of his childhood experience in care. She said, that my mother was categorically denying, that, Jim had ever been in care, but I knew this wasn't true. She asked me, if I had a copy of "the twenty seven pages" in order to show, that, Jim did not have the good relationship with his mother that was being professed, by his relatives in Edinburgh. I told her I didn't have a copy and, that I also didn't think, in this case, that they would be sufficient anyway. I knew that Richard could carry out his threat, because the law in Scotland was different to the law in both England and Eire, which was in the EU. I also knew, that time wasn't on Nula's side. Jim's condition was deteriorating and the last thing Nula needed was another stressful court case for custody of Jim. I agreed to send a fax stating, that, Jim, and I, had both been in care, Jim, once with me, and myself, alone, at about the age of seven. I said that I would swear an affidavit to that effect, and would be willing to appear in court, as a witness, if required. I said that Nula had been a totally loving and supportive wife to, Jim, for many years and did not deserve to be parted from him in their final years together. I later received a text from Nula saying, that she had Jim in the car with her, (Richard and Maureen claimed, that he'd lost his passport,) and was on her way back to Dublin with him. I was a borderline diabetic at this time, keeping my blood sugars down with diet and exercise, but the stress of this incident pushed them well over the limit and I had to go on medication to lower them again. Jim went into Gasgoine House, Cowper Care, soon after this unfortunate event and Nula was given social housing, a half hour's travelling distance from the home. I was relieved, that both Jim, and Nula, now had a settled situation and, that Nula could finally get some respite herself and all the support she desperately needed for Jim's care. As Nula had a large family in Ireland, as well as good friends, I felt she would also be well supported in her personal life. I allowed some time for the situation to settle and planned to go and see them both. In July 2009 I telephoned, Nula, on her mobile and was surprised, when she finally answered it, as she always kept it on voice mail. She told me she was with Jim, and would speak to me, when she got home. I said I would ring her about ten on her landline. I kept phoning all evening and got no reply. The next day, I telephoned the home to see, if anything was wrong. I was told that Nula's sister, who was a doctor, was coming over, (presumably from England) the following day. The nurse said that any conferences would take place in Nula's home, or off site of the care home itself. I just assumed, that it was something to do with Jim's treatment, but I was puzzled, as to, who the doctor was, as I didn't think Nula had a doctor in the family.

Chapter Eight

Jim's Move to Chorley Wood

I received a phone call from my brother, Peter, saying that Jim was in the Sunshine Care Home, Highview, Chorley Wood and that he had met with, Nula, who had arrived the day before. Peter said the home was like a five star hotel and had every facility, and, that he would visit Jim, at the weekends. This was the first time, that Peter had ever met, Nula: he was pleased to be of some support to her and be able to visit Jim. I can only assume that, Nula, was planning to move over to London, in order to be close to her daughter, who lived in Clapham and would also be of some support for her. As, Carol, also lived in Ferncroft Avenue, and had a flat in Dolphin Square, Nula would have the support of, Carol, and her friends also. As Jim had only gone to Eire, because of the tax breaks, being given to artists, and, because my parents had retired back there, it seemed perfectly okay that he returned to London, which had been his home for a very large part of his life. Peter, and his wife, Paula, visited, Jim most weekends and everything seemed to be fine and settled, until I received another text from, Nula, saying, that she was very angry with, Maureen, as she said, that she would organize the funding for Jim's home, but hadn't done it. Her text came at the same time my mother was diagnosed with terminal stomach cancer. I sent a text back saying for her to do it herself, and to take some control of the situation. I received a further text saying the person responsible for the finances of the home was asking if the family could help with the funding. Aware the family, were not in a financial position to help, I told her to explain this to the home. I also suggested she speak to the relevant charities, who could possibly help. I later learned that she had gone to see my sister, Angela, and asked her, if she would speak to the different charities. Angela said that she had, and had come unstuck, as she couldn't answer some of the questions they were asking. She offered to let Nula use her house, while she went up to Edinburgh to look after my mother, but Nula didn't take her up on the offer. I told, Nula, that I didn't think the home would put a terminally ill, sick, vulnerable resident out on the street and that I was sure some resolution of the situation would be found. I received a further phone call from, Nula, saying that she was at her wit's end, and was just thinking of giving up.

Chapter Nine

My Visit to Edinburgh

My mother was diagnosed with stomach cancer in February 2010. My sister, Angela, advised, Maureen, to draw up an itinerary to avoid the prospect of several people arriving together and overwhelming my mother, which my sister did and sent to all the siblings by text. The itinerary included two visits by my brother, Raymond, two by Maureen's son, Georgie and his girlfriend, trips to St Andrew's for several days break in a hotel and was clearly designed to block, Angela, Peter, and anyone else, Maureen, and my mother, didn't want to visit her. My mother's capacity to hurt my sister, Angela, at this critical time in her life, in the way, that she did, was absolutely abhorrent to me, though not surprising. I allowed time for the initial shock of it all to settle, knowing, that my mother was in the very best of hands and would be well cared for. My sister, Maureen is Head of National Cancer Support for Macmillan in Scotland and, Richard's brother a doctor, is in a top medical position in Scotland. I looked at the itinerary for when I had holidays at Easter and saw one small window, between 4th April (Easter Sunday) and 7th April. I telephoned my mother to say, that, if it was alright with her, that I would come and visit her then. She was absolutely delighted and I told her, that I didn't want anyone to meet me at the airport, as I would take a taxi to where she lived. She rang me back and said, that she had booked dial a ride and would come with them herself to meet me, which she did. I was, initially, shocked, when I first saw her; she had let her hair grow white and had lost a lot of weight. She had aged and was not the fighting fit woman I had last seen four years ago, as my father lay dying in Craigavon Hospital. She had with, Maureen's help, a special Sunday dinner all prepared and cooking in the oven for my arrival. Although she was as ill as she was, she was very much in control of her own life still and had all her wits about her. We spent our time together and made our peace, which, in the circumstances, was good for both of us. She was strong and courageous, still self- willed, and without any signs of self-pity, whatsoever. At one point she told me, that, if she had done anything wrong, she just tried to make amends for it in other ways. I do believe, that both my parents were very sorry for what had happened between, Jim, and them, and that the action they took was a knee jerk reaction in response to what he had said in his "twenty seven pages," and, that they never, for one second, ever thought, that it would result in the damage to him, that it did. I also believe, that they themselves ended up as victims too, because of that argument, because of their age, and, because of their own vulnerability, and the fact, that they could not forgive themselves, as parents, and it took its toll on them too. With the help and support of my son, David, Angela, Peter, and his wife, Paula, all got to see my mother, before she died on, 3rd of August 2010 and they all made their peace and said their goodbyes. She, like my father, had made all her own funeral arrangements, and paid for them, and was buried with my father, in Armagh Cathedral's Cemetery. I don't think either of them could have coped with Jim passing away before them, because, deep down, they were good, decent people, for all their bravado.

A poem for my mother
(23rd June 1923) (3rd August 2010)

This morning at 11am
A service was held in the place of your birth
But not for you a funeral dirth
But a gathering of song, prose and mirth.
The end you had, you didn't deserve
But you faced it with courage, strength and reserve
You're back with your own, in your own home town,
And today, with my father,
They will lay you down.
You have come full circle today,
Sixty six years with your man,
And now, an eternity of listening
To the Rubáiyát of Omar Khayyám

You loved to live your life
And lived the life you loved
I hope it's rich and full in that place above.
You are the last of your generation
Finally laid to rest
I hope you find yourself
Reunited with the best
And when Thyself with shinning Foot shall pass
Among the guests Star-Scatter'd on the Grass
And in thy joyous Errand reach the Spot
Where I made one- turn down an empty Glass.
The Rubáiyát of Omar Khayyám

Chapter Ten

Jim Moves to Courtlands Lodge

On 30th July 2010, I telephoned the home in Chorley Wood to ask after, Jim, and was told, that he had moved to Courtlands Lodge in Watford, on 16th July, as there had been a problem with the funding. After a lot of telephone calls to the care home in Dublin, and the home in Chorley Wood, to try to ascertain exactly what the problem had been with the funding, I discovered that, Carol, (Nula's sister who was a doctor) Maureen, and Nula, had had a meeting with the home in Dublin, and advised them, that they had obtained a place for, Jim, in Chorley Wood, which could provide the better one on one care, that they believed he was not receiving in the home in Dublin. The Chorley Wood home told me, that Nula had assured them, that there would be no problem with the funding, which would be following soon. As the home knew of Carol's involvement in Jim's move and spoke with, Maureen, on the telephone, they accepted Nula's word with regard to the funding and admitted, Jim, into the home. I rang the home in Watford on 3rd August 2010 to advise them, that, Jim's mother had sadly passed away and told them, that I would leave it to their discretion as to whether or not they would tell Jim. When I spoke to Courtlands Home on 30th July I was advised, that Jim was still in the early stages of settling in with them, but was settling well. I was advised, that, Nula was away for ten weeks and, that Jim's next of kin was down as, Sian Roberts, Nula's daughter, and Jim's step daughter. I advised the home, that Sian was not Jim's natural daughter, although I knew, that she was very fond of, Jim, and that I also thought, that they should have Nula's mobile telephone number for record purposes, in case they needed to get in touch with her directly. I also asked them to take my telephone numbers, in Spain, and to put me down, as next of kin too, which they did, and to advise me also, if there were ever any change of circumstances in the future. I was also advised, that Jim's stay with them was on a temporary basis of six months, which I found most disconcerting to say the least, as I was aware, that any change for a dementia patient, increases their stress levels and speeds up the dementia. They also have to go through the whole process of getting used to a new environment once again. When I asked why his stay was temporary and what would be the criteria for making it permanent, I was advised, that he could be moved again, if the home could not meet his needs. On 7th August, the day of my mother's funeral, I received a telephone call from my brother, Peter, who lives in Banbury, to say, that he had gone to visit, Jim, and had found him sitting in a dark room at 2pm, unwashed and smelling of urine. Jim had had nothing to eat or drink for three days. This was a totally different picture to the one I had been given the week before. It is possible, that Jim's "window of knowing," was still present and, that he was aware of his mother's passing and was now in a state of grieving. Peter spoke to the member of staff on duty, who advised him, that Jim refused to let anyone go near him to wash or dress him and, that they couldn't force him to eat or drink. Peter tended to Jim's needs that day and he and Sian had a meeting with the care home manager, when she returned from holiday. She agreed with, Peter, that Jim should never have been left in that state, and assured him, that it wouldn't happen again. Peter was satisfied with the reassurance that she gave him, and asked her to put him down as next of kin too. He also advised her, that he would be visiting Jim, every weekend, work permitting. I also learned from Peter, that Jim had been unceremoniously removed from Sunshine Homes, at Chorley Wood, and, that Sian Roberts, and a social worker had gone round several homes for him, and had decided, that the home at Watford was the most suitable. Sian and a friend drove, Jim, to the home in Watford, and one week later, Sunshine Homes were telephoning to ask, if Jim's furniture could be removed from the room, as it was needed for another resident, (presumably one with no funding issue.) Peter went to Sunshine Homes and collected Jim's furniture. When he enquired, as to why Jim had to leave the home, he was told, that it was due to an issue of funding. No one seemed to be able to clarify exactly what the funding issue was, but I was later advised, that it had been applied for too late, which was, allegedly, the responsibility, that had been delegated to, Maureen. I was so incensed, that Jim had to experience yet another traumatic change of circumstances at the hands of the same three people involved in the "Edinburgh fiasco," that I wrote an open letter to the Times Newspaper, on 16th August I sent a copy, with a covering letter, telling them, who Jim was, and the television work he had done for them, as a freelance film director, to the BBC and ITV Grenada.

Chapter Eleven

Nula's Texts

(Exact transcriptions) 15th October 2010

Marg, why r u rubbishing me to James' care home? I am doing all I can for, James both emotionally and financially, when did you last visit him, or send him a card! Please don't do that again. I am under huge stress myself. I don't need your bad mouthing me to care home staff. The only person who helped is Maureen and Peter. Maureen has paid my travel and telephone bills and text me every week. Pete visits James and telephones to tell me how, Jim is. Nula.

My reply to above text from Nula

You accused mum of playing all her children off against each other and that's just what you've been doing too. My only concern is Jim and his care. Have easier mind now, Peter is involved, he has more than you on his plate, but he's blood and its thicker than water in the end, and he cares, that's what really matters in the end.

Nula's reply to my text

Where have you been? You've never visited him once. I'm stuck in Ireland broke. Would you take over care of James?

My reply to Nula

The home is giving his care, it was easier and cheaper for you to make a half hour visit from your home in Dublin than have the chaos and stress you, Carol, and Maureen, not me or Peter, were responsible for.

Nula's reply to my text

They were not giving him care it was a geriatric home not able to deal with dementia! Instead of slagging me off, visit, Jim and you'll see what condition he's in. All I've ever wanted for Jim is the best care, what have you done for him in the last year? I'm the only person who really cares for Jim. The care home was appalled by your slagging me off. They know who cares. Please don't text me again, I've enough stress.

My text to Peter

Won't be in contact with Nula anymore, will leave things to you. Contact me if you need to. I'll ring the home from time to time love Margaret.

My text to Nula

I'm only interested in the stress, Jim has undergone during three moves to three different homes in less than two years and the way those moves were handled by three people, who should know better, having finally offloaded him on to, Peter you abandoned him for ten weeks. How much stress would that give, Jim? There was an outcry about a cat in a wheelie bin and you have the nerve to think you're the victim.

(cc of above text forwarded to Peter)

Nula's reply to my text

You, as a family, have abandoned Jim. I've never loaded him off to Peter, I never met, Peter in the 18 years, Jim and I were together. The first time I met Peter, was in the care home. You should, as a family, be united and visit your elder brother, who was always good to you all, shame on you. What have you done for Jim? You haven't even visited him, shame on you, I've no shame. I've always been there for James.

My reply to Nula

And you, Carol and Maureen got him his place in Chorley Wood and are responsible for the mess you expect everyone else to take on. It's poor Jim, not poor you! I thought you were his family and sensitive to his having been in care as a child. Wives cope with much more than you, with less whining, they're motivated by a sense of love and duty. Reassuring to know there's no cases of dementia in Dublin, is it because they've all been transferred to London?

My text to Peter

Think the "mind fuckers" have come out of mourning, as "mum's now at rest" it can't be her, who's disturbing the peace! Take care, keep in touch Margaret.

Text from me to Nula

Does "your friend," Carol, know you're broke or that there was a funding issue? What has she done for Jim? He'd be better off without her involvement or, Maureen's in the first place. With hindsight, I'd let Richard do what he threatened, then, Maureen, "who doesn't like Jim," could visit him and you could visit Jim. Maureen and Richard in Edinburgh and Carol could go too, Jim would love that old friends united. (cc to Peter)

31st October I spoke to Max at Watford Care Home and he told me they put a portable TV in, Jim's room, as I suggested which was helping to settle him. Jim also has a DVD player in his room and Max said they'd play DVD's of his work, as a film producer, if I could get copies of them. Max said, Jim still thinks he's working and I agree, as he would always carry his battered brown briefcase with him, everywhere he went, containing the film script he produced of "Against the Tides," after the court case, that he'd never been able to make. It was at this point, that his mind became blocked and was the onset of the dementia from which he is now suffering twelve years afterwards. I did write to the BBC and ITV asking them, if they would send complimentary copies of Jim's work to the home, but I don't think they have done so.

In the meantime, I sent, Jim copies of his article, "Walk on the Wildside," which was in BBC Wildlife Magazine (May 1984) and which was shown as part of the QED series on May 16th 1984. I also sent him a copy of the write up in the Manchester Evening News, 15th September 1989, covering his Grenada TV documentary, "The Way We Love Now," as well as his own wedding to his second wife, Sophie Brotherton- Ratcliffe, at Belmont Abbey near Hereford. I noticed that the Panorama Programme covered the issues of the anti-psychotic drugs for Alzheimer patients and were sending the message, that the quality of care needed to be improved and the use of the drugs would be cut by two thirds by next year, 2011. As many television presenters are now openly talking about relatives, who suffer with this terrible disease and there are advertisements now raising the awareness of the public to try to spot and acknowledge the early signs of dementia, I am pleased, that television is playing its part to support both the patients and their families, who have to deal with the distress and anxiety, that accompanies this cruel disease.

Humpty Dumpty Jim,
whatever became of him?
Had a row with his dad,
that drove them both mad.
His dad's now dead,
his mother too,
that's the damage a family row can do.

Article in Manchester Evening News
15th September 1989

Double take for bridegroom Jim

FREELANCE TV director Jim Black, who marries on Saturday has had twice as many wedding problems as most bridegrooms.

For in addition to ensuring that everything runs smoothly on his own big day he has spent many hours meticulously planning coverage of the marriage ceremony of Gary Hegginbottom and his bride Hayley for the Granada TV documentary The Way We Love Now.

The young couple's classic white wedding took place twice at St Thomas's, Norbury, Stockport last Saturday — once in private and once for the cameras.

Black, in his forties, hopes he will require no re-takes when he ties the knot with 30-ish Sophie Brotherton-Ratcliffe in the even more august surroundings of Belmont Abbey, near Hereford.

He tells me: "After sitting through theirs twice I really should be word perfect."

But unlike his film subjects the Blacks will not be jetting off after the ceremony to a romantic honeymoon.

All leave has been cancelled until the end of the series in October, when they hope to snatch a few days in Italy. Buona fortuna.

BLACK: No honeymoon

"He uses that one when he can't find his false teeth"

Thank you to the Manchester Evening News for giving permission to print this article.

(9th April 2011) Jim is now settling well into the care home in Watford. Peter, and Paula, still visit him and I, occasionally ring to see how he is.

(26th September 2011) I rang the home to see how Jim was. I was told Maureen, and Nula, had been to visit him and took him some nice food goodies, that he thoroughly enjoyed. He now needs help to go to the dining room, but the good thing is; that he is still going there. He has his good and bad days, (don't we all) but at least he is settled where he is and there are plenty of family and 'friends' in the London area, who are close enough to visit him.

(12th December 2011) I have sent Jim, a Christmas card with photos inside, and from time to time I also post him presents. He always loved Christmas and I'm sure the home will make it very special for all their residents, who have by now become Jim's friends and companions. I expect he will be visited by, Peter, and Paula, and other members of his family and I hope it will be, as happy as it can be, in the circumstances, and, that he will have another happy and peaceful year in 2012.

Chapter Twelve

Friends in High Places

Nula told me, that Carol married again to an academic but has still retained Jim's family name. Perhaps, because that's the name she's known by in all her professional and social circles. Her CV is certainly most impressive, as is her own willingness to work long past the age of retirement, thereby practicing what she so ably preaches, as well as boosting the coffers of the taxpayers and her employers, the Department of Work and Pensions. It was with some dismay and disappointment, but not surprise, that I read, Carol, and David Frost's, recommendations in the Government Sponsored Review for GP sick note reforms, which has, unsurprisingly, proved unpopular with both the House of Lords and most of the medical profession, to which Carol belongs and, which I have always held in highest regard for the tremendous good work they do.

As for accountability, it is not those in the highest echelons who are ever held to account for their actions, but the healthcare workers at the lower end of the ladder, who fear losing their jobs, if they do not carry out the recommended reforms, that are expected within the benefit system and to the employment and support allowance. If asked the question, "Does power diminish?" In this particular case, I would unhesitatingly reply, "Yes it does, and it has." I think Willy Russell's, "Blood Brothers," and, "Boys from the Blackstuff," by Alan Bleasdale did more to promote the awareness of long term unemployment on mental health, and the health of the country, than this latest government review, because both writers focused on the health of the individual and the country, rather than on how much it was costing the employer, the government and the taxpayer. It's the attitude to the facts and the statistics, as well as the political will, that is important, not the facts and statistics themselves. The one in five, who find themselves taken off long term sickness benefit (and onto jobseekers allowance instead,) at a saving of 3billion a year to the government, can take some comfort in the knowledge, that having "friends," in high places didn't benefit my brother, Jim, either. Education is a great social leveller, unemployment is also a great social leveller and death is a great social leveller. As Mark Twain said, "there are only two certainties in life, Death and Taxes." In my opinion, Carol, as a medical professional, would have been less diminished in my eyes, if she had used her education and experience to prevent the former, rather than to save the latter. When those in high places suffer a nose bleed, because the air is so thin up there, the blood falls on the less fortunate, weak and the vulnerable.

"La salud no lo es todo pero todo es nada sin salud."

Translation of above:

"Health isn't everything, but everything is nothing without health."

"Oh come with old Khayya'm, and leave the wise,
to talk one thing is certain, that life flies,
one thing is certain, and the rest is lies;
the flower that once has blown forever dies."
Myself when young did eagerly frequent
Doctor and saint, and heard great argument
About it and about: but evermore
Came out by the same door as in I went.

Rubáiyát of Omar Khayyám

I understand that another review has been commissioned to report on the self-perpetuating interests of the old boy network, which is also self-serving; this should prove to make interesting reading in these harsh economic times, and I am certain, that its recommendations, if acted upon, will do more to improve the health of the nation, than the government sponsored review, by Carol Black and David Frost, of sickness absence in Great Britain, and may well save both the government and the taxpayer a lot more money at the same time.

Well, Jim, I have attempted to tell your story that you are unable to tell yourself, as openly and as honestly, as I could, but I will let Soren Kierkegaard, have the last word.

Life is understood looking backwards
But it must be lived forwards

A poem for my Brother Jim

All your life, you did aspire
To reach the great heights you did desire
The perfect home, the perfect wife
And the perfect family life
You set your goals you made your rules
And never would you suffer fools.
Cruel nature did intervene
To cast a shadow o'er your dream
Your blood line was to end with you
A most cruel blow that is true
But your other goals you did achieve
And in yourself you did believe
But if aiming for perfection
Check the wind is blowing in the right direction
To fly your kite good and high
Check the others standing by
Should your string become entangled
You risk your dreams becoming mangled
As down to earth your kite is brought
Along with all the dreams you sought
Tis best to fly your kite alone
On your own secluded hill
To let it rise to do your will
And all your hopes and dreams fulfil
Perhaps in another place and time
There will be no obstructions to your line
The way will be clear and you'll run free
Seeing images of happiness and joy for all eternity.

By your sister Margaret

Article in BBC Wildlife magazine May 1984

*Thanks to Martyn Colbeck for the use of his photographs.
Thanks to the BBC for granting permission to re-print the
BBC Wildlife Magazine.*

Pussies ...
Beware the lady with the scraps

Because if you are a wild city cat
and set up a symbiotic relationship with this person, you can expect
your next visitor to be the neuterer, if not the exterminator.
Film director Jim Black
describes his quest for a truly untamed moggie with all its parts intact.

BBC WILDLIFE MAY 1994

I did not like cats. I knew nothing about cats. Yet I had readily agreed to direct a film about cats. I think it was the sniff of a good story rather than any kind of self-confidence that made me accept the job from Ted Poulter of London Scientific Films.

Ted was producing the film for BBC's QED series. The idea was to make an entertaining natural history programme that would examine the behaviour and the lifestyle of some urban feral cats. Ted's production deadlines had the flexibility of a cast-iron cage, but on the other hand, with its excellent natural history team LSF would more than compensate for any deficiencies on my part.

I looked up the word 'feral' before being briefed by Jeremy Bristow, my researcher; I felt I owed him that. My pocket dictionary told all: "Feral: wild, untamed; uncultivated; brutal." A wonderful set of adjectives for my favourite cartoon character, the street-wise alley cat. The auguries looked good.

Bristow's face bore clear signs of strain as he told me that the feral cats in London's Fitzroy Square had all been neutered and that as this colony was intended as the main subject of the film, we had a problem. "What's the problem?" I inquired innocently. He eyed me with suspicion. Surely I would know that neutering changes certain fundamentals of cat behaviour: they don't fight, they don't spray their territory, they don't mate, they don't lactate. His bottom line was obvious: they don't make good television.

Bristow had already scoured London for a suitable group of unneutered feral cats. Although there were many colonies in London, some in wonderful locations such as Pall Mall, the British Museum, Covent Garden and Fulham Broadway railway station, each colony had been trapped and neutered by cat welfare groups. In other places the cats had been trapped and gassed by pest control firms.

Only one location looked really promising. This was a two-storey derelict factory in Camden—a building which stood out starkly in the midst of a nine-acre wasteland of rubbish, scrap cars and abandoned railway arches. Total dereliction—at once wild, untamed, uncultivated, brutal. A perfect setting for the nine or more unneutered feral cats living among the detritus.

The temptation to centre our film around this group of ferals was overwhelming. Yet even here on this wild side of the city we would need to shoot quickly, in view of the constant threat from neuterers and exterminators. It was perhaps this pervasive pressure that sowed the seeds of a new structure for the film we were about to make.

It was fast becoming clear that we could not, and indeed should not, tell a bland, idealised story of the group behaviour of a single colony. To do so would be to ignore many new and significant components of the feral cat's ecology. A truthful appraisal of the feral cat's lifestyle would have to include the major human inputs that impinge upon the cat's natural existence.

The primary human component of the feral cat's ecology is the cat-feeder. Many, if not most, feral colonies are fed regularly by kind-hearted people. Typically, the feeder is elderly, lonely and female. To begin with, she feeds one or two 'strays', perceiving them to be hungry, miserable and unwanted. A symbiotic relationship soon develops between the 'unwanted' cats and the lonely old lady. In time, other opportunistic feral cats drift in for an easy meal. In this way a local colony numbering anything between four and forty cats becomes established.

Such a colony going about its natural business will defend its territory, mate freely and produce offspring. All things being equal, the colony's population growth will be a function of the food supply obtained from feeders, scavenging and hunting. The main factors limiting growth are road accidents, disease and a high level of kitten mortality.

But in practice all things are rarely equal. The colony is visible, exposed and vulnerable to human attention, some of which is benign, some less so. Man's perceptions of the feral cat phenomenon appear to be influenced by the cat's instinctive behaviour as well as its natural problems: pungent odours produced by toms spraying urine to mark out their territory; noisy cat fights over territory and mates; caterwauling during the nights when queens are on heat; distressing sights of diseased cats and kittens. Such natural occurrences can reflect an image of the feral cat as a problem, a health hazard and a pest.

It is hardly surprising that cats living wild in a big city like London will occasionally fall foul of their human landlords. In many cases pest-control firms are paid to exterminate entire colonies. It is a situation that has prompted interest groups concerned with the cats' welfare to promote a 'humane solution' to the 'problem'.

These groups uncritically accept the proposition that the feral population is too high, and in London they actively lobby local authorities for funds to enable them to manage and control the cat population in their area. Groups such as SNIP—Society for the Neutering of Islington's Pussies—have succeeded. SNIP now has the council's blessing and financial support for the wholesale neutering of the borough's pussies. Wider support for a nationwide neutering programme comes from groups such as the RSPCA, the Cat Action Trust and the Universities Federation for Animal Welfare.

In the course of our filming we pressed these groups to produce reliable figures for London's feral cat population, as well as for the UK as a whole. We also felt it important to know whether Britain's feral cat popula-

Above and opposite top: Jake, a 'whole' tom and the star of *A Walk on the Wildside*, prowling his erstwhile range in a derelict factory in Camden. The documentary ends with Jake watching his home fall to the demolition squad.
Opposite below: The cats, mostly neutered, of Fitzroy Square, and Sammy, right, an intact interloper. He was later captured by neuterers, but escaped.

tion was stable, growing or declining. But no one knows the UK's total population. The most statistically credible estimate places the figure at anything between 123,000 and 1.2 million. Whether this is rising, falling or stable seems to be anyone's guess, since no one has monitored the figures over time.

Figures apart, the neutering campaign has strong arguments behind it. Certain feral cat colonies can cause problems—for example, those that take up residence near a hospital or a factory. Here the case for neutering does present a logical alternative to total extermination. It is argued that returning a small number (usually about six) of neutered cats will prevent other cats from taking up residence. Total extermination would simply create a vacuum which other feral cats would fill up eventually.

But in London, certainly, the neutering programme does not discriminate between problem colonies and the rest. All feral cats are considered to be legitimate targets for castration and spaying. Moreover, it is easy to persuade the feeders to cooperate with a pre-emptive neutering programme, particularly when it is presented as an alternative to extermination. ▷

BBC WILDLIFE MAY 1986

243

In the light of this army of feeders, neuterers and exterminators, I wondered whether natural forces could be viewed as meaningful components of the feral cats' ecology? Was I perhaps witnessing what amounts to the enforced domestication of the street-wise alley cat, a character whose presence has always been accepted with tolerance, if not outright affection, around the streets and squares of London.

There is little doubt that the neutering activists share with the feeder a form of maternal concern for the welfare of the feral population. In so far as their activities deny natural procreation, they form yet another human component of the feral cat ecology. Taken together, the human compulsion to feed and the consequent compulsion to neuter add up to a symbiotic trap for the less wary feral cats. I was beginning to form a lasting respect for those alley cats that spurn the concerned attentions of humans, thereby remaining free to pass on their genetic qualities for survival.

Top: Jake, on his Camden rounds.
Left: A trap set by the Society for the Neutering of Islington's Pussies (SNIP).
Right: A natty 'jellicle' in Soho.

Surprising as it may seem, the urban feral cat has survived as part of our British wildlife for at least 1,500 years. Some central London colonies have been firmly established for centuries. Among these groups, the distinctive black and white markings of T S Eliot's "jellicle" or "clubland" cat are as prominent today as they were in his time. Traditionally, Britain's towns and cities have offered the alley cat the essential elements of survival—food, shelter and a place to breed. Currently, however, it is the latter element that is most successfully being denied.

Perhaps it is the choice of urban habitat that provides the feral cat with the key to free procreation. At one extreme, the smart addresses in central London offer an easy living, but dependence on feeding-ladies makes it a soft target for neutering. At the other extreme, such as the derelict wasteground in Camden, survival of the fittest is the name of the game. Here there are no feeding-ladies to focus attention on the free-living feral. Subsistence is gained from opportunistic scavenging and the spoils of the hunt. The battle for survival is a close-run thing, but at least in a site such as this, nine cats in as many acres of dereliction present an elusive and unpredictable target for human interference.

We called our film *A Walk on the Wildside*, dedicated to the alley cat—long may its character survive.

A Walk on the Wildside will be shown as part of the QED series on 16 May at 9.25pm.

www.ingramcontent.com/pod-product-compliance
Lightning Source LLC
Chambersburg PA
CBHW032033150426
43194CB00006B/259